W9-BCA-275

The KNOW-and-DO Manager

by Lynn W. Whiteside

Parker Publishing Company, Inc. West Nyack, New York

The author wishes to thank Mrs. Jean Overeem for her special effort and interest, for her after-regular-working-hours typing, proofreading and valuable suggestions.

PARKER PUBLISHING COMPANY, INC.
WEST NYACK, N.Y.

Fifth printing .... February, 1970

LIBRARY OF CONGRESS
CATALOG CARD NUMBER: 66-23361

PRINTED IN THE UNITED STATES OF AMERICA

51670—B & P

WHAT THIS BOOK CAN MEAN TO YOU

The KNOW-and-DO manager introduces you to "a manager's mighty seven C's," shows you how to get on top of your present job and how to master greater future leadership responsibilities.

This original total management concept is distinctive in its practical application, since all you need do is study the pattern to be applied and start using it on your present job. You'll move ahead with more confidence as you find you can identify your actions as a KNOW-and-DO manager.

You will learn how to use the first three of the manager's mighty seven C's. They are: communication, cooperation and competition. On-the-job practices point out example areas of performance excellence in which the growing manager must learn to excel.

Veteran managers will agree that the first C, "Communication," the exchange of ideas, giving directions, getting people to listen, understanding others and being understood in return, constitutes a must skill for the successful manager. This book tells you how to sharpen your communications, some dangers to watch for and ways to make personal contacts more productive.

The second mighty C is to give and get "Cooperation." You will receive helpful ideas on how to use general supervision "how-to-do's." The jet age manager can't afford to be held back by the regimented practices of an older generation's management thinking. Today's complex economy requires the successful manager to find and use people's hidden cooperators.

The third mighty C is to promote the "Competitive" spirit. "The KNOW-and-DO Manager" details basic appeals to emotions, the meaning of individual and group reactions. You will also discover how to prepare people for changes, get more effort from people, and how to stimulate improvement.

The fourth mighty C is "Conceive" which reminds the ambitious manager of the requirement for "look-ahead" planning of details, their administration, some ways to prepare for emergencies and the need to allot time to think about better ways to do the job.

The fifth mighty C is to "Carry-out" specific job actions. Here you can learn some ideas on how to fully use an organization; thoughts on building teamwork; ways to implement policy and maintain discipline.

The sixth mighty C is "Check-up." A proven, job-tested tool for achieving this good manager essential is described. If you are having trouble correctly evaluating a subordinate's performance, in helping him develop or getting the job results you want, give careful attention to the sixth mighty C.

The seventh mighty C is to "Convert." Learn about the five power sources which undergird the whole performance capability of the successful manager. To be useful, values from these strength areas must be converted to on-the-job benefits. You will find some pay-off keys in the suggested development and use of all these five skills, qualities, or abilities.

The first power source includes social relationships, reasoning, decision making, judgments on when to compromise, and how to use proven tools for problem solving. Second, the importance of evident expected results, setting an example and making yourself available to support subordinates. Third, balance in carrying out your administrative assignments and developing superior understudies; the right way to delegate your obligations, up, down and to the total organization; some guides to selecting and training subordinates. Fourth, how to fill and use your knowledge tank to solve on-the-job problems; getting more from experiences, ideas, facts, thoughts. Fifth, your attraction for others as a practical motivator; how to manage so that others get a personal return from their efforts; how to avoid the destructive power of ego-involved issues or fault-finding criticism; "watch-fors" in both the open and closed minded individual. Your personal "pull" as a manager is determined by your total pattern of actions, not isolated gimmicks.

You should read "The KNOW-and-DO Manager" with intent: adapt its practical guides to your own personal improvement on your current job. If you do this you can expect a satisfying and progressive future in the fascinating job of management.

CONTENTS

Chapter 1: The KNOW-and-DO Manager's Success Pattern

As a member of a select group which is limited to ten to twelve percent of our nation's work force, you have a right to be proud of your achievements.

A manager at whatever level he may be in his organization should feel that he is somewhat special. He is a decision-maker charged with the task of keeping the people reporting to him unified and moving ahead in an ever more productive society.

What's It Worth?

The personal and social satisfaction you quite properly feel at having reached this out-in-front position is supplemented by additional, tangible rewards such as higher salaries, special privileges, and more pleasant physical working surroundings.

What You Must Do

For all these good things you have paid and are continuing to pay a price. Managers accept a life of tension as part of this cost. You are always working against a deadline which doesn't permit time to check and recheck facts to make sure that the action you are taking or recommending will leave you feeling comfortably assured that the results you must have will be forthcoming.

Pressures Are Generated Because:

As a manager, you must act. July 26, 1861, General George B. McClellan was appointed to the leadership of the Union's Army of the Potomac amid great popular acclaim. Because of earlier victories over the Confederates, he was referred to as "Little Mac" and "The Young Napoleon." Great things were expected from the liberator of West Virginia; but, just a little more than a year later, he was removed from his command because he couldn't come to a decision to attack Lee's Army which numbered only one-half that of his own. As Bruce Catton writes:

> McClellan was always going to make his big move in just two or three more days—as soon as the rain stopped, as soon as so-and-so's division joined him, as soon as this or that or the other thing was all ready. The two or three days would pass, the rains would stop, the other things would work out right but nothing would happen. Never could he bring himself to the point of action.[1]

In contrast, General Grant won Lincoln's commendations because he was willing to fight when the situation called for it.

A *second* source of tensions result because each manager, as one of the few in a favored spot, expects competition from individuals within the majority. This is one of the strains on a leader's everyday life; and the higher you rise on the scale as a manager, the more rarefied the air and the greater you feel the squeeze caused by a short supply of desirable jobs in the face of a rising demand.

Third: Another stress cost you pay is illustrated when your wife asks, "Why can't you take a long weekend with the family the way that John Jones does?" Frequently, not only what you would like to do, but what you ought to do for the family must take second place to the demands of your assignment. Your job working time often cuts in on a golden opportunity to help Johnnie with his algebra, and the pressure isn't reduced any when the "Mrs." fails to sympathize with your management ambitions.

Fourth: An additional penalty, closely related to "shorting" the family, which you pay is the many long hours of intensive effort you spend without any special recognition. Most management jobs are so complex that your boss can't take time from his own responsibilities while you lead him step by step through the often agonizing trail of how you reached a difficult conclusion. Your knowledge that he must bank on you lights another fire under the pressure boiler.

Finding the Answers Is A Solitary Function

This illustration was cited by writer John B. Cooper, " 'Decision-making is a lonely business,' said Clarence B. Randall former head of Inland Steel Com-

[1] Catton, Bruce: *This Hallowed Ground,* p. 168

pany and advisor to Presidents, 'and the greater the degree of responsibility, the more intense the loneliness.' " It is human to wish to share the risk of error and feel the comforting strength of outside support. But the strong man, the one who gives free enterprise its vitality, is the man who weighs thoughtfully the entire range of available opinion and then determines policy by relying solely on his own judgment. Mr. Randall recounted this story about P. B. Armour of Chicago:

> In the early days of Armour & Company, Mr. Armour had an admirable plan for training second and third echelons in the techniques of management. He organized about a dozen men into a junior board of directors and, from time to time, submitted important company problems to this group.
>
> One day, after a particularly lively discussion, a young man said, "I move that we go ahead with this." There was a second, and then Mr. Armour as chairman of the meeting called for a vote. Every man said, "Aye." Whereupon, Mr. Armour said, "The motion is lost." and went on to the next order of business.[1]

When asked later about the propriety of this action, Mr. Armour said, in effect, "Sometimes we count the votes, and at other times we weigh them."

This example shows that, in the final counting, the responsible individual must decide on his own what is to be done about a company's important problems. The final accountability can't be delegated to a group or committee.

You Prove Your Metal on the Tough Ones

A leader must remember that to retain the respect of his followers he has to make the hard decisions.

One example from ancient history and another from modern times illustrate the tragic results of weak leadership. In 702 B.C., King Hezekiah of Judah, feinting illness, entertained the Babylonian king Berodach-baladan in Jerusalem. After Hezekiah had displayed his treasury and weapons of war, the two kings plotted an alliance against Assyria, at that time the ruling empire of the world.

When Isaiah, the Prince of Prophets, charged Hezekiah with cowardice, duplicity, and actions inviting retaliation from Assyria because he failed to meet his problem squarely, the king's answer was, "This will give us peace and security in our time." He discovered how wrong he was when only months later the Assyrians were at the gates of Jerusalem.

In our generation, Neville Chamberlain, Prime Minister of Great Britain, made three trips to visit Hitler in September, 1938, in an effort to appease Germany's aggressive expansionist demands. On September 30, 1938, he signed the Munich Pact with Italy, France, and Germany, which gave Hitler vital areas of Czechoslovakia. As he stepped off the airplane in London in 1938 the British Prime Minister echoed King Hezekiah's "Peace-in-our-time" words of 702 B.C. Chamberlain's refusal to make the hard decision, his failure to face up to his responsibility, only hastened the opening of World War II because within six

[1] Cooper, Joseph D.: *The Art of Decision Making*, pp. 119-120

months Germany broke the Munich agreement, and the conflict started in September, 1939. Notably, in both these historical instances, the faint-hearted leaders passed from history, rejected by their followers.

President John F. Kennedy made the hard decision of a great leader when, in a dramatic television address to the nation on October 22, 1962, he announced a U.S. Naval and Air quarantine against the delivery of all offensive weapons being sent to Cuba. Kennedy's challenge was so tough, and so direct, that the world's diplomats began to maneuver to keep the two major powers from gun-barrel confrontation. There was no doubt after the American President spoke that U.S. Naval Forces would shoot, if necessary, to keep Russia from shipping more offensive arms to Cuba.

At least twelve of the twenty-four Russian vessels which were headed for Cuba when the blockade began turned back. For a tense week the world waited with baited expectations while the United States put the quarantine into effect and kept its armed forces in combat readiness. Finally, Khrushchev offered to remove the missiles, and Kennedy agreed to lift the quarantine and not to invade Cuba. On this basis, the crisis which actually began October 24, 1962, at 10:00 A.M. EDT, came to an end.

Managers Are Individualists

Even if you are a manager of limited experience but average sensitivity, you have observed that your fellow managers exhibit a wide range of personal qualities. This heterogeneous group includes individuals who like people and those who seemingly do not; some who understand people and many who do not; those who demonstrate a capacity for over-riding others and individuals who stimulate willing effort through their influence on others. Among the classification of business leaders are those who have superior mechanical abilities but are largely devoid of administrative skills. You can be a successful manager without a sympathetically warm feeling for others if you understand them; and if you know and use the abilities, skills, qualities, and tools of a good manager.

As a student of people, you may have observed managers who have a wealth of inner warmth for others but fail to express it. Still others may be woefully deficient in anticipating or meeting the reactions of those reporting to them. In spite of evident handicaps to leadership, every one of these managers can be a success on his job.

Deeds Mark the Man

What is the common secret essential? Remember this, it is not what you are but what you do. It's how you use the qualities you have to gain the respect of all with whom you work—associates, peers, subordinates.

One of the best ways for you to create this favorable personal regard necessary to your becoming an on-top manager is to act with confidence. A statement easy to make, but you may well ask, "How do you do it?" First, know what you are doing. Don't try to perform in the dark. Educate yourself. Then, be ready to accept personal responsibility for your actions. Keep in the forefront of your thinking the fact that you are an important person.

KNOW-and-DO

In our economy, opportunities abound. Every manager who applies himself can see many a combination of factors which are just waiting to be exploited. If you make yourself into the kind of manager who sees these openings and drives ahead with evident vigor, you will carry many others along with you. What you are doing by such actions is to convince others that an opening, an opportunity, does in fact exist even though most of your followers may not see it. *For thoughts are seeds of future deeds.* Therefore, you will get better results as a successful manager by finding a way to display confident, on-the-top leadership.

Look Back Only for Future Improvement

The power to dismiss mistakes is as valuable as your foresight in profiting from them. All managers have a reservoir of personal values, acquired through the years, which might be placed in the category of such things as love of country, belief in motherhood, and professed dislike for sin. Here are the kind of rules we live by, and little short of a monumental catastrophe will cause us to change these fundamental personality affectations.

In a healthy minded way, we hammer our actions, even our mistakes, to fit into the mold of our unchanging beliefs. Normally, we are better managers if these deep-down principles are not scarred by on-the-job errors, because excessive worry reduces a manager's effectiveness. However, in the area of management techniques, action consequences should be evaluated and corrections made from experience. As you decide to make these improvements, among the first requirements are: to know what is happening to you as an individual; something about the way in which you come to the conclusion to do the things you do; a knowledge of how you affect others; and what you can do to control and steer your impact upon those with whom you work. It is not practical in most instances to expect a mature manager to change his personality, but all of us can do a better job by making full use of the basic temperament we have cultivated.

Better Managers Are A Must

You, as a manager of the future, will find all of the old problems of the past plus the challenges of the dangerous new crises ahead. Among the new difficulties which cry for original thought and, as yet, have unsuccessful solutions are: *First,* ballooning population growth, both national and world-wide. *Second,* rapid strides in communications which encourage the have-not peoples of the world to demand a better shake. *Third,* merciless domestic and foreign competition for markets. *Fourth,* meeting the shortage of skilled workmen. *Fifth,* encouraging the development and effective use of more and better machines. *Sixth,* throwing off the pall of high taxes. *Seventh,* coping with increased government buying, interference, and control of enterprise. *Eighth,* determining how to best use a limited money supply for productive purposes. *Ninth,* how to most beneficially use a better and better educated population.

While you wrestle with tough new problems, you still hold the primary responsibility to conduct your business affairs so that your enterprise not only operates at a profit but grows as well. Management is much like riding a bicycle —you either move yourself and your organization ahead, or you fall over.

In the face of all the myriad obstacles which the modern manager faces, you should take some encouragement from the fact that, *It is always well to bear in mind that the margin between success and failure is generally very narrow.*[1] The best professional golfer is only a few strokes better than many weekend pleasure seekers. The runner who draws the attention of the crowd is only a split portion of a second faster than the also-rans. So it is with you as a manager; striving to stay on top and to improve with your job, you must have that small edge.

Meeting and Beating Your Competition

To be a winner in management, you need to know, as one of the first requisites, as much as possible about the environment in which you work. For instance, some thirty years ago, the lower and middle levels of managers could get by with the fairly simple duties connected with organizing and directing a group of employees so that acceptable production was maintained.

Today, you as a manager must accept as a part of your assignment the need to continually work for your own personal improvement. You must quickly learn that it is to your own advantage to know something of the materials you use, and the technical detail of the process you supervise. You must be alert to the reactions and special interests of the people reporting to you. It is frequently important that the manager know something of packaging and marketing; and, because the company has community responsibilities, the manager often finds

[1] Rautenstrauch and Villers, *The Economics of Industrial Management,* p. 72

it advantageous to exert some leadership in civic, political, religious, and public school affairs.

In picking one single change which represents the most drastic deviation from management practice of a generation ago, the greatest innovation is the current acceptance within organizational ranks of the need for working toward improved job performance by managers at all levels in business and industry.

No longer is management a profession into which people just happen to drift. The superior college and university graduates are eagerly sought by corporations with job offers as enrollees in training courses for business leadership. Most larger companies have developmental programs for their managers, and many small organizations also promote some activities in this area. As evidence of this wide-spread interest, just one professional society for training and development lists 1,975 firms and organizations with thousands of individual memberships.

Plan Your Attack

To get the most from your self-development efforts, you need a plan for progress. Undirected, unplanned, hard work is not enough. If such were the case, the beavers, the bees, the ants, would rule the animal and insect kingdoms, and the Hebrew savior Moses would not have had to lead the Israelites out of Egyptian bondage.

Few managers make the grade who have not put forth special effort to prepare themselves for the time when the big promotion or just the right job opens up. A KNOW-and-DO manager must be constantly thinking, alert to opening and closing mental doors, and giving answers to problems one after another as situations arise which require a decision. By study to keep abreast of the developments in your profession, and by patient testing of the flood of often contradictory, academic or unfamiliar information about the important job of professional management, you can gain a significant edge over your competitors.

In meeting the complex requirements of the management job today, you must have back-up support. Thus, it is important that you bring your subordinates along, lean on them, and encourage them to use their unique abilities. An alert, progressive, growing, producing unit, group, department or plant is the best recommendation for a manager who seeks to widen his personal margin of competence.

A Manager Does Things

The general manager of the local operation of a large, multi-plant manufacturing company was a far-sighted executive who realized that an important part of his job was to develop future top-management people. One program for this purpose, in which he directly involved himself, was that of providing special growth opportunities to a small, carefully selected group of younger managers, with a sprinkling of non-managers of potentially high caliber. The detailed administration of this improvement effort was assigned to the management development director.

Since the training program was a corporate-wide endeavor, the general manager periodically reported in person, verbally, to a headquarters committee on significant action and results achieved. In preparation for such a report, the general manager called the management development director into his office to discuss the director's most recent written report.

Fully conscious of his boss' interest in this program, the management development director continually checked with subordinates and watched the progress of this group carefully. Thus, he was thoroughly confident that he was on top of every detail the general manager might ask about. To a question by the general manager as to what should be stressed, the director answered, "*First,* the changing personnel in the selected group, promotions out of and additions to the trainee listing. *Second,* the direct use of top-line managers to suggest how the art of managing might best be developed by the members of this selected group. *Third,* exposure of those chosen to the management problems, personnel, and practices in different departments through attendance at staff meetings other than those held in their own units. *Fourth,* the developing managers work on a choice project, its analysis, and their recommended solution to a knotty management problem which could be in their own or another department. *Fifth,* personal interviews with trainees and superiors, plus specific examples of actions taken to meet the particular needs of individual program enrollees."

As the general manager nodded approval, the management development director continued, "We have plans to make use of the special talents represented in the group; for instance, to have the industrial engineer explain to the selectees the concept, progress, and finalizing of a manufacturing plan; to have the financial specialist discuss product pricing and overhead controls." The director added, "One of our problems is to increase the individualized nature of our management improvement opportunities for the members of this group."

The general manager interjected, "Two things disturb me. First, this group is not as high-powered now as it was before all these promotions that you have pointed out; and, second (related of course), we have too many people on this list without a college degree." Then, waiting a moment, he added, "You had better give some attention to these latter items. Thanks for coming in."

From this brief and sketchy example of a typical management conference between a superior and subordinate, we can determine several helpful guides which will be useful to you as managers in staying on top of your jobs.

Areas of Action

Every manager is charged with the primary duty of seeing that problems don't crop up and, if they do, of solving them. A standard pattern to help you meet this requirement assists you in becoming a better professional manager.

In our conference example, both the general manager and the management development director were operating in three distinct categories. These can be designated as *generalist, specialist,* and *personal* leaders.

The Generalist

In the generalist classification, you should consider all of the manager's performance KNOW-and-DO requirements which must be handled by a successful leader whether he is supervising a manufacturing crew, a group of engineering technicians, directing your finance department, or happens to be the general manager of your company.

Examples of the Generalist Duties. Such things as the value of a challenging assignment, the excitement of the successful job performance, the personal stimulation to an ambitious manager when he is given opportunities to prepare himself for tomorrow's heavier responsibilities, are valuable tools for the KNOW-and-DO manager, whatever his present station in his management organization.

Success as a professional manager of the future will demand more imagination and individuality than has been required in the past. You need to practice brain-stretching exercises to visualize new and better ways of moving your company and yourself ahead.

Whatever your management job, you must exhibit enthusiasm and work to create this quality in those reporting to you. As Emerson wrote, *Nothing great was ever achieved without enthusiasm.* So it might also be said when the leader and his followers have this motivator in action, you have one of the most important KNOW-and-DO management qualities going for you.

Operating as a generalist, the good manager cultivates ideas. You must appreciate that these are the "stuff" which makes the future. Ideas are too easily lost. When one pops up, nourish it and protect it, until it can be carefully examined.

As a KNOW-and-DO manager, improve your natural gifts and don't forget to encourage your subordinates to do the same. The expanding and honing of these qualities will help you to better interpret the shades of gray between the clear black and white, right and wrong, which add to the difficulty of correct decision-making as you progress up the management ladder.

The good manager's KNOW-and-DO performance is not entirely confined to the more effective uses of people, since there is also a need for understanding and using fundamental cost and efficiency procedure or methods. However, people, and how he works with them, will determine his success or failure.

The Generalist at Work. The example of the meeting between the general manager and the management development director clearly showed the participants' concern with a broad look ahead. Also evident was the training program's targets for accomplishment, the importance of time, plus a stressing of the company's organizational goals in an understandable fashion.

Further actions of value to a manager, regardless of his job assignment, were the management development director's acceptance of the importance of permitting individuals to develop their most valuable skills. This fact was also confirmed by the general manager with his approval of the program and the feature of drawing on the special talents of the group. In the reference to organization and its values, there was agreement upon unity of specialization as an aid in reaching an objective, but the general manager quickly switched to the importance of the individual improving himself.

Another quality, skill, and ability, which the meeting itself illustrates, is that of communication. No one interested in professional management disputes the importance of increased attention to the exchange of ideas not only between all levels of management but also between management and employees. For better understanding, face-to-face discussion usually gets the best results.

The manager demonstrated the application of the generally accepted principle of sincerity of interest in the subordinate's job and respect for other's opinions, which are helpful management tools in securing willing cooperation.

The Specialist

This is the next fundamental for the KNOW-and-DO manager. In each specific management assignment, we find singular functional duties which must be performed.

The actual details of just what is to be accomplished will differ with the particular job, but all directional task responsibilities should be included in these three broad duties: *planning, action, and measure of results.*

It is difficult to conceive of a management assignment which you could properly handle without setting some targets for accomplishment; that is, keeping clearly before you what is expected from your group, section, department, or plant. The professional manager must also look ahead, think, and secure what is needed to meet his job requirements. These essentials include the people with the necessary skills, appropriate materials and possibly a continuous source of supply, efficient processing, and the equipment and machines to produce a competitive product or service.

A manager's on-the-job actions are concerned with carrying out plans previously made, correcting and developing new ideas, and meeting emergencies. Most organizations establish policies or rules as a guide to secure consistency at all levels throughout the supervisory structure. These relatively permanent, broad, general, directional guides include instructions in handling routine types of situations, such as employment and termination procedures, vacations, reporting absences, and numerous other similar occurrences. As time passes and an organization grows, the area covered by policy expands, forcing the supervisor to be alert to new developments.

One of the professional manager's most rewarding job experiences is that of providing assignments which challenge the subordinate's growth potential. This enables the superior to give his attention to duties which are more likely to result in furthering his own desires for a better job as well as creating promotional opportunities for a well-prepared, follow-up man.

Management actions which further mutual understanding among all employees tend to reduce the need for disciplinary actions. A good supervisor should attempt to learn as much as possible about the people under his direction and use this knowledge with patience, understanding, and consideration. Skill in giving just the right kind of orders can provide the essential motivation for an ambitious supervisor to fill his role as the catalyst which makes things happen.

Another important functional duty which is essential in all management assignments is follow-up, a means of determining results. As a professional supervisor, you use this necessary control medium to develop subordinates as well as to determine that the job gets done. Producing so many pieces or things in a given period of time does not necessarily develop better managers, so the forward thinking superior finds some means of interjecting man-growth into his "Measure-of-Results" methods.

The Specialist at Work. If we examine this superior-subordinate discussion as it relates to the management development director's specific assignment, three distinct functions become apparent. *First,* the director had spent some planning time on the program. He indicated attention to creativity and working toward established objectives. *Second,* the actions outlined seemed to be in accord with his superior's thinking about what should be done, and the details followed a logical pattern toward a satisfactory training accomplishment. *Third,* the "Measure-of-Results" feature of his specialist role was evidenced when the director volunteered that one of his problems was to further individualize the program. The general manager established some additional goals for his subordinate when he directed greater attention to improving the quality of the people selected for training. The boss was specific in stating that the group members should have more formal education, preferably, a college degree.

The Personal Leader

Personal Leadership is a third grouping of performance qualifications in which you as a successful professional manager must prove yourself. While it is a difficult KNOW-and-DO area requiring self-discipline and even personality redirection, it is also a more manageable area because the ambitious supervisor can learn, use, and develop his talents as a leader without restrictions or special approval.

Evident intelligence, personal drive, administrative skill, general knowledge, and leadership attraction were five distinct behavior practices discovered in proven managers through interviews, tests, opinions, and performance analysis. However, of equal validity is the fact that each of the five listed qualities make sense to an experienced supervisor as goals to attain. For instance, it would be difficult to find a veteran KNOW-and-DO manager who would dispute the importance of the knowledge and performance necessary to meet the *Evident-Intelligence* requirement, since the exercise of judgment and decision-making is an often repeated action in his normal workday.

Personal Drive is likewise beyond dispute as a requirement for successful leadership. This quality as related to professional management can be called "the urge to accomplish." In part, this exercise of initiative springs from an individual's attitude and in part from his recognition of the opportunities for pay-off actions.

Administrative Skill, as practiced by the KNOW-and-DO manager, includes planning, directing, controlling, and every-day maintenance of productivity in striving toward established objectives. This skills category is characteristically the most tangible and easily measured gauge of the supervisor's performance. Therefore, a knowledgeable professional manager should use care to avoid placing undue importance upon the "doing" part of a subordinate manager's job in appraising his total performance.

In the *General Knowledge,* leadership strength section, you can verify practical utility by on-the-job application. Such proof is apparent when a manager solves a problem by drawing upon his stored fund of knowledge which has been accumulated from many sources over an extended period of time.

In the *Leadership-Attraction* strength category, you should think realistically of the importance of human relationship in the job situation. As was true in the discussion of the other qualities, abilities, and skills of the KNOW-and-DO manager, this is an area where you can improve your on-the-job performance. As you attempt to build up your personal leadership performance, remember that wisdom is knowing what to do next, skill is knowing how to do it, and virtue is doing it.

The Personal Leader at Work. This management requirement is also evidenced by demonstrated on-the-job performance. In the conference of the general manager and the management development director, the first power source is used for an example. Alertness and intelligence could be seen in the lucid account of program activities given by the director and also in the closing statements of the general manager.

The second power source, *Personal Drive,* is shown by the work which the director and his associates exerted to help make the program a useful improvement tool for the prospective top-level managers.

The third power source, *Administrative Skill,* can be thought of as the knack of fitting things into their proper places. In our conference example, the logical procedure of the discussion suggests that the two managers exercised a measure of discipline in the balance-required area.

The fourth power source, *General Knowledge,* is a fascinating one because it often goes unrecognized. However, all good managers use their knowledge tank every day, when they draw upon stored-up experience, reading, ideas, and information to meet on-the-job problems. The director undoubtedly drew upon his past study and experience in originating, checking the details, and guiding the training program. The general manager "came up" with the college-degree requirement because his information reservoir alerted him to the fact that general education was valuable to a top manager.

The fifth power source is the attraction for others which enables you as a manager to obtain the willing cooperation of all your associates. Some may call it "personal magnetism," others "empathy." It stems from your total personality and how you use it in your contacts with other people. In our superior-subordinate conference example, this quality could be noted in the general manager as he listened to the director's report and in the way he directed further action in improving the group's quality. This is an intangible but powerful management requirement, difficult to put down on paper; but extensive discussion of all these management tools will be found in the succeeding chapters.

The Success Pattern of a KNOW-and-DO Manager

You are in an enviable position for which you pay a price in tension, pressure, isolation, and in making tough decisions.

You have a right to maintain your own personality, but you must earn the respect of others. You can do this by studying your job, establishing self-confidence, and learning from experience.

Better managers are necessary for the future. To be a winner, you must follow a plan. Your progress schedule must be based upon superior performance in three areas: as a generalist, as a specialist, and as a personal leader.

Chapter 2: Know What You Are Doing

An interesting question asked of fifty-three eager young employees recently promoted into their first management job was, "Is the ability to effectively communicate with others of more value to you on your present assignment, or do you think it will be of greater importance in the higher-level management position you expect to occupy in the future?" The question was asked as part of a written developmental review session; therefore, one person's answer did not influence another's. Significantly, every man, without exception, answered that communicative skill, the ability to get thoughts across to others, was in their judgment essential to leadership success and of equal importance at all levels of management.

Supporting their conclusion on the importance of communication, some time back it was determined by a survey that members of the Young Presidents Organization normally spend better than three-fourths of their working time in direct face-to-face conversation with people, talking about production, sales, finance, community, public relations, personnel, general administration, and miscellaneous affairs.

Most experienced managers will concede that you must have an understanding between yourself and other people if you expect to direct subordinates, get production, and accomplish results. Thus, you should be vitally interested in anything which is of such evident and universal importance to a manager. For self-improvement, you might ask, "How can I add to my performance score in this area?"

Identify Your Target

The German dictator Hitler, with the greatest armed might ever assembled by a single nation at the time, in 1939 and the early '40s directed his forces to the East through Poland, West through France, North into Russia, and South into North Africa. Charging around in all directions probably was the chief reason for his inability to win the war. No doubt history will confirm that the Austrian house painter did not have a progress plan of what he wanted to accomplish, no sensible estimate of the possible cost, and no realistic assessment of the value of a victory.

As a manager, he was a flop. The later, widely publicized plot by his generals to destroy der Fuhrer, although it did not result in his assassination because of a last minute change in schedule, was successfully engineered because Hitler failed to communicate with his essential subordinates. Again, he failed to recognize a leader's need to keep informed. It seems certain that if he didn't know about the broad defection this event portended, he did not have a finger on the pulse of his organization, thus typifying the expression, "If you don't know where you are going, any road will get you there."

Communication Aids—Knowledge of the Jobs You Supervise

A veteran manager earns respect from his subordinates if he can very quickly determine why a key machine on the production line stops running, look at a balance sheet and spot the figures that are out of place, or grab a slide rule and calculate why a structural design is faulty. Subordinates admire this evidence of know-how from the boss, and quite often the superior enjoys performing such tasks; but, the manager must make a careful judgment as to where he can best spend his time.

The technical experience gained by a manager coming up through the ranks often supplies detailed knowledge, particularly if the individual is mechanically inclined. However, in a rapidly changing technology, some effort must be exerted to keep current; and the question arises, "What is best for the company?" The level of management also must be considered since the higher the rank, the greater the variety of technical operations reporting to higher management. The kind of work and numbers of people also make it difficult to set a positive rule for all situations.

Mechanical Ability at the First Level of Management

In most shops if you are the supervisor immediately over the workmen, knowing how the jobs should be done will give a distinct advantage over a fellow supervisor lacking such knowledge. You can go ahead with greater confidence to improve your proficiency in planning, budgeting, and working with personnel. This assurance also allows you to exercise a reasonable control with a minimum of time-consuming effort.

However, even here there is a danger of placing too much emphasis on technical details. If the supervisor isn't careful, his position can degenerate into something approaching that of a mechanical troubleshooter. At best, it must be recognized that repairing tools and doing the work which should be performed by other employees takes time away from the prime function of a manager—to direct the work of others.

As a help in handling this judgment problem, a manager should consider:

Using Specialized Staff Support

An employee working outside the production organization, either management or non-management, with the assignment to assist the line production supervisor can concentrate his attention upon his specialty. Preventive maintenance can help avoid breakdowns in the area of machine repairs. Production control and planning specialists can aid the manager in budgeting and setting objectives. Personnel people can assist the manager with information on policy interpretations and customary practices.

In each of these examples cited and in many others not mentioned, specialized staff help can be valuable to the company. As in all good things, however, there are some disadvantages. For instance, a strong-minded, willful staff man can short-circuit the line manager's communications by assuming authority to direct the production employees. A staff man's function is to advise the line manager and direct production employees only when specifically requested to do so by the line supervisor whose accountability for results cannot be passed on to anyone else.

If staff assistance is not wisely used, the development of a line manager can be hampered. Often the easy course for a supervisor is not to stretch his brain for the best answer to a difficult problem, but rather to rely on the advice of a convenient staff specialist.

The respect of subordinates and, likewise, a manager's ability to effectively communicate with those reporting to him, depends upon how the boss handles his need for specialized help. This is true whether we refer to a first-line foreman or any other management position up to and including the chairman of the board.

General Guides on Technical Know-How

In the broad look at *his* future in *his* own profession, a manager should remember that he is supposed to direct the work of others, not perform the operations himself. It is often said that a professional manager should be able to direct an operation even though he is not familiar with the specific technical details. However, the question continues to arise, "Can an engineering design supervisor successfully manage a group of draftsmen without being able to read a blueprint or handle a slide rule?" The correct answer to such a question can be both "yes" and "no" because it depends, among other things, upon the level of supervision. Generally speaking, the further away the manager is from the actual workmen, the less real need he has for detailed technical knowledge of the job. The chairman of the board, president, and plant manager obviously are unfamiliar with most of the operations for which they are responsible. In fact, the vice president of engineering who is never without his slide rule may be expressing a lack of full commitment to management as a profession. Subconsciously, he can be alibiing: If I fail as a supervisor, I'll still be able to go back to my old job.

The size of the organization also has some relationship to the question as does type of product or service. The level of skill of the workmen, physical layout of the operation, and many other contingencies could have some bearing upon the amount of technical knowledge the manager must have to properly direct those employees reporting to him.

Balanced View

These unknowns are the reason why *A Balanced View* is a necessary factor to consider in your attempts to improve your performance in the total management job. In most situations, the amount and way in which the manager gets the technical knowledge he needs must be left to his own best judgment. As resource material for more dynamic exchange of ideas between yourself and the people who make your views a reality, it is a manager's responsibility to consider such mundane things as liquid capital, floor space, and equipment needs. While such items are not as exciting nor difficult to properly manage as people, they have their place in your total job problem. They should not be overlooked even though the human animal is the focus of your greatest attention.

Another area in which you as a manager must allot some of your time, energy and judgment is the personal evaluation of your own performance. In this endeavor, you may find it helpful to consider these questions:

- What recent successes have I had, and why?
- Where have I made mistakes, and why?
- Just what am I trying to accomplish?
- Do I take time to consider the most essential actions to take?
- Am I attempting to find better methods of achieving results?
- Would a budget or job performance standards be helpful?
- What do I know about the people and operations of associated departments?

- Are there some new ways to stimulate others to think, work, and produce more?
- Am I overlooking some outstanding performance by employees which deserves special recognition?

Possibly one or more of these questions might suggest to you some place for the use of balanced judgment.

In mulling over these questions, an interesting fact is noticeable: all are directly related to people, each of whom is a complex mixture of qualities, abilities, skills, and energies in amounts which make him an unique personality. The manager's challenge is to communicate with this individual so that he has the opportunity to deliver products and/or services at the top quality and quantity of which he is capable with willingness and enthusiasm.

When you as a manager wholly accept and act on the knowledge that your future is better served if you learn more about, work more with, and get along better with people, you are less likely to hear your boss say one day, "You have been weighed in the balances and found wanting."

It's Easier to Communicate with People You Know

A potent medium for improving your management performance is to acquire a thorough knowledge of the individuals under your direction. Such an understanding is necessary to properly guide subordinates, meet their wants, and effectively exchange meaningful understandings for better job results. The most evident and practical reason for a manager to know his subordinates is so that you can make full use of their most valuable skills at every opportunity. Complete information is also necessary to enable the alert supervisor to exhibit leadership skill in recognizing, guiding, and directing the special personality quirks as well as strong and weak characteristics which exist in all those reporting to him.

It is only when a manager really knows his subordinates that he can make full use of the activating power of individual recognition. Since people are different, to get the greatest benefits from rewards they should be given those things which have the greatest appeal to them. If one of your staff subordinates does his best work in supporting shop people, put him there as much as possible. Assign people where they deliver best and willingly.

Having set forth this requirement as somewhat of a key to the use of this series of good management tools, some attention should rightfully be given to suggestions as to how the supervisor may best "gain a thorough knowledge of the individuals under his direction."

One of the first things which you as a supervisor must do is to satisfy yourself that you have a clear picture of the working characteristics of your organization. To gain this needed knowledge, you will find it helpful to ask yourself these questions: Is the general performance climate "results oriented," or is it toward a social club atmosphere? Is the exercise of initiative a natural way of operating, or is this vital quality stifled? Is there an inclination to help each other, or tension caused by backbiting? Is there enthusiasm for the work, or lack of it?

The only way to get answers to these questions is by first-hand, on-the-job observation and action. Most experienced managers will agree that it is in these contacts with people reporting to you that a supervisor either makes or breaks his career as a professional leader.

Because talking with individuals and groups of subordinates is so important, the manager must be well prepared for these encounters.

Expressive Episodes

Exchanges with your associates provide an opportunity to learn from the other person as you, at the same time, reveal something of yourself to them. For this reason, it seems proper to term personal contacts *Expressive Episodes.* Such interchanges should not be thought of as a single conversation or event since they may well encompass a series of contacts or incidents. For instance, some of you are no doubt familiar with the biblical story which tells us how the great King David, ruler of all Israel, strangely restless just before sunset on a balmy spring evening, strolled slowly out across his Jerusalem palace roof. As he idly gazed over into a nearby government housing project, it was no accident that his eyes fairly "bugged out" when they riveted on a sight carefully prepared for the king's regular evening saunter. David saw the luscious female Bathsheba spread out in an inviting posture, dressed in nothing but her birthday suit, beside the otherwise deserted community swimming pool. In the fading light, the alluring female stretched and rolled on the pool side like a sensuous panther. This was the beginning of an expressive episode which Israel's king bungled. If David had correctly analyzed the planned intent of the original incident and the events which followed, the history of the Hebrew kingdom would have been different because his enthrallment with Bathsheba caused him to abandon a lifetime management plan which had raised him from an unknown shepherd boy to the throne of the mightiest empire of its day. The king lost the respect of his army and his people; he neglected his administrative duties and even the training of his sons. Unquestionably, the happenings which started on that quiet spring evening marked the beginning of the decline in Israel's fortunes which led finally to the destruction of the nation in 586 B.C.

Among other things, the biblical king failed to concern himself, as many unsuccessful managers do, with a key question; "What makes people do what they do?" At times the answer is, "Logical thinking." But, contrary to the operating practices of many supervisors, subordinates and superiors are often more influenced by their feelings than by rational thinking.

What People Work For

If you really want to be a KNOW-and-DO leader, then nail down prominently, where you will be reminded frequently, an important axiom; namely, *People work to get what they want.* And the priority of these desires usually goes in this order: *First,* food and shelter, the immediate necessities for existence. *Second,* future security, some assurance against becoming economically destitute because of lack of money, poor health, old age. *Third,* association with your peers and acceptance by them. *Fourth,* gaining self-esteem, self-confidence, personal status. *Fifth,* creativity, a chance to fulfill what the individual thinks is his complete potential.

These desires are, of course, very general, and they vary widely with individuals. However, the ambitious manager can usually be confident that, when good wages tend to assure employees plenty to eat and wear and a place to live, the incentive to work harder for just more money alone tends to be less and less attractive. It is then that he works harder willingly for something higher on his value scale, possibly security for old age, sickness and hospital benefits, job security, total economic safety. In recent years these have been important demands in every major union contract negotiated by industry's highest paid workmen.

After passing this point, the potent energizers are highly personal needs, such as a feeling of belonging, association, acceptance by others, mutual exchange of friendship and love, self-confidence, independence, achievement, competence, knowledge, status, recognition, and appreciation. They represent a different kind of motivator in the sense that they are never satisfied. For instance, a person can consume only so much food and shelter. After reaching the saturation point, their motivation weakens. A recent advertisement by a sales incentive company in the *Wall Street Journal* posed this interesting idea when it announced, *Men will work harder for status than they will for cash. If you want proof, call the E. F. MacDonald Company.* A manager on his way to the top can't overlook the notable difference between the physical and intangible personal activators, and the fact that the latter must be constantly renewed. They seem to feed upon themselves. When an individual earns compliments and recognition, he strives to gain further compliments and recognition.

The boss, struggling to do a better directional job, must realize that interference with or denial of these wants kills initiative, the creative spark, and an employee's willingness to strive for a better total job performance. The resulting frustration of employees can cause indifference, hostility, and antagonism. At the very least, his attention is directed away from his job toward some activity which fills the want void created by the circumstances of his work.

By talking with subordinates frequently about job details, the boss lends importance to the subordinate's assignment. A recent report in the newspaper announced the resignation of a U.S. Senator's administrative assistant. The subordinate said, "My job was not challenging, and the title was merely a high-sounding designation for a handler of office affairs." The Senator, speaking of his subordinate, said, "He was a good man and a capable staffman. I'm sorry he left the staff." This seems to be an example of a breakdown of relationships due to neglected communications. In this situation both superior and subordinate lost, and the damage could have been avoided by attention to and more conversation about the job between the two principals. The lack of importance which the subordinate attached to his job could have been corrected if the boss had clearly spelled out his understudy's accountability in his work.

Your superior has a better chance of achieving what is expected from your personal leadership if you are informed and make use of the goals, objectives, and targets for the unit, the department, section, group, or crew. You will also be more likely to make your full contribution to the efforts of the organization if you know where your company is trying to go. This knowledge enhances your ability to give and spring back, compromise and hold tight in accordance with your best judgment in the interest of your organization. "As the Duke of Wellington once remarked, Napoleon planned his campaigns just as you might make a splendid harness. It looks very well, and answers very well, until it gets broken; and then you are done for. Now I made my campaigns of ropes. If anything went wrong, I tied a knot and went on." [1]

Healthy Mutual Dependencies

Better communications and increased understanding comes about if both superior and subordinate realize that each contributes to the total team effort. You can encourage better total performance if you let your key subordinates know that you look to them for support. Many times, particularly in the technical area, special recognition for unusual talents pays off in new machines and methods which mark your crew as live-wires in the eyes of your superiors and the entire organization. It is not just coincidence that most companies get the biggest majority of suggested new ideas from a very small number of departments.

As a manager interested in values to be obtained from better communications, here are some suggestions for finding your best men. *First,* look for the individuals who express a belief in the importance of their work. *Second,* discover those who find a challenge in their job. *Third,* find those who exhibit enthusiasm and strive to get out of the ruts of habits and customary procedure. *Fourth,* another key tip-off to watch for is the individual interested in his own self-improvement. These will be the people to watch, help, and give opportunities to stimulate their special talents.

[1] Cerami, *How to Solve Management Problems,* p. 120

Imitating the Boss

One of the factual realities of organizations is for the followers to imitate the leader. Cartoonists have long used this theme to give a humorous turn to what most knowledgeable observers recognize as realism. Normally overlooked is the fact that the superior at whatever spot he may be found in the management line generally has very little conception of just how much influence he exercises over those reporting to him. Indeed, the subordinate does not often realize himself that a mannerism, a bias, a way of talking with people, a priority order of doing things has become a part of his way of supervising until a careful objective look reveals that he is largely a replica of his boss.

Thus, when you carry out your exchanges in the expressive episodes, one of the first things you must appreciate is the weight of your influence on the subordinate. For instance, you, as the boss, can do your organization a favor if you can restrain the natural human impulse to expect the people reporting to you to do the job exactly as you would do it if you were in the subordinate's place. Such close control restricts individual creativity, hampers new ideas and the development of better ways of doing the job. You will find as you grow as a manager that the greatest return to your company will occur if your boss also improves as a manager. Experience shows that your company will not get real payoff results for itself as an organization from a subordinate improvement program unless the superiors also grow. The boss must become involved. Management development is not an activity for which you can hire a consultant, approve some program that he advocates, and then sit back and wait for the phenomenal results. If top management is not willing to take an active part in the development program, then the company will be the loser. This is not to say that the individual manager cannot improve without his boss' support. In the past many good managers have raised their status and position on their own, and an even greater number are doing it today. You are your own best investment, and I believe we all know that experience has shown that the thing to which we devote the greatest attention usually returns the favor. Growing as a manager is a personal matter, and one of the make-or-break payoff areas is in the expressive episodes.

You're on the Right Track

You're on the right track when your subordinates are free and candid in their discussion with you. This is the proper atmosphere for a productive expressive episode. Recently, a prominent management consultant reported an experience in which the president of a large company with extensive operations in all sections of the country became suspicious of how a pet management plan of his, call it *X*, was working. The consultant, a college professor, was called in and, during his briefing for a tour of all the nation-wide facilities, the president explained that the announced purpose of the trip was to be educational for the professor. In reality, the president wanted to check the real workings of plan *X* since his curiosity was aroused because invariably all reports coming to him were glowing endorsements of what was being accomplished through its use. The consultant found that without a single exception those who were supposedly benefiting from the plan seldom recognized it when a casual inquiry was made. After more searching questioning, the descriptive brochure detailing the workings of plan *X* came out of a buried file cabinet with admittedly no use ever having been made of the president's pet. Obviously this president has a tremendous communications barrier, and this is certainly *not* the climate for effective expressive episodes.

Such a miscarriage of information is not limited to top management. The same management consultant also related the case of a safety training program. The action phase of this effort was to have the first-level foreman hold a short monthly crew meeting at which he stressed various parts of the company's plans to encourage safer working conditions. The worthwhile endeavor degenerated to the point where a staff man prepared material intended as a speech for the foreman, but this alleged manager was always too busy to make the presentation and simply attached some glowing statistics to the written material as evidence of results and sent it to his superior each month as mission accomplished.

If you are going to grow to be a KNOW-and-DO manager, it is up to you to set the tone so that those reporting to you can and will be honest in their expressive episodes with you.

"Go" Tests for Your Expressive Episodes

First, your subordinates are obviously glad to discuss their real job interest. As the boss, you recognize that when a supervisor talks about the detailed performance of an individual or the step-by-step results of a process you are getting the straight "dope." *Second,* the people reporting to you have pride in their work when they freely volunteer new ways of doing things. Enthusiasm for the job portends a fruitful expressive episode. *Third,* conditions are right for a good expressive episode if subordinates want to discuss real job problems. *Fourth,* when you are the kind of manager who reflects a willingness to help subordinates with a problem, your expressive episodes will be worthwhile. *Fifth,* when those reporting to you can continue their normal work tempo if you unexpectedly appear in their work area, relationships are right for the expressive episodes.

"Scrub" Tests for Your Expressive Episodes

First, an extreme "no go" for a manager's expressive episodes is the "silent treatment." In this situation, subordinates ignore their superior's presence as much as possible. Nobody seems to care whether he is there or not. Further, nobody has a problem to discuss with him. His acceptance is so bad that nobody even wants to tell him their troubles. *Second,* you are misinformed by those reporting to you. Whether this is intentional or not, it is fatal to a successful expressive episode. A first step in correcting this situation is to carefully determine whether the fault is an honest error, just carelessness, or deliberately misleading. *Third,* subordinates waste time gossiping. Spotting this warning signal requires some alertness on your part, because the real intent is often camouflaged, often by a phoney job problem. While this is usually just a nuisance, it serves to hamper the value of an expressive episode. How many times have you felt compelled to listen politely while a "motor lipped" associate rolled on and on, relating innumerable details, or bringing in irrelevant comments, important only to him? *Fourth,* watch your expressive episodes when your sudden appearance on the work scene causes a nervous flurry of increased activity. Such a reaction usually suggests that subordinates feel that there is something to be hidden.

Changing the Expressive-Episode Atmosphere to "Go"

First, you must set your own thinking straight by honestly reminding yourself that really lasting results cannot be accomplished if you approach this critically important management function as a simple manipulative technique. Frankness begets frankness, so be a mature enough manager to be more than just a clever operator as you strive to improve your expressive episodes.

Second, think specifically of who you want to talk with and what you want to talk about.

Third, be sure that you have clearly in mind what you want to accomplish.

Fourth, it is helpful if you can get favorable attention at the start of the expressive episode. Depending upon what your past relationship has developed, you should try to encourage the other person's "want-to-listen" interest. Often this might be a friendly "hello," a remark about a notable accomplishment of the person. Anything which recognizes the other's importance is effective, but let's emphasize again that it must be sincere.

Fifth, don't let disagreement upset you. Often the only way you can get full value from your subordinate is to hear him out. Even if you have anticipated his objections and can logically show him some genuine benefits through agreeing with the point of view you are presenting, don't be too quick to try to prove your point. In your impatience to get the job done, it is very easy to build future trouble for yourself by brushing aside the other person's thoughts, suggestions, ideas, and objections as of no importance.

Sixth, if you want to be a KNOW-and-DO manager, show by your actions in the expressive episodes: that you consider the other person important; that he has a right to his own view and his personal opinions; that he should express these thoughts and have them seriously considered; and, if it is decided to act contrary to his views, be sure he is told your reason why it was necessary.

Selected Types of Expressive Episodes

As a growing manager, you will find it valuable to use expressive episodes:

1. To keep others informed;
2. To get needed information;
3. To give directions;
4. To make a required correction;
5. To build another's confidence.

Reasons Why Better Managers Keep Others Informed

While you are working on your job to develop yourself into a KNOW-and-DO manager, it is a tremendous aid toward this goal if you can have others look to you for leadership. Since the leader is the person who knows "what is going on," it is in your own interest to keep subordinates, superiors, and all associates informed.

As a good manager, it is not enough to simply build your own prestige. In addition, you must have the support of others. Your subordinates, superiors, suppliers, and buyers make judgments about you, based in large measure upon what they see and hear. The ambitious manager will make sure that these people, important to him and his company, get correct, timely, and up-to-date information. Keep in mind that a man's judgment is no better than the information in his possession.

Another important reason for the manager to give out information arises because, as you take the time and trouble to advise a person about the company, something interesting regarding the department, some future plans, difficult problems, or other items of news in which the listener is interested, you are saying to him, "You are an important person, worthy of my special attention." From this position, it is only a short step to looking to you for sound advice and leadership.

Many people outside the competitive business world distrust management, not because of what they know, but because of what they think. Even some employees, not only workmen but some lower-level managers as well, are cynical of management's motives largely because of faulty, little or no information. Therefore a final important reason for using expressive episodes to pass out information is to avoid distrust, dissention, misunderstanding, and hostility.

Your Guides for "Pass-On" Information

As a growing manager, you should use information in your expressive episodes to *first,* build your personal prestige; *second,* guide the thinking of others; *third,* create in your listener's mind a cooperative bias; and, *fourth,* avoid misunderstandings.

Be an Interesting Informer

Prepare yourself by, *first,* knowing a great deal about a lot of things which have a bearing on your current job assignment. If you are a finance manager, be an expert on such things as costs, budgets, capital assets. As a manufacturing supervisor, be up-to-date on schedule controls, the latest planning methods and incentive possibilities. *Second,* have some side-line specialties on which you can contribute authoritative information. Some of these special areas can be trends of the total economy, your local school system, taxes, politics, art. Any important interest area in which you make yourself the person to talk with helps you meet the information pass-on guides. *Third,* use what you have. Don't hide your enthusiasm for your favorite subject. You will seldom oversell in passing on information.

Store Up Ammunition

Numerous studies, surveys, and experience show that most successful managers are inveterate readers. As a growing supervisor, keep up on the latest news through newspapers, news magazines and trade publications. Don't overlook your plant papers and newsletters. Be alert in staff meetings. When you attend a lecture, don't just sit there. Take notes. It is a good habit even if you find after reviewing them that the speaker failed to say anything new.

It is just as much fun and a lot more worthwhile to read something lasting and useful than to spend the same amount of time watching a worn out TV plot unfold. You'll find that a really engrossing side-line will serve as a self-disciplining help.

Cautions in Talking

A knowledgeable manager picks up many items of a proprietary nature which can be of substantial value to a competitor. Be on guard against hurting your company. A *second* item to watch is the use of good judgment and proper taste. Most likely you shouldn't tell about the traveling salesman's latest adventures with the farmer's daughter at a women's club convention. *Third,* endeavor to make your comments serve one of the "pass-on guides" or some other beneficial purpose. *Fourth,* make it factual; an expert cannot afford to become known as a faulty informer.

Expressive Episodes Can Give You Need-To-Know Information

A growing manager can use some "listening between the lines" in his expressive episodes to uncover signs of future trouble. When a manager has a behind-schedule production output, a material shortage, or a difficult "must-be-handled" personnel problem, it is not helpful to have the boss say, "You shouldn't have gotten yourself into that position," even though he is right.

When you know about a developing trouble situation before it happens, you can correct it and add to your reputation as a management winner. You should use these methods to avoid trouble. *First,* make a checklist of possible problem areas. This can be tools, equipment, materials, improper methods or deficient subordinates. *Second,* take corrective action or develop alternatives if it is temporarily impractical to avoid the difficulty you have uncovered. Often different tools, idle equipment, or substitute materials can be used in an emergency. Improper methods can be adjusted if they are discovered in time. *Third,* deficient subordinates can pose a much more difficult problem because just finding the source of the trouble often tests your metal as a manager. Some of the "may be's" are:

1. *Misplaced, misassigned, lack of skill.* The correction in such instances might be transfer or training.

2. *Non-cooperative attitude.* This means you should make a greater effort to plant your own want-to-help concept in the mind of those employees reporting to you. Avoid fault-finding, but see if there isn't a better and easier way for the subordinate to do his job.

3. *Hostile attitude.* See if you can take some of the blame for what may be bothering the subordinate who is performing below an acceptable standard. It might change his thinking if you encouraged him to bring any unusual job situations to your attention. You might try giving such an individual more job accountability.

As you endeavor to become a better professional manager, don't overlook the value of expressive episodes as a test of your working atmosphere.

Using Expressive Episodes to Give Directions

Lord Tennyson immortalized six hundred plus British cavalrymen in the poem titled *The Charge of the Light Brigade.* This action was a part of the battle of Balaklava in the Crimean war in which Lord Raglan, the British commander-in-chief, for some unexplainable reason allowed his direction to Lord Cardigan, the commander of the light brigade, to become so garbled that the six hundred disciplined horsemen rode into a death trap in a futile attack upon the whole Russian army. Looking backward over more than a hundred years, it is difficult to understand why the two lords did not engage in less restricted expressive-episode exchanges to save some soldiers' lives and turn a stalemate into a victory.

On your job as a manager, of course, you could not get the blind obedience which characterized the cavalrymen at Balaklava. However, you are required to direct the activities of those reporting to you.

While you would like to have your subordinates' willing cooperation, it usually seems that people automatically resent having their superiors tell them what to do.

Overcoming Boss Resentment

Often the way in which you give directions will directly affect the subordinate's performance on the job. This is an exchange between a first-level manager and his subordinate Joe. The manager said, "Joe, move all the stock out of Crib 27. Take it over to Section 18." That is a good, clear order, and Joe went ahead and carried it out. While he was doing it, these thoughts went through his mind, "I just moved that stock in yesterday. It took me all day to get it in there. What is the matter with this guy? Doesn't he know what he is doing? Does he think that all I have to do is 'move-it-in, move-it-out, move-it-in, move-it-out?' It's a wonder we ever get anything done with bosses like him running the place." Joe was getting paid for doing the moving job, but he certainly wasn't happy doing it. Why? Most likely because almost everybody likes their work to have a purpose. Undoubtedly, Joe would have cooperated more willingly had his boss said, "Joe, move all the stock from Crib 27 over to Section 18. We need the area where Crib 27 is located for a new multimillion dollar contract which is going to make everybody's job more secure." People feel better about following directions if they are aware of why their job needs to be done.

Telling subordinates *why* also increases your acceptance as the boss by those reporting to you. Here is an on-the-job example. Charlie, a maintenance manager, told Sam, an experienced electrician, "Go to the supply room and get one-hundred feet of 1″ conduit and lay it under this fresh concrete so the finishers can complete their job." Sam went to the supply room and found they were out of 1″ conduit but had plenty of ¾″. Having made many similar installations in the past, Sam thought, "The machine going in there will only use a four-horsepower motor—maybe at most a five—so ¾″ is large enough. I'm sure Charlie wasn't thinking. Maybe I should call him, but then he always bites your head off when you question an order. I'll just go ahead. He'll never know the difference." So the ¾″ conduit was used to do the job. The next day, when wiring workmen attempted to string two #6 wires through the newly installed conduit, it wouldn't go. This set off a rash of recriminations as to whose fault it was, which went all the way up the management line to the superintendent because this was a rush job for a newly developed machine which required a fifteen-horsepower motor, making the heavier wires essential. The fact that the job had to be done all over again was not only expensive but also did not help Charlie's stature as a manager; in fact, the whole supervisory line suffered from reflected blame.

Proper give and take in the expressive episodes between Sam and Charlie could have built an understanding and respect between superior and subordinate so that this mistake would not have happened.

You should remember that the manager and those reporting to him are a team. Each must take a portion of the accountability for the successful carrying out of an order.

Effective Expressive Episodes Help in Correcting Others

One of your most distasteful jobs is correcting subordinates. Many managers avoid taking this kind of necessary action until their whole organization is weakened. Here's an illustration. John, a department head, got along well with Jim, a lower-level manager in his department. The two enjoyed bowling and socializing together away from work. Jim did a good job for a couple of years and then began to take his duties very casually. He came to work late, quit early. He frequently asked for time off and reported sick. One subordinate said, "Even when he is here I feel it is an imposition to ask him for a decision."

John had worried and watched Jim deteriorate and had even made a few good-natured attempts to bring his concern to Jim's attention, but with no success. As a department head, John was aware that employees and other managers on Jim's level were asking questions of each other about his pull with the boss. John evidently had not used his expressive episodes as a positive tool to keep Jim from drifting into intolerable work habits. Also, you realize that John should have used personal contacts to correct his subordinates after conditions became so bad they could no longer be overlooked.

When you use expressive episodes to correct a subordinate, *first* be fair by recognizing good performance, attitude, and other exceptional qualities as well as pointing out errors. *Second,* be firm by making sure that your responsibility as a superior is understood. *Third,* be prompt by meeting the unpleasant situations before they get worse.

Expressive Episodes as a Means of Building Self-Confidence in Others

The greatest reward which you as a manager can derive from the proper use of expressive episodes is improved team coordination and cooperation. When you talk with associates, therefore, one of your important objectives should be to build up their feelings of assurance. To establish such an atmosphere of well-being, you should help the important people you contact get rid of their feelings of fear, and relieve emotional tensions which cause them to perform at less than their best.

For instance, one Friday afternoon, Henry, the department manager, said to Jeff, a bright, hard-working young production operator, "Starting Monday morning at 8:00 A.M., you are the supervisor of the eleven-man crew on the second floor." Jeff didn't sleep well over the weekend; came to work on Monday morning game but hollow-eyed. The very first thing, he assigned the wrong men to the key jobs; materials didn't come out right, machines failed to operate properly, the trickle of production which did come through was misweighed. Henry strolled casually through the second-floor operation about midway in the shift, noted Jeff sweating profusely. He walked over and remarked, "Don't take it so seriously. The company won't go broke if you fail to get out a single ounce of production." As this idea soaked in, Jeff felt better. Henry walked on across the floor and, while Jeff couldn't hear, he said to first one and then another of the workmen, "Help the young fellow out. He is a good man." As you can well imagine, Jeff was soon on top of that job with a smoothly operating crew, setting production records time after time.

Of course, this exact solution will not work in all circumstances, but it does illustrate some important principles about building a subordinate's confidence. Henry, with seeming deliberate intent, threw Jeff to the wolves when he assigned him to a job which was temporarily over his head. The boss' brief comment to the young supervisor steadied him, served to give him some feeling of security. The response which Henry received when he asked the operators to help Jeff tells us that the department manager had used his past expressive episodes to build strong personal leadership cooperation.

In your job of directing the work of others, frequently a top-performing subordinate falls down in his work for no apparent reason. At such times, be careful about following your first impulse to let him have it. Remember that if you are going to be a good professional manager, you'll be working at it for a long time, and some of your most effective progress can be made in a sincere and carefully handled expressive episode.

A Growing Manager Is Always in Command

As a growing manager you must:

1. *Be strong in the ability to exchange ideas with other people.*
2. *Have a plan for progress, know something of its costs and what the rewards may be.*
3. *Either have or be able to obtain an understanding of the technical jobs under your direction.*
4. *Maintain a balanced view of your total job with people in the forefront of your attention.*
5. *Appreciate the importance of knowing people so that you can talk with them for productive results.*
6. *View personal contacts with people as expressive episodes.*
7. *Know what people work for.*
8. *Recognize the mutual dependencies of people.*
9. *Realize that, whether knowingly or not, subordinates imitate the boss.*
10. *Be alert to a hard-core barrier of people who can destroy free communications.*
11. *Know when your expressive episodes are working.*
12. *Know when your expressive episodes are not working.*
13. *Know how to change the expressive episodes from "stop" to "go."*
14. *Know where and how to use expressive episodes to inform, and their value.*
15. *Know how to get need-to-know information.*
16. *Know how to use expressive episodes to give directions and overcome resistance to authority.*
17. *Know how to get help in directing others.*
18. *Appreciate the value of using expressive episodes to build a better performing organization.*

Chapter 3: How Your Success Depends On What Others Hear, See, and Think

Time after time, the Israelites whom Moses adroitly liberated from Egyptian slavery rebelled against his leadership. One such occasion holds a significant lesson for an aspiring KNOW-and-DO manager.

This event occurred after Moses had successfully brought his people through the management tests posed by shepherding an undisciplined mob of former slaves during the critical Red Sea crossing, withstanding attacks by the murderous Amalekites, and cajoling timid peoples through the howling wilderness with little food and water until they arrived at Kadesh, an oasis on the northern Sinai peninsula and the gateway to Palestine, the homeland of their dreams.

At this point, like any good leader, the Hebrew savior decided to scout the competition. Moses made what appeared to be a good choice of spies to ferret out the difficulties which might be expected during his proposed invasion by selecting one man from each of the twelve tribes. However, the hero of the Israelite exodus had not learned that a manager's success depends upon how others evaluate what they hear, see, and feel. Moses placed the success of the entire venture in the judgment of these twelve tribal representatives. And he was unprepared for the veto report by ten of the twelve based upon what they saw and heard. The dissenters described the land as very productive—a veritable garden spot, flowing with milk and honey—but defended by a race of giants, well armed in great walled cities, which the Hebrews would not be able to subdue. In fact, these Israelites of little spirit were so frightened by what they saw that they described themselves as grasshoppers when compared to the people of the country.

You can learn another good management lesson from the fact that Joshua and Caleb, the only two spies who recommended an immediate attack, saw and heard the same peoples and things as the other ten, yet viewed them differently. If you are going to be a better manager, *first remember your leadership success depends upon how others react*—and this can very well be not necessarily what you intended to convey. And, *second, individuals always see the same things differently.*

Moses at Kadesh was unaware of these essential leadership principles and almost lost his life when his followers rebelled. The very people who had benefited from the great Hebrew's managerial judgment threatened to stone him when he insisted on invading Caanan as recommended by Caleb and Joshua. Moses did escape the wrath of his followers, but the aftermath of this episode was thirty-eight years of homeless wandering in the wilderness by the Hebrews with repeated insubordinations which suggest that the great Hebrew manager never did fully learn to cope with the two leadership communication essentials of *individual reactions* and the *differences in interpretation* which people place on the same experience.

As a manager you will never have to face possible stoning; but if you gain a KNOW-and-DO management position, you must remember as you sit in an important meeting with associates that a subordinate on whom you are depending strongly for support is thinking first of his own interests. If you are to be a real leader, then it is up to you to make sure your subordinate sees something of value for himself in accomplishing your goals.

Listen to the Other Person

Don't attempt to give out a message without special consideration for the receiver. For the purpose of illustration, picture a manager named "Al" with an experienced milling machine operator named "Cliff" under his supervision. On this occasion, Al said to Cliff, "You'll get better quality and more production if you slow down your table speed and take a deeper cut." The operator came back with this quick rejoinder, "Oh, yeah?" Al thought to himself, "Cliff just doesn't understand what I am suggesting." So Al proceeded to clearly, concisely, and in minute detail explain what he knew about metal, the angle of cut, the power of the machine, and why the shop must have more output. All this time Cliff was standing there looking bored. The manager thought, "I never realized that this guy was that dumb before." So Al motioned Cliff aside, shut down the machine, set the cutter, and started it up to show the subordinate what he meant. When things happened much as Al had explained, he turned to Cliff with a patronizing smile and, with a superior hitch to his shoulders, continued his rounds through the shop. During the next week, scrap from Cliff's machine tripled, cutter blades were used by the dozens, and a drive motor had to be replaced. The operator took the following week off and, when he returned, requested a transfer to another shop.

Let's use the same situation with a different manager named "Bill." Again, the episode started with Bill saying to Cliff, "You'll get better quality and more production if you slow down your table speed and take a deeper cut." Again, the reply came back, "Oh, yeah?" Now, Bill did not assume that Cliff's reply necessarily meant that the operator didn't understand. He realized that it could mean numerous other things. In similar situations, Bill has learned by experience two things: *First,* that to find out what a subordinate really means, a manager must listen when the other person talks; and, *second,* that coldly logical reasoning frequently fails to bring two independent people's thoughts together because personal emotions are usually fully as important.

From Cliff's quick reaction, Bill decided he should use more care in handling this situation. Thus he asked, "You are getting good maintenance on your machine, aren't you, Cliff?" The operator was quick to defend the performance of the mill, declaring that it was one of the best in the whole shop. Then the manager asked about the material and how the quality was running; and again he received an enthusiastic endorsement. Bill followed by asking Cliff how he thought quality might be improved and quantity increased. Now, with the operator and the supervisor both in accord on a cooperative project, they were able to conclude that "slowing down the table speed and taking a deeper cut" might be worth a try at least. Needless to say, it did increase production, improve quality, reduce scrap, help an operator and a manager find new interest in their jobs, and create a better relationship between Bill and Cliff.

Personal Exchanges Are Colored by Bias, Prejudice, and Preconceptions

Managers, workmen, employees and people generally develop their own pet ideas, quirks, beliefs, and traits. In growing as a better manager, it is an advantage to you to be alert for evidences of these "performance influencers" in others. You will probably never do much to change others' fixed ideas, but you can use good leadership judgment in dealing with these personal peculiarities. For instance, some executives like to work in their shirt sleeves, while another equally successful manager has a strong conviction that the dignity of the job requires the supervisor to wear a jacket at all times in carrying out his duties. Some top managers don't approve of a manager wearing a sport coat to work. Still others always wear white shirts and feel that all managers should do likewise.

Perhaps you have heard a successful manager say, "I don't trust a guy who makes an effort to look me in the eye when I talk with him. He is trying to hide something." Still another manager says, "You can depend on a fellow who looks you in the eye when he talks. He is a straight-shooter." So how is an ambitious manager, struggling to be a better on-the-job performer, going to meet these barriers to good communications?

First, you must find out what these beliefs are, how many, and how strongly they are held by the people important to your success. *Second,* you must yourself to guard against making wrong decisions based upon purely emotional judgments. Here is one area in which you can make real progress. You don't need anyone's permission to make a self-improvement. Watch yourself and avoid mannerisms which you find objectionable in others.

Where the Message Comes From Makes a Difference

A somewhat cynical observer of management communications once said, "At the top of the list and most important is who says it, next in order is how it is said, and lastly and far down the scale is what is actually said." This apparently implies that the "boss is always right" and fortunately much of the time he really is—otherwise most business organizations would not be successful.

An ambitious manager must at all times consider the source as he evaluates what should be done in response to the wide variety of communciations he receives. You should find out who among your associates is most likely to cry "wolf" the loudest without reason. "Peg" the experts in a particular area, learn to sift facts from fiction. You can't afford to become known as a supervisor who goes off half-cocked on important projects.

Use Another's Specific Interests to Gain His Attention

When two intelligent people are introduced they usually start casting about in their conversation for mutual acquaintances or compatible job or experience situations as they seek to know more about each other.

On your job as a manager you should not be handicapped by lack of knowledge of your associates. You must be able to appeal directly to the individual's interest arouser. Hobbies, special opportunities for service, money, easier ways to do a job, and personal prestige builders often carry special appeal when used with the appropriate people.

President Woodrow Wilson kept the United States neutral in World War I by declaring that we were "too proud to fight." "We were the most unselfish nation on earth" until the German's made the fatal mistake of inflicting the atrocities of unrestricted submarine warfare upon U.S. citizens and ships. Mr. Wilson was not only a good manager but an idealist as well. When it became necessary to enter the war, he insured the attention and support of all crusaders by declaring that this "was a war to make the world safe for democracy." Mr. Wilson's sincerity was evident when he wrecked his health in a valiant attempt to gain support for the League of Nations as a means of tempering the selfishly designed provisions of the Treaty of Versailles.

This example illustrates the power of a specific appeal to the interest of those whose support you need, and the importance of honesty in attracting another's interest. A manager on his way to the top should never try to manipulate people; that is, cleverly coerce them against their will to gain his own and the organization's objectives.

General Guides in Making Your Exchanges More Meaningful

First, in getting a better understanding, recognize clearly that this is a human problem. All the mechanics, techniques, good deliveries, and interest arousers will not overcome distrust between the participants. *Second,* don't let your personal feelings mislead you. A growing manager must often "set his sentiments aside" to get and give right communications. *Third,* look behind the words and phrases for real meanings. When the boss said to a key subordinate, "Check those records out with the Department Heads" and the manager addressed replied, "Oh, I would rather not; I am afraid to talk to that much brass" does he really mean it? What should the boss do? This requires real communications because it can be a turning point in the subordinate's development and a valuable future guide for the boss. A superior may be betting his chips on the wrong man. After considering his past contacts, most managers should insist upon this training exercise. Some cold sweat is good for all of us.

The Manager's "Giving-Out" Obligation

Manager Ed had been having a particularly bad year. As the supervisor of an indirect service department, he had been forced to cut his personnel in half at the beginning of the fiscal period to meet an overhead cost target to a direct labor decline. Ed spent the next six weeks in the hospital with a heart attack. When he recovered, his wife had a narrow squeeze with major surgery. One of his children had been involved in a serious automobile accident; the other three children were attending college where expenses seemed to mount daily. On a day in late September, Ed was required to discharge a key subordinate because of participation in a messy sex case. After this was handled, Ed's boss asked him to come into his office for a conference. This harassed manager's perceptive superior encouraged Ed to talk while he listened with interest to the subordinate's views on politics, religion, the value of a college education, the general economic situation—all of which were subjects of special interest to Ed. After this pressure relieving conversation, the boss told Ed as he left the office to stay in there "pitching" because next year had to be a better deal for him.

This superior was actively fulfilling his management "giving-out" responsibility when his subordinate needed it badly.

In striving to be a better manager, you need to develop the sensitivity shown by Ed's boss which enabled him to provide support for his subordinate at an opportune time. This is effective communication at its best and shows a superior manager's mastery of the hardest and probably the most important single skill of a leader.

The episode between Ed and his superior also serves to illustrate a "giving-out" management fact that many supervisors fail to appreciate: namely, transmitting and receiving impressions between two or more individuals is a total personality projection. Getting into detail can either speed or hamper the interchange of significant relationship information depending on tone of voice, past contacts, degree of exhibited interest, and all kinds of behavior which carries meaning.

Shakespeare knew how important it is for a leader to be able to interpret the subtle actions of others as evidenced in the famous passage from Julius Caesar concerning Caesar's possible assassination by conspirators, "Let me have men about me that are fat; sleek-headed men, and such as sleep nights. Yond Cassius (one of the plotters) has a lean and hungry look; He thinks too much; such men are dangerous."

While the most common means of communication are oral or written words, you should not forget the importance of a smile, a shrug, a frown, or an emotionless demeanor which can convey approval, disagreement, or disinterest. You should remember also that instructions, hints, and inferences are potent instruments for securing action or passing on ideas. Each of these communications can have its meaning influenced, depending upon where it originates. For instance, a smile from the boss may carry a different meaning from the same reaction by an associate or a subordinate.

The Difficulty in Getting Your Ideas Across

After you as a practical manager accept the fact that the total personality is an active tool for exchanging thoughts and ideas, you must appreciate the difficulty of clearly relating your specific thinking to others. Experience suggests that when a supervisor's thoughts are intangible, that is, not capable of concrete proof, he cannot get the complete picture he has in mind over to the person with whom he is trying to communicate.

The greatest of all leaders, Jesus Christ, worked and lived with his twelve disciples for three years. During this time he constantly taught them by parables, demonstrations, examples, and an exemplary life; yet it was only after his crucifixion that any of the twelve finally caught a glimmer of what the full meaning of his life on earth was intended to be.

While it must be admitted that good communication is difficult for you as a manager, this fact should only add zest to the challenge because the harder you try, the closer you approach reaching complete understanding. And when you do score, it gives a real sense of satisfaction.

General Helps for Effectively Putting Over Ideas

In communications, an atmosphere of mutual confidence is helpful in getting through to the other person. Such a climate can only be obtained when you respect those reporting to you, and you in turn have earned the esteem of your subordinates. For instance, when the boss, after reading a detailed letter, says to his secretary, "I believe this second paragraph ought to be a part of the first one," Miss Competent replies, "No, that is a different thought. One paragraph would be grammatically incorrect, and besides, two paragraphs make the letter look better." The boss reluctantly grunts, "O.K." They are communicating.

Miss Competent would not have dared to contradict the boss if he had not earned her respect as a fair-minded manager. On the other hand, the boss would not have accepted her correction unless past performance had convinced him that he could safely put his confidence in her judgment on such a question.

Mutual respect in one area is the basis for smoothly transferring confidence between superiors and subordinates into all segments of their relationship. This is a must for putting over ideas; for, even with the best intentions of the sender, the receiver's attitude can short-circuit the meaning of the message. The recipient may distort or intentionally forget instructions; he may fail to read or retain written information. All such actions can hamper the free flow of information up, down, and across the organization, and most likely frustrate proper teamwork.

Writing, as a Manager's Helper

As in all facets of the complex job of directing the work of others, preparation for your key contacts is of primary importance in reaching the goals you set for yourself. The ambitious supervisor should remember that, in communicating, nothing is as valuable as writing. Of course, every time you need to say something to a subordinate you do not sit down and write him a note. To the contrary, most managers talk better than they write and accomplish more in face-to-face conversation. However, the more clearly you have in mind what you want to accomplish and how you expect to do it in a specific contact, the better the chances of success. For pay-off results on this score, nothing beats putting it in writing first.

As a manager you write to make your thoughts clearer to either yourself or others; therefore, the most helpful writing ought to be simple, direct, and easy to read. For this purpose, Albert M. Joseph, Executive Director, the Industrial Writing Institute, suggests six principles: *First,* prefer short, familiar words; *second,* keep most sentences short and simple; *third,* prefer active verbs, avoid passives. (As an example, "The supervisor turned off the punch press" not "The punch press was turned off by the supervisor.") *Fourth,* use a conversational style; *fifth,* get people into your sentences (I, we, they, you—not it); *sixth,* know your subject.

Mr. Joseph further stresses the need for managers to state their conclusions first. For instance, "Every employee will put more vim and vigor into his job when he is convinced that the airplane will not fly without the part he is working on." Next, think and use some of your own logic in explaining how you arrived at this conclusion. For instance, "I did this and John Jones turned out twenty gadgets, eight more than he ever did before." As a helpful manager, you should also suggest how your idea can best be put into practice. Finally, Mr. Joseph finds that too many supervisors dilute their writing style by worrying about rules. Modern writers have made sentences ending with a preposition and beginning with "and" or "but" entirely proper. He says, "You can even use sentences that are grammatically incomplete, if you're skillful enough. Sometimes, anyhow." [1]

Be a Receiver

Your attention must not be directed entirely to the display- or giving-type communicators, that is speaking and writing, because like most supervisors you need to spend at least equal time on the acquiring- or the getting-type of communicators, such as reading and listening. If you don't do this, there is a danger that you may become one of those "who think too little, and who talk too much." Acquiring is the communication category which you may find most difficult to practice because you must use greater self-discipline. To get full value from thinking, reading, and listening, you can't, as some wag has said, "Talk until you think of something to say" or turn the pages of a book while woolgathering.

While you read, be alert for worthwhile material. If it is your book, mark it up, underline, make marginal notes. Start and keep a file of useful references and information. Review periodically to avoid missing valuable helps.

At all levels of management, you will find by experience that your best source for learning to know and properly size-up the people important to you is to listen when they talk. To be a real leader, remember that the other person usually has something worthwhile to say.

If you want to do a better job in the acquiring communications category, DON'T:

[1] Joseph, Albert M.: "How to Write Better," Reprinted *Business Management* (formerly *Management Methods*), 1960, Management Magazines, Inc., Greenwich, Conn.

1. Prejudge the material or the speaker—give each a chance to be heard;
2. Forget to discount your own prejudices and biases;
3. Be big "I" to the point that you think you have all the good ideas;
4. Fail to make some notes. Most people who can talk can give you something of value. As the saying goes, "Even an old blind pig will pick up an acorn now and then."
5. Let your attention be distracted by competing noises, pet peeves, or the difficulty of the material being presented.

Environmental Factors in Communication

After you are well checked out in both giving and getting information, you cannot safely overlook the setting in which you attempt to communicate. One important factor is *timing*. For example, telling a subordinate about a difficult job you want him to handle the next day while he is on his way to the door, trying to get home because his wife wants to go out for the evening, will receive a different reception from the one you will get if the same details are given just before the work is to be done.

A second consideration is the *physical situation*. Noisy or quiet, public or private, each has an effect upon the meaning attached to a personal contact. As an illustration, if you just take the trouble to find a quiet place for your conversation with an associate, this lends importance to the exchange.

A third environmental factor which you need to consider as it affects communications is the *social tone or relationship* of the individuals and working group. Where many people are closely associated physically on the job they enjoy the advantage of a more personal understanding but also the disadvantage of open exposure to personality clashes. The first situation is an atmosphere conducive to clearer comprehension; the second, naturally a hindrance.

A fourth illustration of an intangible but significant consideration in communications is whether or not *the method of passing out information* follows customary practices. For instance, if your organization has for years used memos to notify managers of such changes as appointments to new positions, promotions, and job realignments, then without notice you start relating information verbally, some confusion almost certainly will result.

The Exchange Quintet

The popularly dubbed "hot-line" telephone connection between the White House in Washington and the Kremlin in Moscow is an effort to avoid permitting a war between the Soviets and U.S. to start because of lack of communications. If better exchange of information had been possible in the early 19th Century, the Battle of New Orleans, fought January 8, 1815, would not have been necessary because British and American commissioners had signed a peace treaty at Ghent, Belgium, Christmas Eve, in 1814. The rights of freedom of speech and press were considered so important by our founding fathers that these fundamentals of communication were written into our Constitution's first amendment.

For you, as a manager seeking to get on top of your present job and move up to the next higher level of directional responsibility, communications is probably the single skill of greatest practical value. If doubts arise in your mind that you may "over-train" yourself in communications, remember the following questions: Can a team score too many points in a ballgame? Can an individual receive too much education? Can a person have too much good health?

As a hold-over from the closely directed practices of management generally followed up to a century ago, many managers still tend to think of their job as communicators in terms of telling subordinates what to do. This is only one of the requirements in this area. The others are to: inform those above you, inform those on your level, and recognize and use the uncontrolled flow of information.

Get On the Boss' Wave Length

If you expect to succeed as a professional manager, you must keep your superior advised in the manner in which he wants to be informed.

In improving your leadership, you can all benefit from a knowledge of how Nehemiah, staff assistant to King Artaxerxes of the Persians, handled this problem back in 444 B.C. The ancient manager was concerned about the destitute condition of his people, the Jews, who had returned to Jerusalem from Babylonian captivity under Ezra's direction in 539 B.C.

The king's staffman learned from travelers that his homeland city still lay in the ruins of Nebuchadnezzar's leveling of 586 B.C., with his relatives hopelessly eking out an existence, hiding in Jerusalem's rubble from marauding surrounding peoples. The once proud rulers of Palestine were objects of contempt to their murdering neighbors.

In spite of Nehemiah's very secure and lucrative position in the king's court at Susa, he decided he must provide some leadership to his oppressed peoples. Notice, however, as a good manager he did not act hastily. Laying plans for four months, he finally chose the most opportune time to take the first step—which was to gain his superior's permission to go to Jerusalem.

When the Jewish hero made this critically important contact, notice the things he had going for him: 1. The great Queen Esther (a Jew) was with the king; 2. Nehemiah had built up an outstanding record of service in the king's interest; 3. Nehemiah allowed his superior to observe by his worried facial expression and outward demeanor that he had some troubles. In getting Artaxerxes to inquire what was his problem, the intelligent Jew avoided asking a favor and also assured himself of a sympathetic listening superior.

The king's staffman was so successful with his boss that he not only was given permission to go to Jerusalem but, in addition, was supplied a military escort, finances, plus requisitions to the Persian keepers of the forests and national stockpiles to give Nehemiah the materials he needed to rebuild his city's walls and get the Jews started back toward a national entity.

When you have a really big project on which you need your superior's approval, your plans and approach should be as carefully thought out and executed as those of the great Jewish hero. Much of the time, however, your upward communications are concerned with day-to-day contacts with your superior. The success of these exchanges depends upon how well you are able to first learn his way of thinking. All managers have a personal thought pattern; your superior may first want to know how much money is involved, the number and skills of people, what equipment will be necessary, what is the worth of the idea or proposal, or is it a proper activity for the organization. These and other items or combinations may be important to you as a subordinate to study. As a tip, if your boss' background is finance, very likely money and budgets will be important; if it is manufacturing, processes and tools; engineering, probably design and planning; personnel, then people and skills may take priority.

Second, find out your superior's likes and dislikes, strengths and weaknesses. It is only practical common sense to try to avoid being one of the people on his disliked list. Promotions come more easily if you get along with the boss. Most likely he will not change, so possibly you had better make the adjustment.

Third, does your boss want most to build an organization—show a great profit—produce the finest quality product? Knowing something of what causes him to do the things he does, finding out what his ambitions are, will help you communicate with him.

Fourth, your superior has a special way of operating. All managers do. It may be a tendency toward quick decisions or slow; delegation of such things as detailed personnel affairs, structural planning, writing procedures, or checking salary scales. He may want all information in chart form, written or verbal; whatever his preference, you should make it work.

Find Out What the Boss Expects of You

As a KNOW-and-DO manager, simply following a written job description is not enough. You must be able to determine when your superior wants a full report, and when he just wants some ideas. You must find out when a casual request is an order; when suggested further thought really means "dig in," and when it means "file the idea."

Second, many things about your job tie back to *your superior's special interest*. If housekeeping is an area where he sets standards, you had better see if there is something in your job which needs special attention. You must meet the boss' requirements for types and frequency of reports, whatever they may be.

Third, *look for signs of miscommunications*. If you are consulted for ideas in connection with organization changes and the final decision is contrary to your recommendations, you had better try to find out what happened. You may have a problem in this area if you are overlooked when questions on your specialty arise. The boss naturally works better with an understanding subordinate who doesn't require the "hard-sell" to produce the kind of support a superior must have.

What Do You Report?

When King Saul of Israel sat under the tamarisk tree at Gibeah, growling about the successes of David, the man he considered his enemy, Doeg the Edomite reported to the ruler, "I saw the son of Jesse, in flight from your wrath, stop at Nob, the Priest Sanctuary. Ahimelech, the chief priest, gave him food and the sword of Goliath as a weapon." Israel's king welcomed the report because it gave him a reason and a place to vent his rage against the man he hated. This is not to suggest that your superior needs or wants information in order to cut up someone in the organization, but it does illustrate that as a subordinate you should give the boss what he requires to succeed in the job he wants to accomplish.

If the sequence of production operations needs rearranging for greater efficiency, if you have discovered a sales pitch which works well, if you find the answer as to why the overhead costs are out of line, or if you have what you think is a good idea for a new product design, your superior should be informed.

A caution—don't wear out your welcome; remember the boss must listen to some other subordinates, too, so don't try to monopolize his time.

How Do You Report?

Here you must be governed largely by your superior's wishes. If he is away from the office or unavailable, and you want to get an important decision as soon as possible, writing up the facts and your recommendations so they will get his immediate attention when he returns may be a good idea. Writing also allows you to clarify the details in your own mind while they are current. Your reports will be made either orally or in writing. Each has advantages and disadvantages, and your good judgment should determine which best fits your situation.

The advantages of the oral report: First, the information can be more quickly passed on. Second, it gives an opportunity for immediate questions and answers. Third, any needed additional or supporting information can be supplied.

The disadvantages of the oral report: First, a record of the information is lost. Second, the very ease of this means of communication encourages careless preparation. Third, such information cannot be easily and accurately circulated to others.

The advantages of a written report: First, it tends to force the communicator to be clear, correct, concise, and complete. Second, it encourages you to organize the material so that it flows in a logical sequence to a conclusion and your recommendation. Third, it provides a permanent record.

The disadvantages of a written report: First, because it is difficult to prepare, it may discourage you from passing on important information. Second, a delay may nullify the value of your report. Third, writings can become so voluminous that they cause a flood, and then your reports lose their value.

Be Able to Tell Others What You Do and Why

As an experienced manager on an assignment with which you are thoroughly familiar, you usually do not find it necessary to keep a log book of detailed activities to be performed. However, all managers must calendar special or unusual duties, engagements, meetings.

You must be able to tell others—such as superiors, associates, key subordinates—what is required in handling your job. This is difficult for several reasons. *First,* all management jobs tend to become individualized. They grow like the person who holds them. Even in an organization that has written job duties, over a period of time the manager accumulates added duties. Often another supervisor with related responsibilities acquires some duties of his associate by common consent because the two of you agree that it is more efficient. *Second,* as a manager, when you become more familiar with your duties, you also tend to be more adept at handling routine happenings and your speed picks up unconsciously. When an unusual event takes place, you find time to handle it without difficulty, and it is forgotten. *Third,* whether consciously or otherwise, most managers are secretly convinced that "nobody can handle my job as well as I can." This basic attitude makes you reluctant to reveal all your secrets which give you a comfortable dominance of the job. As a manager, you also have a personal pride in your achievements and may feel that telling others how you work will destroy some of your personal luster as a top-flight manager. *Fourth,* as a manager with KNOW-and-DO ambitions, you have your time well taken up. In the hustle and bustle of handling your regular duties, you find little time to analyze just what you are doing and why it is necessary.

You Gain When Others Know Your Job

Think of the time you have saved by deciding to delegate a check-up chore which not only relieved you for other work but developed a subordinate. How many times have you thought about the use and need for reports and concluded a better, easier, and quicker way to pass on the information to the needed source? Have you recently studied your way of talking with a subordinate and decided to change? These are some benefits that you can get from self-appraisal if you study your job to the extent that you can tell others about it.

In preparing yourself to report to others, you will find spots where your organization can be improved. Possibly through shifting of duties, better assignments, or the elimination of unnecessary activities. Such an exercise uncovers valuable skills which those reporting to you may not have been using to their greatest potential. This preparation provides you with the information you need to give a deserved promotion, which is the most promising way for you to develop a key subordinate; someone who can take your place, and thus not hamper your own advancement. Your company gains from insured, competent management continuity.

The Manager as an In-The-Middle Communicator

Whatever your place in the management of your organization, instructions, directions, information, and orders must be passed down to those reporting to you. You also have the obligation to relay the results of these communications to your superior.

When your boss says, "Tell your crew not to report until Tuesday of next week; we are only working four days per week until further notice," you will not immediately rush out shouting this unwelcome news without some careful thought, if you intend to advance as a manager. You will want to know some reasons for the change in schedule, probably tell those involved individually, and consider what may be good about the situation.

When your superior's direction has been carried out, even after the exercise of tact and your best judgment, some of your subordinates will blame you if they don't like what they hear.

If the working group threatened to strike because of the short work-week, you must tell your boss, and he thinks (whether he says it or not), "You didn't tell the men the story correctly." This is not an unusual situation because you must implement policies, carry out disciplines, and maintain production continuity in accordance with the directions of your superior and be sure that higher management is informed of important feed-back from the results of these instructions. Even after your best efforts in some respects, you will be the "fall guy."

Your Horizontal Communications

A somewhat different brand of performance is required when you contact suppliers, those responsible for maintenance of your equipment, staff supporters, and customers. While each of these exchanges will vary with circumstances, such as your need for his services and his need for your business, the common denominator is that your direct-line authority is missing. As a last resort for the modern professional manager, you can order a subordinate to do a job in a certain way and he will do it, at least after a fashion. The independent supplier on whom you depend doesn't have to follow your orders. Communication in this area puts a premium on persuasion; and, to get results, you must make a greater appeal to their interests. If you are able to meet the challenge, you will be developing as a better manager.

The Grapevine—Uncontrolled Communications

"Did you hear that the XYZ Company has bought our plant and will be bringing in all new personnel to operate it?" This kind of story can spread throughout a large organization in a matter of hours and cost thousands of productive dollars while employees gossip. Why did the news start and keep going? Because of a lack of information. The grapevine thrives on some of the barest of rumors. It can reveal proprietary company information, wreck personal reputations, and cause detrimental animosities; so you, as a growing manager, need to be concerned about such communications.

Because in every group there are people who like to talk, probably no organization is free from the spread of unauthorized information. When the company management releases an announcement such as, "The current loss of sales may not mean a slow-down of production unless we are not able to introduce a new line because of competition," here we have something on which the grapevine can start to work. Ambiguity, half-truths, uncertainty, fear, and hostility cause gossip to thrive. In striving to be a better manager, you should not worry much about who passes on the rumor. Almost everyone does at times. You can more profitably concern yourself with what is circulated; and, if it is harmful, see that the facts are known as an effective rumor stopper.

Using the Grapevine as a Management Tool

This transmission system is ready and just "panting" to be used. It has the second advantage of being as rapid a communicator as any organization can establish. Third, the system has tested and proven customer acceptance.

Thus, you as a manager might want to see what reaction the employees will have to, say, a proposed shift change starting at 7:00 A.M. because of the heavy traffic at the present 8:00 A.M. starting hour. Just plant that with the right secrecy and before lunch time you'll have an answer. The same idea can be used in getting an impression of what will happen if you tighten smoking rules in specified areas, or if you shift personnel from one assignment to another. Since you know the grapevine works, you might as well make constructive use of the system.

To Improve as a Manager, You Must Fully Accept That:

1. *People see the same thing differently.*
2. *A help in establishing mutual teamwork interest is to listen.*
3. *Communications are affected by bias, prejudice, and opinions.*
4. *It is important to you as a receiver to consider where the message comes from, and as a sender what the receiver's interest may be.*
5. *Communications are a human activity.*
6. *While exchanges are difficult, mutual respect will help.*
7. *Better writing habits will help communications.*
8. *You must receive as well as give.*
9. *You must consider the environment in which you attempt to communicate.*
10. *As a manager, you are required to communicate—downward, upward, from the middle, horizontally—and to recognize, regulate, and use the unauthorized grapevine.*
11. *You must meet the boss' requirements.*
    a. *Understand him.*
    b. *Know what he expects.*
    c. *Know what and how to report.*
12. *You must be able to tell others what you do.*
13. *At times both those above and below you in the organization may blame you for their troubles.*
14. *You must keep important associates happy with your communications.*
15. *Rumors and gossip in an organization are natural. And by good management, you can reduce their destructiveness and even obtain some values for yourself and the company.*

Chapter 4: The KNOW-and-DO Manager's Future

One of the most evident facts of management life in the economy of our nation is that methods, equipment, and operations change, jobs and whole skills are eliminated, and new ways of doing things constantly arise, even within a relatively short time period.

This phenomenon has special significance for the ambitious manager because: *First,* it means that you as a progressive supervisor should encourage these technical job improvements. Invite and make early use of all modern methods, machines, tools, and equipment. *Second,* you must recognize that your future as a manager can best be promoted by learning to work effectively with people rather than studying the mechanical details of the jobs you supervise. *Third,* you can actively further your success by fully appreciating and preparing yourself with a broad look ahead. In your speculation of the future, give appropriate weight to your technical and people management responsibilities.

A Get-Cooperation Philosophy

Val, the vice president and general manager of an extremely successful, large manufacturing concern in a highly competitive field, was talking with Jeff, the operating manager, about the importance of getting a higher volume of production when Jeff blurted out, "I'm behind schedule because I can't get those 'so-and-so's' working for me to do their jobs." Val went to the blackboard on the wall of his office and, as Jeff watched, he drew the familiar, triangular organizational chart with the general manager at the top and the sides of the triangle spreading by management echelon wider to the bottom, broad baseline where the word "employees" was written. Then Val drew a line around the side of the pyramid with an arrow to indicate that the triangle was turned upside down. The general manager then said, "All of us should think of ourselves as supporting those employees who get out the product." As he walked back to his desk, Val remarked, "With this philosophy the employees are not working for us, but we are working for them. Thus, our job becomes one of helping all other employees to do a better job."

Ways to Help Subordinates Do a Better Job

The freedom of the American colonies from British rule was accomplished through the willing cooperation of the French with General George Washington. As the Revolution approached a climax, Lord Cornwallis and the British army had been chasing a combined French and American army in Virginia under the French general Lafayette. When Cornwallis decided to establish better sea communications with General Clinton, British commander in New York, by moving to Yorktown, Virginia, near the mouth of the Chesapeake bay; Comte de Rochambeau, commander of a French army, and General Washington with the American army combined forces and closed off any movement by Cornwallis on the land while Comte de Grasse with a French fleet of twenty-eight ships of the line cut off escape and provisioning of the British from the sea. Timing his attack for maximum effect, General Washington forced Cornwallis to surrender October 19, 1781, which for all practical purposes brought the war in America to an end.

Willing cooperation and freedom are magic words for the modern manager. The most important *first step* for you as a manager to take in earning the common benefits of the united efforts of your unit, group, or organization is to *make sure that the people reporting to you know what they are supposed to do.* The French and Americans at Yorktown demonstrated that, in spite of distances and the diversity of forces, each was aware of what needed to be accomplished, and their close and timely cooperation won the victory.

You can assist your subordinate by intelligently checking his knowledge of his job. Show your interest in what he is doing, ask questions, observe, suggest possibilities of actions, and when necessary correct.

Second, an alert on-top manager will *use special care and good judgment in giving directions* so as to permit all the freedom practical to encourage subordinates to use their own initiative, imagination, and ingenuity. If a person freely chooses his own course of action, he also accepts personal responsibility for his work. Such an attitude will help to build strength in depth on your productive team. Because of your position, you can command a form of obedience, but you can't command cooperation. This must be earned.

Third, as a creative, thinking manager, make sure that you continuously try to *give all possible opportunities to every member of your team to apply his highest talent.* Nothing helps a person produce as well as the personal recognition of his own unique talents, whether this happens to be the skillful use of machine tools, special ability to make personal contacts, mathematical calculations, or report writing.

A *fourth* way you can help those reporting to you to improve is to *make sure that each person knows that his job is important.* Make-work or busy appearing chores are universally resented. One way to emphasize the importance of a job is to let the individual see how his efforts contribute to the ultimate product.

Whether an employee exerts his total capabilities toward his job or simply goes through a set pattern of motions in robot fashion depends largely upon his superior. A robot does what it is wound up to do. It lacks intelligence, initiative, resourcefulness, and any sense of responsibility. People have human qualities, and the successful manager makes use of them.

Setting a Climate for Performance

Cy Jones was an aggressive, young, rising executive responsible for the spinning room in a manufactured fiber plant. On his shift were fifty operators, all women, about equally divided in groups reporting to two supervisors named Charlie and Slim. This department was one of those that you read about but seldom see, for the fibers from the machines were continually high in quality, quotas were met on time, machine maintenance and material waste costs were consistently lower than other shifts and comparable operations, wage costs were in line, there was a minimum turnover of employees, absences from the jobs were never a problem, and more suggestions for process and even plantwide improvements came from this crew than all the rest of the factory combined.

The division manager naturally was interested in this stand-out department, so he asked Cy what his secret was, and this good manager replied, "I suppose it's the atmosphere that Slim, Charlie, and myself create. We believe that you've got to give people a chance to build their own sense of security by developing their self-confidence through successes on the job." Cy continued, "I think you can see what I mean if you have time to let Slim show you how he is helping a new girl, who just reported for work, become a cooperating member of our team."

While Cy went about his other work, the division manager watched Slim show the new operator how to clean a spindle. Then he let her go through the details while he corrected her mistakes. This went on until the girl performed the job without a hitch and smiled at the supervisor confidently. Slim didn't ease up but immediately demonstrated the flow control valve, the speed of the spindles, the unloading operation. The division manager remarked to Slim that he could see that he was much too busy right at that time to be bothered. The manager told Slim he would see him later, and started to find Charlie. As he went through the department, it was notable that none of the employees seemed concerned that the big boss was there.

Charlie was able to give some more details of the success of the department. He pointed out that the new operator Slim was getting started right was introduced to all the girls working near her. She had been shown the whole operation to the final loading for shipment and invited to ask questions. All the rules and policies were explained, and before she started working the supervisor listed with special pride the high performance standards of the group to which she was assigned.

Later, after the breaking-in period, the new employee would be given a chance to run a larger, more complex unit, encouraged to suggest improvements, and have her ability stretched by learning new skills. Charlie said, "We believe in learning by experience. The operators must clearly understand what they did, how it worked, and what results were obtained."

When the division manager started to leave, he told Charlie, "It appears to me that you fellows have an exciting department in which to work. Keep it up."

You can use the same principles in your management which gave this department the air of "the place to work." Cy and his subordinate managers worked at the job of getting total cooperation. They reduced the production loss due to employee nervousness by helping everyone feel at home right from the beginning. As the operators learned by experience, they took the mystery out of working blind. They encouraged cooperation which tended to wipe out any suspicion that fellow workers might take advantage of them. Individuals lost their fears and worry. There was rarely a tension or emotional blow-up and, in this healthy give-and-take between employees, a proper climate naturally grew up for superior performance.

Fair Treatment from the Boss

Your subordinate looks to you for many things: among them, for his continuity of employment, possible promotions and a variety of accompanying needed satisfactions such as increased pay, more responsibility, station in the organization, prestige, plus many personal and social benefits from his work assignments and company arrangements. It is worthy of note that all surveys of employee opinion show that by far the majority of workmen place high on the list such things as "good boss" or "fair treatment from management" as an essential for job satisfaction. It is also true that, since you get your results through the performance of subordinates, you must keep in mind that you can only succeed to the degree that those reporting to you will permit. So, remember these four better-action-getting steps: First, *let your subordinate build his self-confidence* by on-the-job success experiences. Second, *be sure you give him judicious support.* Third, *keep him stimulated by periodic progress reports.* Fourth, *give him information,* with discretion, on the results of specific actions which he (the subordinate) has taken.

Your subordinates, whether managers or general employees, do not expect favored treatment. As mature adults, acquainted with the facts of business life, they feel they are entitled to your respect and good leadership. Wise application of the four better-action-getting steps will help create willing cooperation as well as tap the latent potential which is present in all employees.

Use General Not Close Supervision

Casey was the manager of a crew milling a fine textured plastic for the moulding of figurines. Jonesy was the operator of the original break-down and mixing process on one of the three shifts, and there were seven such units. The milling was accomplished on a machine with three heated steel rolls set at different speeds so that the material in the batches was chewed up and broken down for the refining phase of the operation. The written specifications allowed the operator to use discretion on roll heat from 300° to 500° and allowed batch weights from 250 to 400 pounds. Over the years, by general common consent, all operators set the roll temperatures on all rolls at 300° and batch sizes at 300 pounds.

The plant product inspector notified Casey's department head that his unit consistently put out better quality and greater volume than any of the twenty other production crews. When Casey's boss commended him for these exceptional results, his answer was that he had an excellent working crew. However, Casey wasn't exactly sure why they were so outstanding. Tracing back through the cycle, Casey found that Jonesy was real proud of the fact that he used his own judgment on roll temperatures and batch sizes. The operator freely discussed with his supervisor the original instructions which Casey had given him which were, "Make this job the very best you can. Use your own ideas and judgments. If you have problems, let me know right away."

Jonesy explained that he had experimented with the kinds of material, roll temperatures, weights, and felt he was an expert on adjusting these variable factors. He further revealed that he had talked with the other operators in the locker room and found they were afraid to even mention a change from the 300° and 300-pound standard which everybody had used for years. One brave operator had suggested it to his supervisor but had his ears slapped down with this reprimand, "You do that job the way I tell you, hear? Don't go getting things all upset."

Jonesy was looked-up to by the other workmen because of his freedom to run his job, and he told Casey that it was fun to come to work because he had to be careful to study the material, the heat, and to get just the right amount of weight in each batch.

Casey was using general supervision and his fellow managers were using close supervision.

General supervision is the only answer to the greatest current management problems which finds people more and more dissatisfied with their work because of the lack of a challenge. In our machine economy, computers and other devices which practically think tend to take human judgment out of jobs so that operators can perform their functions almost automatically. And, as our people become better educated, the problem grows.

Advocates of greater regimentation or control by management cite as an advantage that, "It will make people feel genuinely secure and relaxed." The United States, the greatest productive complex of any nation in all history, was not built by secure and relaxed people.

You must put high on your list for becoming a better manager the practical application of the general management philosophy. When an executive says to his secretary, "Here are some names which I jotted down while attending that conference at the state capitol. Please make me a mailing list with titles and whatever else will help make a personal note from me effective." That's general supervision.

Your Attitude and Permissiveness Can Cultivate General Supervision

To get the benefits of general supervision, you can't be mentally lazy and think of all people in a gob. Inept managers have probably done more than any other single force to cultivate the idea that "all people want something for nothing." In many cases, employees have been forced to accept this lower priority choice. To be a better manager, you must believe that most people want to be useful. Surveys show that a majority like the results of our system, and they remain individuals in productivity, in desire for personal opportunity, in their wish for recognition. Your job as a KNOW-and-DO manager is to stimulate and offer chances to each to develop their own personal potential.

The only way that regimentation and close supervision as a basic management practice can be made to work and get results is by creating fear. Subordinates stimulated in this fashion are loaded with liabilities at the start. For instance, if employees are going to do a better total job, some changes in performance are needed; and the very improved methods—as in the example of Jonesy and the plastic mill—that should be installed most likely will be stifled by the subordinate's fear, which in turn is created by poor managers. Actions generated by fear are seldom permanent, but require repeated attention from the supervisor and resemble the dope addict's problem in that the doses must become progressively stronger and stronger as time goes by to get the desired results. Not only is the fear stimulant less productive, but it is also an intensifier of personality conflicts which contribute toward making the manager's job much more difficult. It should be noted, too, that fear certainly does not help the subordinate to work toward making his job a meaningful career or in getting satisfaction from it.

In seeking to obtain better cooperation, as an alert manager you can get some tips from the excellent accomplishments of the organization which is called Alcoholics Anonymous. This group has succeeded in changing thousands of people without the force of authority. The basic requirement underlying the AA recovery plan is that the people to be helped must take most of the responsibility for changing themselves; and the volunteer change agents, like managers, must be helpers rather than manipulators.

General supervision as a method of handling the supervisor's directional job is in accord with the modern management thinking of such authorities as Rensis Likert and the late Douglas McGregor. Any additional tapping of the valuable ideas and effort which can come only from the enthusiastic support of employees will add immeasurably to a greater volume of better on-schedule production at lower costs.

People Really Like to Work

Employees sometimes vehemently declare that payday is all they are interested in, but these same people may see money *as a measurement of progress, symbol of prestige, bulwark against disaster or an end in itself.*[1] However, in assessing the value of work as a human essential, you should notice how rapidly retirees decline in health and vigor without something to do. We even hold clinics to prepare people for retirement, largely to avoid the shock to a person who has nothing to do. Notice the increase in "moonlighting" (the holding of a second job) when an employee has time on his hands. You have possibly noticed, as do all experienced managers, the increased tension in your crew on occasions when the workload declines to the point that people don't have enough to do to keep them busy. Isaac Watts' admonition, *For Satan finds some mischief still for idle hands to do,* seems to have been confirmed by a recent riot at a Federal Job Corporation project in Kentucky. The news reported that a New York youth in residence at the location defined the cause of the trouble in these words, "Man, we don't do nothing here. That is the whole trouble. I want to be a mechanic but they say there is no room in the mechanics class. Man, there is nothing to do here." [2]

Closely associated with the desire of most employees to have plenty of worthwhile work to do is their pride in being on a winning team. They look to you, their boss, to be their spokesman with higher management and to lead them to achieve goals which will enable their performance to stand out as some-

[1] Gellerman, "Motivation and Productivity," p. 139
[2] *The Wichita Eagle* and the *Wichita Beacon,* August 22, 1965, p. A2

thing special and distinct. Throughout history, armies and fighting forces have used banners, flags, and special names to cultivate and reward the winning-team idea, which is a natural human desire.

If you are going to be the kind of leader that productive subordinates follow, you cannot be neutral or middle-of-the-road minded. You must clearly commit yourself to support those from whom you in turn expect support. You must be the buffer for those reporting to you. You are the decision-maker for your crew, department, or section. If mistakes are made, you cannot alibi and let the subordinate take the heat. This protective kind of action helps you earn the respect which you must have from your subordinates. You will most likely want to pick a private time and place to discuss with those reporting to you the mistakes that have been made and endeavor to reach a better understanding to avoid a recurrence of any specific difficulty.

Information as a Cooperation-Getter

To aid the get-things-done employee, you should have as many conversations as practical to clarify the details of a subordinate's job, to further, "See eye to eye on the what and how of his duties. To achieve this shared viewpoint, the two of you should sit down and talk about the work to be done, the standards by which it is to be measured, and the major problems involved." [1] As the superior, you have an obligation to see that those reporting to you are aware of the practices, rules, policies, and the expected performance of your section as it relates to the total organization.

It is in your personal contacts with the subordinate that you open the wellspring of new ideas, new methods, and better ways of doing a job. The employee quickly learns whether you welcome an understudy with original proposals or prefer him to leave the thinking to you. By the very nature of a business organization's structure, it is what you, the boss, think is most important which gets done first; and it will aid the subordinate if you let him know what duties you consider should have primary attention.

Constructive Control of Conduct

John, the manager of a large company's printing and reproduction department, found reasons to suspect that some employees on the night shift were sleeping during working hours among the large rolls of paper in the supply room. In thinking about the situation, John determined the priority order of importance in the problem: 1. Danger to the employees because of possible shifting of the rolls of paper; 2. Bad effect on working morale of the others in the department; 3. The loss in efficiency.

[1] Quinn, "Sure-Fire Ways to Stunt Your Subordinates' Growth," *Personnel,* January-February 1963

John told George, the night shift supervisor, that he would like to try to handle this disciplinary problem without making policemen out of managers. Because of the danger, they agreed that the area where the rolls were stored should be fenced off in stout wire with a gate locked and key retained by the manager on duty. However, John thought they should also use this incident for some education in cooperation.

Within the following two days, John and George together checked with the local, independent printing firms on prices, quality, and ability to meet output requirements. These figures were compiled in chart form which showed that the work their department was doing could be performed outside the plant at slightly less than the cost in their own department.

John presented this resumé to employees on all shifts, in factual fashion, as information of interest to all of them. The very next day orders started rolling out of the department at noticeably increased tempo, and the people on the job made sure that any slackers knew they intended to keep the work in the plant. Over a period of time, some "no-goods" decided to leave and, in a case or two, others were asked to leave; but the overwhelming majority supported their management, and efficiency went up amazingly.

From this example, you should get: *First,* the managers took precautionary action to insure the employees' safety; *second,* John and George used an educational approach rather than abruptly raising a rules barrier which the employees could use to convince themselves that they were being treated unfairly; *third,* the specific conduct requirements were tied to something that all employees understood—their safety and jobs in their department; *fourth,* John and George did not attempt to pry into the private lives of employees but limited their concern to on-the-job difficulties. An off-the-job practice could have had a bearing on the case; but, as George Odiorne states, "The corporation alone apparently has the strength to make a bargain with its employees that permits a man to retain his uniqueness as an individual at the same time he earns his money . . . Managers must see the relationship as an economic one." [1] *Fifth,* in positive, constructive control of conduct, you must remember that the superior can play no favorites. You can't close your eyes to violations of clearly understood, proper conduct. If employees understand that you will move quickly to support right actions and just as fast to do something about wrong conduct, the total superior-subordinate relationship will be improved.

Working Effectively with People

As a present-day manager, you will be a success because of *how* you supervise rather than specifically *what* you direct. As a true leader of people, a technical assignment will not upset your professional ability to perform as a

[1] Odiorne, *Michigan Business Review,* March 1965, p. 31

manager. You may need time for special study and organization, but the tests of your performance will still be how well you make decisions, solve problems, and motivate others. They are key factors in any manager's success.

Meeting these problems should pose a fascinating challenge for you, partly due to management's broad scope. The breadth of your responsibilities is illustrated by the fact that *every manager has five entities to serve.* Keep in mind that each is primarily a personal relationship. *First, the customers*—business must be responsible to those who buy its products and to their needs. You must exhibit interest in the customer's problems and conscientiously work toward providing solutions rather than maintaining a "Hands-off" attitude which in effect says, "This is your problem alone." More emphasis on service is evidence of a realization of this responsibility to the customer. Chrysler Corporation's 5-years or 50,000-miles warranty on their cars is an example of the trend. When the auto dealer calls you to find out how the car you recently purchased is operating, he is taking a step toward a personal relationship. It is good for his business.

Second, as professional managers, *you also have an obligation to the owners of the business.* Most people agree that because investors provide the necessary capital for a business, they are entitled to a fair return on their money. However, the mutual interests of both the operating directors and owners are better served if you make the effort to convince the investors of your competence and stewardship as a good manager. Specifically, the stockholder is more willing to accept the plowing back of earnings into the business rather than paying them out as dividends, if he has confidence that his company's managers are building a better future investment for him as the owner.

A *third* factor important to the business, which you must satisfy largely through your personal relationship efforts, *is the community.* More and more frequently, managers are called upon to provide leadership in such things as the Chamber of Commerce, Red Cross, United Fund, YMCA, Boy Scouts, Salvation Army, and other types of worthwhile public services. In a broad forward look at the present and future of corporate citizenship, it appears that this is the area in which the stewards of business enterprises have the best opportunity to meet what Peter Drucker calls the first social responsibility of the manager today, which is, "To make understandable to the layman—the educated people who are outside of business and necessarily ignorant of it—what it is that business does, can do and should do, and what it is the manager is doing." [1] And it just may be that meeting this responsibility will determine whether the economic system as we know it can survive.

M. J. Rathbone, recently retired chairman of the board and chief executive officer of the Standard Oil Company (New Jersey), said before the Wharton School Alumni Society:

[1] Drucker, *Managing for Results,* pp. 226-227

> We know perfectly well that business does not function by divine right but, like any other part of society, exists with the sanction of the community as a whole. The interests of the community are in turn expressed through governments. As a business manager, I am absolutely certain that we must keep in touch with the point of view of a great many people. To do this we must tune in on public thoughts and attitudes and insofar as possible, consider them in our decisions and actions. And the larger and more complex the business, the more essential such tuning-in must be.[1]

As a professional manager, you have a *fourth* boss which can be very demanding; that is *the employees.* Probably the most deadening burden on our nation's economy today is the serious decline in the enthusiasm which people have for working at their jobs. Automation, the size of organizations, the stepped-up pace of living, and increased population concentrations are just a few of the factors which can be blamed for contributing to dehumanizing the individual's employment environment. The lessening of job interest has spawned pressure groups and spotlighted spokesmen who are unqualified to speak on these really complex questions, plus an outwardly benevolent but nevertheless disturbing governmental interference. All of these intrusions have made the manager's job of building a healthy relationship with employees more difficult.

The *fifth* personal relationship which you have as a manager *is with suppliers.* Almost all manufacturers, wholesalers and retailers depend upon a person or organization for a critical portion of the products which keep them in business. Valuable on-time scheduling and meeting quality commitments at a fair price are important to all businessmen. These essentials are largely based upon confidences built up by mutual respect between the parties. If the supplier and the supplied understand each other, it can result in wiser capital expenditures for inventory, new equipment and maintenance, and more precise sales targets with the total long-range business planning made easier for both parties.

With these five basic relationship requirements as an aid to your better understanding and operating as a manager, you are now ready to study suggestions in areas for working more effectively with people.

One of the first things you must strive to do is to spend more time with the people vital to your success, including those reporting to you, your peers, and superiors in your organization. You can learn from an action which sales managers as well as the telephone company continually stress, that is the value of spending more time "selling." One test showed that a group of salesmen actually spent only 23% of their time selling their products.[2] Likewise, don't be a manager who stays in his office and listens to reports that subordinates want him to hear. Instead, be the kind of supervisor who finds out for himself.

Since getting along with, understanding, and working with people are necessary to your future as a professional manager, you must spend as much time as possible in the best laboratory there is for developing leaders—that is

[1] Golden, L. L. L.: "Not by Divine Right," *Saturday Review*, Sept. 18, 1965, p. 129
[2] Gray, *Psychology in Human Affairs*, p. 553

with people. Human reactions, the give and take of personal exchanges, and noticing how different individuals respond to and perceive stimuli can result in more meaningful experiences if you have read, studied, and understood management theories and principles. Such knowledge and experience can result in a know-how which will not become outdated as machine technology changes.

Integrity is a basic success quality in dealing with people. If the supervisor is a "stinker," he ought to be an honest one. It is essential for you to be yourself if you are to establish integrity. Don't attempt to be something you aren't. You will find it more difficult to change your personality than to adapt your management practices to your own sincere self.

Increase Your Ability to Persuade

Jack was leading a conference in which he hoped to get general agreement from the twelve participants on a proposed company-wide training program. Each member in the meeting was his own boss in the sense that there was no direct line authority of one manager over another, although different management levels were represented.

Jack opened the meeting by saying that general criticism had come from customers because of the poor quality of their pots and pans. The inspection department representative broke in with, "Most of the trouble is on the punch press and in the dipping operation." This caused the manufacturing shop representative to alibi that, "The purchasing department was buying too cheap a grade of steel." This accused department vowed, "The people that personnel sends you fellows don't know a tub from a skillet." The conference leader interrupted to remark that, "It looks like everyone has a stake in this problem, so let's quit blaming each other and see what can be done about correcting the situation." Then, as everyone settled down, he asked for ideas on what could be done.

First one and then another suggested more attention to his own specific section: manufacturing, more care in use of dies and machines; inspection, to tighten their specifications, and so forth. Jack wanted to know, "Isn't there a way that all departments can work together on this difficulty?" This caused some thinking, and in the sparking of thoughts back and forth it was suggested that a general "better-quality drive" throughout the company should be promoted. From here on Jack's course was smooth sailing because he could get everyone to take a direct part in the program with activities and rewards to each individual and section.

Several principles applicable to managing for cooperation are illustrated by the above incident. *First,* everyone in the meeting was influenced to Jack's viewpoint because all honesty felt included as a team member. *Second,* each participant felt he was getting something for himself out of the decision which was reached. *Third,* each person felt some pride in their total organization as a wide-awake outfit.

How You Can Get Better Cooperation on the Job

First, the people reporting to you are distinct personalities, a combination of the way they see their experiences, their respect for you and other authority generally, their willingness to follow directions. Your best course is to *deal honestly with those reporting to you at all times and on all occasions.* Tell your subordinate what you like or dislike about his work. He needs to know, wants to know, and has a right to know what you think of his performance.

Second, it is only natural that your subordinates ask, "What am I getting out of doing my job the way that I do it?" You must answer this question in terms sufficiently attractive to gain and maintain the individual's cooperation in the total team effort. In order to meet his requirement, you will have to *know a great deal about the subordinate,* his job, and how to communicate effectively with him.

Third, to keep subordinates cooperating, *you must give them something to look forward to.* Sometimes this may be a live organization, one that is going someplace. As Gibbons wrote in *The Decline and Fall of the Roman Empire,* "All that is human must retrograde if it does not advance." It is more practical if you can make progress something to look forward to, an on-the-job interest, but possible outside activities should not be overlooked—either for the subordinate or the company management. Often employees take pride in their company if its officials are active in unselfish, good citizenship causes.

When you fully accept and practice the general laws of cooperation, you necessarily display an attitude which is expressed by words and actions toward your subordinates. This attitude has many facets:

1. You recognize the interdependence of all employees.
2. You think, act, and talk about success.
3. You are constantly alert for new ideas.
4. Others become noticeably more important to you.
5. You stress team problems rather than your own personal difficulties.

Your Future Lies in Learning to Work with People

1. *Machines, tools, equipment, and methods change, but people remain* just people.
2. *Managers should think of their jobs as serving subordinates.*
3. *Help those reporting to you by:*
   a. *seeing that they know what to do*
   b. *giving practical freedom to perform*
   c. *letting them use their talents*
   d. *making their job important.*

4. *Make your crew, section, or department "the place to work."*
5. *Make it possible for your subordinates to:*
   a. *have on-the-job success experiences*
   b. *see that you will give them judicious support*
   c. *get periodic reports, and*
   d. *review the results of specific actions.*
6. *Practice general supervision rather than regimentation. See that your management thinking doesn't consider people in a gob.*
7. *Remember that people like challenging work and will give better co-operation if they are informed.*
8. *Constructive control of conduct is an educational process:*
   a. *watch for safety hazards*
   b. *don't make arbitrary rules*
   c. *make conduct requirements understandable*
   d. *don't pry into people's private lives*
   e. *play no favorites, support right actions and condemn wrong ones.*
9. *You have a management relationship responsibility to*
   a. *customers*
   b. *owners of the business*
   c. *the community*
   d. *employees*
   e. *suppliers.*
10. *Your best laboratory is working with people. Always be yourself.*
11. *Increase your persuasive ability by:*
    a. *getting everyone into the act*
    b. *giving something to all, if possible*
    c. *awakening pride in the total group.*
12. *Get better cooperation by:*
    a. *keeping your subordinate up-to-date on how he is doing*
    b. *giving those reporting to you something they want*
    c. *giving your subordinate something to look forward to.*

Chapter 5: The Hidden Urge

"Challenge is the core and mainspring of all human activity. If there's an ocean, we cross it; if there's a disease, we cure it; if there's a wrong, we right it; if there's a record, we break it; and finally, if there's a mountain, we climb it." [1] These words of James Ramsey Ullman, written about *The National Geographic*-sponsored American Mount Everest expedition, express the competitive desire to excel which you must have to reach the top in your job as a professional manager.

Without an urge to outstrip anything which stands in your way to becoming a better manager, you will not make the necessary effort to study, think, practice hard judgments, and endure the pressures which are an everyday requirement of a really top-flight, guiding decision-maker.

A strong manager's competitive "will to win" can help you immeasurably in meeting your current and future leadership problems however difficult the situation.

The Biblical history of Saint Paul illustrates his matchless spirit in contending for Christian converts in the face of tremendous odds. Something of his passion for success is evident in his writing when he said:

> I made myself a slave, a Jew, came under the law, worked outside the law, became weak. I have become all things to all men, that I might by all means save some. . . . Do you not know that in a race all the runners compete, but only one receives the prize? So run, that you may obtain it.

[1] *National Geographic Magazine,* July 1965, p. 9

This is not to say that you must brutally trample all opposition in a "dog-eat-dog" struggle up through the ranks of a business organization. Far from it. Earning a leadership position requires many additional qualities besides competition, such as good judgment. In satisfying the competitive requirement, it is often necessary for you to make personal sacrifices in handling job assignments so that you will be better prepared to move to a position of greater responsibility when the opportunity arises. While you as an individual manager are doing your best, you must respect all other good managers in the organization who are themselves endeavoring to advance in their profession. Such an atmosphere results in the creation of a winning team from which managers and employees alike can benefit. When you work in this fashion, your organization has a greater continuous volume of quality production at lower costs which means more contracts, more business, more jobs, and more openings for advancement. Your out-front position will be won because rival organizations were not as efficient in "running so as to win the prize."

Success Is First an Idea

Author Cameron Hawley has his creation, Cash McCall, make some appropriate statements, such as:

> I'd left the United States with the idea that the American businessman was a pretty awful character—cold, materialistic, nothing but a money grubber. But when I stacked him up against what I found around the world, he looked like a fairly decent character. The longer I went, the more I began to feel that same way about the whole American idea. All right, maybe we had turned company worship into something like a national religion, but could anyone argue that it didn't work? Look at the results. Could anyone say that we hadn't created the best way of life that the world had ever known? [1]

And the people most essential for making this economic system work are that small select group which you represent, the business managers. After a special kind of management experience, Cash McCall said:

> It was the most exciting thing that had ever happened to me . . . probably sounds ridiculous to make the comparison, but it was something like mountain climbing—all the preparation, every detail so important, knowing that if you slip once you're done. Then you make it and you're up there on top. Once that's happened, you're never quite the same again—you never get it out of your system.[2]

Avoid Unfair Competition

If you put everything you have into your job, it can be a daily experience in exhilaration; however, you need to be alert for damaging, unfair competition.

1 Hawley, Cameron: *Cash McCall,* p. 355
2 Ibid., pp. 357-358

The vice president in charge of public relations for a large manufacturing organization, call him "Speck," was discussing an employee hiring program with the director of industrial relations, named "Wilford." Because the skills needed were not available in the labor market at this time, Speck suggested that, after a careful selection, a training program should be started. Wilford immediately volunteered to see that the vice president's idea was carried out. Speck had a second thought, however, which caused him to remember that the manager in charge of training, Cedric, reported to another vice president. With a caution to the industrial relations director to hold everything, he called his associate vice president and briefly outlined the problem and his idea for a solution, requesting that Cedric be allowed to sit in with them on the details of arranging the training program.

You might well consider that Speck's actions were unnecessarily cautious, but this is necessary to encourage company-wide teamwork. Not only must you protect the supervisors in your own organization from harmful internal competition, but you must do all you can to see that relationships throughout the organization are kept honest.

It was a very natural reaction by Wilford, as a good, aggressive manager, to strive to add to his duties and authority by invading Cedric's area of responsibility. You will find, however, that such actions lead to retaliatory sniping and bickering which distorts your own judgment and prevents your getting the cooperation from others which a good management team must have. Speck fortunately was an experienced administrator and recognized the danger in time to bring the proper associate managers into a necessarily joint endeavor.

This is not intended to say that under all situations Wilford would have been entirely wrong. For example, if Cedric had known of the need and failed to take supporting action, then some carefully controlled internal competition from a logical rival would have jarred the delinquency out of Cedric, the complacent manager. If properly guided, a hungry supervisor striving for added authority provides zest for a true professional manager's work. As reported in *The Wall Street Journal,* November 26, 1965, President Johnson made some use of such administrative tactics:

> McNamara spreads his wings beyond the defense realm, irking other bureaucrats.
>
> Some officials bristle at his take-over of announcement of stockpile sales plans. "He's not really running the thing," one critic insists. McNamara slows supersonic airliner development more than civil aviation men like. The Pentagon chief has even ventured into aiding Appalachia, with a study of job effects of oil vs. coal competition.
>
> McNamara's nondefense activity is largely Johnson's doing. LBJ aims to throw a war-need cloak around price restraint efforts. He won't hesitate to give McNamara other economic tasks. Business background, plus self-assurance, makes the defense boss a natural choice. McNamara is quite willing to serve as a lightning-rod for Johnson.

McNamara tires of his Pentagon post, no longer finding fresh challenges in it. But that's no guarantee he'll move on.[1]

If possible dangers of competition to teamwork are kept in mind, you can help subordinates cultivate an ardor for the job because, as the intellectual Emerson said, *Nothing great was ever achieved without enthusiasm,* which may be just the thing to add spice to an ambitious manager's work interest. As a leader who might with judgment choose to stimulate internal competition, take some advice from Andrew McCall, the swashbuckler, free-wheeling entrepreneur and grandfather of Cash, who had once said to his grandson, *The only thing that ever worried him was giving another man just cause to think that he had been treated unfairly.*[2] Keep the competition clean. Remember, no house divided against itself will stand.

Using Ambitions to Build Competitive Attitudes

One of our universally shared emotions is ambitions, and individual aspirations are as varied as the people who hold them. In a recently held, special, lower managers' developmental meeting, one of the participating supervisors asked the vice president of the division, "In your own thinking, how important is money as an incentive for superior management performance?" The vice president, a very forthright individual, quickly answered, "If you leave out the money, you lose me right away. That's why I am here." Quite obviously, a manager at such a high level was not motivated entirely by money. He had sought and earned added responsibility because of some dominance of personal ego. Undoubtedly, the vice president certainly looked ahead to further improvement in status. So as a knowledgeable manager be careful that you are not misled into believing that competition for wages alone will bring out the best performance in a supervisor, even though it is universally recognized as a measuring stick. Money is often more of a motivator when it is a challenging comparison with what another manager earns.

In considering how to stimulate a manager reporting to you, watch for shifting emphasis in his ambitions. The most readily recognizable one is that as a person becomes older, security becomes one of the important foci of his ambitions.

Allegiance as an Aid to Competition

In the Battle of New Orleans, January, 1815, Andrew Jackson led frontiersmen in leather jerkins and homespun, New Orleans militia in dress uniforms, some U.S. regulars, a few marines, Baratarians in flashy silk sashes,

1 *The Wall Street Journal,* 11-26-65, Washington Wire Column, p. 1
2 Hawley, op.cit., p. 359

Mississippi horsemen, whites, negroes, mulattoes, Creoles, Frenchmen, and Dominicans. They fought in a common cause. All the members of this heterogeneous army were loyal to a leader who worked fourteen hours a day himself and expected similar devotion from his followers. Upon his arrival, General Jackson set things to stirring in the old city. It was evident that he knew what he wanted and intended to get it.

Undoubtedly British losses of almost thirty times those of the defending forces came from competition between the numerous nationalities to demonstrate superiority over their comrades in arms.

As a manager, if you can generate inspired leadership approaching that which our seventh president demonstrated in winning one of our country's most significant victories, subordinates will compete for your favorable comment.

Most people have common loyalties, and usually one of these is a measure of affection for *my* job, *my* company, and *my* organization. As a manager striving to improve, you can use such a predilection as a valuable motivational force.

Most People Respect a Fair Deal, Even in Tough Competition

Selling life insurance is a highly individualized and strong competitive business. Recently, a young college graduate named Ron started in the general life policy division of a large company. Our young salesman called on Ray and his wife, Nell. He received a very nice welcome. They visited about the purchase of a small policy. Ron returned to his office and worked out a proposal in line with their conversation, and then explained it to Ray. Even though it was satisfactory, Nell suggested they wait a few days before closing the deal.

After a week, Ron checked back with his prospects and, much to his surprise, found that they had purchased the very coverage which he had worked out from Nell's brother-in-law who also sold insurance.

Even though Ron was young in the business and had a legitimate reason to be upset, he very graciously said he was sorry that they had not bought the policy from him but that he was glad they had obtained what he thought was the coverage which best suited them at that time.

Through a series of unusual circumstances, within a month Ray was made president of his company. In that position, as a protection to the organization, a one-hundred thousand dollar life insurance policy was taken out by the company on Ray's life. And you know who wrote that policy—Ron.

Ray realized that on the earlier, small policy (for $6,000), he had not acted fairly, and Ron's courteous reception of this act of bad faith had made a terrific impression. The promotion enabled Ray to make amends, and Ron traded slightly more than a hundred dollars in commission for thousands of dollars as a reward just a month later.

It pays to be competitive, and it also pays to be fair.

The people reporting to you notice how you and others behave when the pressure is really on.

A Strong Competitor Builds Pride

You can learn a management lesson about pride and competition from the Biblical story of Samson, the strong man hero of the tribe of Dan. Before his birth, Manoah, his father, and his unnamed mother sold their friends and acquaintances a legend of how important their son would be to Israel's future. When Samson arrived on the scene, he was already famous with the pride of a significant birth and the expected performance of great accomplishments to come about in the future.

Overloaded with the handicap of his own self-importance, the Danite immediately started to compete for the favor of women instead of the glory of Israel. His parents tried to direct his energies into more productive channels but were disappointed because their son, born with so much promise and schooled with such pride, directed all his competitive urges to physical pleasures and violence.

A few of his notable actions were killing a lion with his bare hands and slaying thirty Philistines in a rage when he found one of his women friends had betrayed him. On another occasion, he caught three hundred foxes, tied their tails together with a lighted torch between each and burned the Philistine's grain ready for harvest. Following this, he killed a thousand enemies with the jawbone of an ass. While visiting a lady friend in the Philistine city of Gaza, his enemies attempted to trap him within the walls by locking the heavy gates, but he picked up the gates and post holding them and carried them to the top of a nearby hill.

Finally, a woman named Delilah used his pride in his physique to weaken and trap him so that he meekly submitted to his lifelong enemies, the Philistines. He died as their prisoner.

Samson, born of great expectations, directed his urge to excel to feats of great physical strength but failed to develop judgment and leadership intelligence.

As an alert and ambitious manager, you can avoid the problems that wrecked Samson's life. Use personal and group pride of accomplishment to further healthy competition by: *First,* helping all subordinates to feel adequate on their job through expressed confidence; *second,* freely commend good work; *third,* stimulate those reporting to you to do their own thinking in developing their jobs; *fourth,* encourage a subordinate's pride in his work by letting him expand his responsibilities and consulting him on detailed practices which relate to his job.

Teamwork Against Tough Odds Makes Competition Fun

The big strike started on a cold February morning with a picket line of largely out-of-town strangers manning the strategic gates into the manufacturing plant. Throughout the day supervisors and some skilled employees climbed the fences or rode through the gates on trains and trucks to get inside.

A later count of noses showed that several hundred had been able to get into the plant. They faced the countless problems cheerfully. Food could be shipped in by rail and prepared in the plant cafeteria; but, there was a question of clothes, a place to sleep, toothbrushes, shaving equipment, haircuts, and communicating with the outside by overloaded telephone lines. Shower rooms were available, coveralls supplied, and other personal items acquired in various ways.

As time passed, there were repeated threats by pickets to storm and enter the plant. This became more real when certain mischievous insiders gleefully threw sacks of a very black mixing compound from plant windows on the opponents outside.

Despite the many handicaps, managers inside the plant operated production lines. One of the most exciting experiences of the entire siege was the personal competition which sprang up between supervisors as each tried to outproduce the other.

Weeks passed and a plant newspaper was published with news of humorous happenings to individuals within the plant. For recreation, basketball games were organized and roller skating became popular. Throughout the many days of relative confinement, no one grumbled, and no suggestion was heard of giving up. Everyone willingly pitched in to help, exhibiting a strong teamwork interest in winning the contest whatever personal sacrifices might be required. When, after due time, a settlement was reached, all those who had been inside went out and home with a feeling of having learned and enjoyed a successful working-together experience.

As a manager striving to do a better directional job, you can get some of the values of this strike experience into your leadership if you can stimulate a unity of purpose among those reporting to you.

Ways to Further Teamwork Unity

First, don't hide the difficulties; obstacles add a needed spark to the striving. *Second,* all management must be continuously in the act. Just words will not serve the purpose. *Third,* leaders must be optimistic and clearly reflect a hate-to-lose attitude. *Fourth,* the individuals must see some personal benefits. *Fifth,* your subordinate alone is a different person than he is as a member of a supportive group. *The Wichita* (Kansas) *Eagle* published a news report November 27, 1965, which illustrates this idea:

> Kansas college students attending a conference to protest U.S. policy in Viet Nam were caught up Friday in the meeting's enthusiasm.
>
> More than 800 persons, including 15 Kansas representatives, crowded the Harrington Hotel here for the conference's second day.
>
> *"The main value is that there is tremendous enthusiasm here,"* said Martha Habetter, Bethel College senior from Reedley, Calif. "This will be carried straight back to college campuses."
>
> "Just talking is worthwhile," said Steve Stucky, Bethel sophomore from North Newton, Kan. *"The ideas passing around—they give you the feeling others are with you."*

To Be Competitive, You Must Use Technical Advances

Most workmen will admit privately that tools, equipment, and machines have increased the nation's productivity and provided more goods and services for everyone. However, as you stimulate fresh ideas and make use of new methods and better technology, you must be ready to meet the frequently raised but impractical charges that automation should be curtailed because it means a shifting and relocating of familiar job skills. Such falacious arguments, that the continued advance of machines will finally put everyone out of a job, have been going on since the start of the industrial revolution. The facts are as Dean McGuire says:

> Automation will probably create more jobs in the long run. This has been the history of innovation since the wheel; every economic advance has added to the stability and income of labor, although it has often brought about immediate and technological unemployment. Furthermore, history illustrates that labor has always fought against such innovations—from the burning and stoning of factories in the industrial revolution through the destruction of the mechanical cotton picker in the Southern States during the 1930's and the objections to automation today—and has always lost, for not even the strongest labor union can permanently delay progress in technology.[1]

Certainly no one can deny the evident and accomplished fact that through the years more and better machines have been created, and that such improvements are a major reason why productivity has increased, thus raising the material standard of living for a greater number of people.

In our nation over the past twenty-three years for which comparable figures are available, investment per production worker employed in manufacturing as a whole has increased from \$5.2 thousands in 1939 to \$21.7 thousand in 1962.[2]

During this same period of time, factory jobs have increased by 4.2 millions, and unemployment as a percentage of the total civilian labor force has declined from 17.2% in 1939 to 5.6% in 1962.[3] These statistics not only indicate the growing use of machines, but, more importantly, the increase in jobs, decline in unemployment, and accompanying improved well-being of more people.

1 McGuire, *Business and Society,* p. 300
2 *Economic Almanac,* 1964, p. 273, and *NICB Road Maps of Industry,* No. 1526
3 *Economic Almanac,* 1964, pp. 32-3, 72

The Wall Street Journal, December 1, 1965, quoted:

> Arjay Miller, president, Ford Motor Co., after a talk before the Economic Club of New York, in reply to the question: "How many people have been replaced by computers at Ford Motor Co.?"
>
> Since we first started using large-scale computers at Ford about 10 years ago, the total employment has not gone down—it has gone up by about 20,000 persons. I might add that of these 20,000, 3,000 are working on the computers themselves. Not only is this a large number, but the jobs involved are highly skilled, interesting and challenging.
>
> I think there's a misconception about computers. In the early days they did, to a certain degree, replace human effort in such areas as the writing of payroll checks and inventory control. Computers have now progressed far beyond this, and are performing tasks that human beings could not do economically, and are thereby creating new work, not only for our computer programmers, but also for the manufacturers of computers . . . More importantly, computers permit us to manage better, and if we do a better job of managing, we shall have more opportunities for growth in employment.[1]

Again, one of your important responsibilities as a KNOW-and-DO manager is to cultivate a free exchange of ideas between yourself and subordinates. You must evaluate their proposals, use the good ones, give credit, and avoid stifling any potentially valuable thoughts.

All managers need to do a lot of thinking, working, and communicating about better, quicker, and more efficient use of new technology.

Some Difficulties in Using Technical Improvements

Years after the installation of diesel engines, railroads still retain unneeded firemen. October 11, 1965, the International Typographical Union and the Publishers Association of New York agreed to a settlement of a twenty-three-day-old strike against New York newspapers in which automation was an issue. *The Wall Street Journal* reported on this date a suit by the *Cleveland Plain Dealer* against Local #1 of the American Newspaper Guild because they refused to handle *New York Times* news service copy. On September 17, 1965, *The Wall Street Journal* reported that the newly merged San Francisco *Chronicle* and *Examiner* and *News-Call Bulletin* in a front page editorial apologized to its readers for the paper's shortened form, riddled with typographical errors and carrying large blank spaces in place of advertisements. The publishers blamed the members of the International Typographical Union's Local #21 for production troubles. It is understood (says *The Wall Street Journal*) that a key issue is a reduction in the number of employees.

What You Must Do

Getting acceptance of productive improvements is a nation-wide problem, but alert, thinking managers can solve it as they have those of the past. Here is a helpful thought:

[1] *The Wall Street Journal,* Dallas, Texas, 12-1-65, p. 16

> Progress in the automation of manufacturing processes and in electronic data processing has, of course, markedly increased productivity and enabled gross national products to grow at a much faster rate than the working population. . . . By itself, . . . , automation will not solve all our manpower problems; on the contrary, ever-increasing attention must be paid to insuring that our human resources are effectively used.[1]

First, as a manager striving to meet this need, you must *be sure you are flexible, adaptable, and imaginative* in trying to find the best means of teaching subordinates to appreciate the advantages to them of the increasing trend toward automation.

Second, you are not insulated from this problem because the rapid improvement of machines means that more and more of management's *routine administrative chores will be eliminated.* A full understanding of this fact can jar a complacent supervisor who has grown comfortable through following a standard routine for years. In such a case, you need to adapt your own thinking first before you can help your subordinates.

Third, remember and use the evidence that *many small, production-increasing changes occur every day without difficulty.* New arrangements of productive processes, movement of machines, and reassignment of people to new and different jobs are normal management changes.

Fourth, prepare your subordinates for a changed situation affecting them as far ahead as practical. Frank discussions on an individual basis are best. Point out the good and bad features. Often transfers to other jobs are possible.

Fifth, you need to be well checked out on the jobs under your direction. Your position in the organization may be at a level which prevents your personal administration of these details because of the number of employees involved. In your case a competent subordinate must secure a clear picture of employee skills affected by the improved methods, including those even indirectly required to change. The age of the individuals on these jobs and the turnover rates will be helpful in making the necessary adjustments.

Sixth, it is only fair to both the new and veteran employees that special care be exercised in adding to your payroll. As well as can be determined, the supervisor should see that newly hired people possess the qualities of flexibility and adaptability, plus the necessary intelligence. A thought expressed by J. F. Burlingame should be considered by the manager as he endeavors to help subordinates:

> With a rapidly increasing percentage of our population acquiring advanced education, it is difficult to believe that members of this group who go into business will be satisfied with spending their daily working hours . . . in pursuits devoid of intellectual satisfaction. It is more likely that they will attempt to curtail the freedom of businessmen or any other group that tries to force such a condition on them.[2]

[1] Mann, "Providing for Present and Future Management Needs," *Personnel,* July-August, 1965, p. 27

[2] Gellerman, op. cit., 95-96

This quoted thought suggests that you review written job descriptions to make sure they are up to date and, if practical, interject specific challenges which might be appropriate.

Seventh, as changes are made, you can at times *be of help to subordinates by identifying any hold-ups to production.* You must study the people, machines, flow of work, and even the union contract in great detail. In every case where you cannot correct the situation yourself, you should be sure that the problem and your ideas for a solution are passed on to your line superior.

Eighth, in meeting these innovations, you should arrange to *make full use of all facilities for training and retraining of present subordinates.* The experienced employees are probably more valuable to the organization than the general class of new people available for hiring. If the employed force can be retained at a stable level, learning costs can be reduced, relationships will be better, and increased unemployment costs can probably be avoided. An added advantage is that such practices tend to attract the higher types of employees.

Get a Little Bit More Effort

All the "must do's" suggested encourage a better over-all job performance, and just a little bit of better quality work from a lot of people "snowballs" the results into sizeable total improvement. Researchers tell us that you as a manager, as well as your subordinates, normally work far under your top potential. You might note a statement by Colonel Lyndall F. Urwick, well-known management consultant, "It is inhuman and as destructive of personality structure to keep an individual in a job which does not demand the best he or she can give as it is destructive of physical structure to keep a child in shoes that are too small for it." [1] It is certainly of mutual interest to you as well as those reporting to you and the organization to try to discover special skills and make full use of them.

An alert boss has a better opportunity to discover these valuable abilities when working with the valid assumption that most people want to do a better job. Again, Urwick has some stinging criticism for managers as he says, "Remarkably little is done . . . about any of the things which might possibly win the worker's interest and enthusiasm as a craftsman, a man of foresight, and a worthwhile member of society." [2] This thought, even if only partly true, certainly reduces the subordinate's inclination to put forth a special effort toward giving a better total job performance.

To whatever extent Urwick's comments fit your method of managing, you should increasingly direct your attention toward trying to find ways of stimulating better subordinate interest and enthusiasm. If you work persuasively at your job, you can show subordinates how meeting the better total job perform-

[1] Urwick, *How the Organization Affects the Man,* p. 4
[2] Ibid.

ance objective can mean more jobs because more and better production at lower cost puts the organization in a better competitive position. Then, too, you can help an employee add to his self-satisfaction by giving him more freedom to use his own ideas in his work.

If you are to provide the greatest improvement help to your subordinate, you must do the specific things on the job which convince the employee that teamwork between superior and subordinate will help him obtain some special benefits important to him.

Good Managers Must Be Tried Under Fire

Some managers have phenomenal success in picking outstanding supervisors for key jobs. There are also many executives who can perform all their other duties well but can't seem to pick a winner as a follow-up man. For instance, Harold had worked for ten years as a production planner for a large manufacturer of a complex transportation product. Competition in the industry was keen. The sequence of operations had a very direct effect upon production costs. Harold had trained himself to analyze a blueprint and picture in his mind just how the process plan should flow to get the greatest efficiency on even the smallest part. His supervisors were impressed with his know-how and would back his judgment over that of any other planner. Harold took a great deal of pride in his reputation for excellence. He often related to his wife how this or that top manager had asked his opinion of how a production schedule should be laid out.

In the normal course of events, some new managers were needed and, with Harold's record, everyone was convinced that he would make a good supervisor. With the full assurance of all his superiors, Harold took some training for the first-level management job. He studied the text material, learned quickly, and finished the course with one of the highest ratings in his group. Then he was assigned to direct people in doing the job he knew so well.

From the very first day on his management job, Harold was a different person. One of the attributes which his superiors had particularly liked was the confidence with which Harold went about his work, but now he appeared nervous and irritable. Where before he had been smiling and pleasant, now he became sour and preoccupied. Jim, his immediate superior, talked with the new supervisor, but about all he could get from Harold was grumbling that he couldn't keep track of everything. After a couple of months, a manager from another department told Jim that Harold's wife had asked him what they were doing to her husband at the plant, that he didn't eat or sleep well, and always seemed worried. Jim had some more conversation with Harold and also his own superiors. As a result, Harold went back to his job as a production planner and within a week was his old self again.

While this attempt at promotion to management failed for a deserving employee, even though outwardly he appeared to have the needed potential, other instances of success in a first-management situation could be cited where individuals had less going for them than Harold.

One reason why Harold failed to handle the management job is that as a successful manager you must have a full measure of competitiveness. *You must:*

1. strongly want to do that job
2. want accountability for the work of others
3. have personal confidence in your judgment
4. put into management the best that is in you.

You can also learn something worthwhile from Jim's action in Harold's case. Not only is a good competitive manager willing to take a chance in stretching the capacity of a promising subordinate, but he is just as quick to make a correction when the plan fails. He always thinks first of what will benefit his organization. Harold might have reacted like a "whipped puppy" instead of being relieved by the chance to get out of a tension situation. In either case, as a good manager Jim was braced for what might happen.

Changes Are a Management Requirement

Each boss should let his subordinates know that he expects them to encourage changes which mean progress. Managers particularly need a measure of the pioneer spirit. However, many supervisors don't mind taking a minor risk or accepting a little more responsibility without too much heat and tension.

When you are an alertly competitive manager, you will be careful not to become too attached to a particular method of operation to the extent that you are unwilling to seriously consider new ideas or procedures. Don't be too quick to say, "It has never been done that way before," or "This is the way we have always operated," or "It won't work."

New ideas are particularly valuable because you are living in an age when innovations literally spring up overnight, outdating technical information and obsoleting equipment before it can be depreciated. Even in the short span of fifteen years, marketing techniques have been drastically changed. Mathematical concepts and computers have revolutionized management controls, financial and otherwise. Today governmental agencies are providing information and services unheard of in years past.

In direct proportion to the increase of all kinds of competition, such as new products, substitution of articles, and dollar choices, your decisions as a manager have become more pressurized. Profit margins are tighter; judgment errors on your part can wipe out an investor's take-home pay by only a small miscalculation. So as a knowledgeable supervisor, you must wisely see the need to get the full cooperation of others. Concentrate on working effectively with people rather than striving to meet the impossible task of personally checking, understanding, and approving all the details of every operation you direct.

Keep Your Good Managers

To remain competitive in today's business climate, your organization must make every effort to keep its most promising managers. You have an obligation to contribute to the values that superior managers see in your company. Good managers will stay with a dynamic and progressive oufit if they think it is going places and holds forth the promise of personal rewards to a person qualified as an outstanding performer in management.

Many factors will work against your best intentions to develop strong management understudies, including: 1. Drastic economic structural changes such as recessions, replacement of products, new technology. 2. The ever-present "hot item," demanding your attention. Your local, time-consuming crisis. 3. The pressure for immediate profits. Some managements still are not willing to spend money on the development of managers for greater future returns to the company. 4. The reluctance of many managers and potential managers to admit the need for some special effort on their part to gain self-improvement. In many cases, this stems from preconceived ideas by those who have difficulty in adjusting their thinking to a changed situation.

General Restraints on a Manager's Freedom to Increase Competition

As you attempt to develop yourself into a better manager, you should recognize these relatively recent handicaps to your freedom to make changes and increase competition. *First, governments—local, state, and national—have increasingly moved into a controlling position.* This outside direction comes about through the taxing and spending powers of these bodies. Mounting taxes to support governments consume many dollars which could be directed more advantageously into capital expansion, personnel or methods improvements. The spending of government funds for purchases always carries strings which prohibit the entrepreneur from using his competitive drive to best advantage, since official inspections, rules, and bureaucratic qualification standards restrict the operation of successful, free-market practices. On many government projects, wage rates are set; and meeting better quality or time schedules do not earn a performance bonus as is true on many private contracts. As a general fact, standardization always hampers competition.

Second, the growth of labor unions' power tends more and more toward monopoly. Unions keep first and foremost the interest of their own organizations. They work for greater economic power and strive for higher wages for their members. This in turn handicaps changes which permit improvements and lessens the benefits of free competition among companies best qualified to render the needed services or products.

Third, the trend by business organizations to expand in both activities and numbers of employees hampers the flexibility needed for changes. As an organization grows, controls increase in the form of more paperwork, needed approvals, and increased pressure to do things as they have been done before.

These are some obstacles which you as a competitive manager must find ways to overcome in making the changes necessary to promote a better job performance by all employees. No doubt this is one of the factors contributing to *the fourth hindrance to change, which is defined as "a breakdown of management ethics."* The most recent, widely advertised case illustrating this point was the conviction of executives of General Electric and Westinghouse along with other electrical equipment manufacturers of price fixing. This was an obvious restriction on competition; but more than that, it tended to destroy the general confidence of people in the professional manager's qualifications to operate a free enterprise in the best interests of all. Peter Drucker writes:

> Because public attitudes toward business and businessmen are fundamentally positive, public expectations with respect to big business and its leaders are rising sharply. As a consequence, public sensitivity to any gap between actual and expected business behavior is heightened. This, rather than any sudden boost in public morality, explains the deep and lasting public concern with the General Electric-Westinghouse price-fixing affair.[1]

To the extent that managers fall in public esteem, the more difficult it becomes for business to effect the changes which you must generate as a competitively motivated manager.

The Challenge To Be a Better Manager

1. *You must be inspired and use competition in discharging your job duties.*
2. *Get excited about your work. Be aggressive, but keep the competition honest.*
3. *Build competition by using:*
   a. *ambitions*
   b. *allegiance*
   c. *a fair deal*
   d. *personal self-respect, pride.*
4. *Unity and competition go together.*
   a. *Unsolved problems tend to cultivate teamwork.*
   b. *All managers must actively promote a unified effort.*
   c. *Leaders must be optimistic and poor losers.*

[1] Drucker, "Big Business and the National Purpose," *Harvard Business Review*, March-April, 1962, p. 50

d. Employees must see some personal benefits from teamwork.

e. Your subordinate in a group is different from the same person as an individual.

5. *Make use of technical advances. Use the "must do's" to get acceptance of changes.*
6. *Strive for a little more effort from a lot of people.*
7. *You don't have a real manager until he succeeds on the job.*
8. *Changes are necessary to a manager's success.*
9. *Develop and keep your good managers.*
10. *Recognize the four broad restraints on your freedom to increase general competition:*

    a. governments

    b. labor unions

    c. the size and complexity of business organizations

    d. any breakdown of management ethics.

Chapter 6: Planning Patterns as a Functional Help to the KNOW-and-DO Manager

Hobe, a veteran of many years of management-development program experience, was hired by a rapidly expanding manufacturing company to initiate a training and education effort for the improvement of the total management force. The ground rules for control of the new training manager were broad and fluid. His boss, Jig, explained that a budget would need to be established, but that the finance department along with all other divisions of the company wanted some action right away and would be inclined to take a liberal view of expense requests. Hobe confirmed that Jig was saying that almost anything within reason could be done if it promised more and better supervisors for all departments.

Since Hobe had only just met the key people in the company's management, he knew nothing of the potential of the present managers, their needs, or even future numbers required except as a very general estimate. Thus, he felt the necessity for more information about the people with whom he would be working.

With such thoughts in mind, he proposed to the plant management council, a group of top managers from throughout the organization, a series of seven lectures to be given to all present managers in groups of approximately fifty. When his suggestion was accepted, Hobe personally reviewed selected material on management fundamentals which a supervisor should know and practice with the management council before it was presented to the total group of supervisors.

As a result of these review sessions and the general lecture series, the new training manager determined that, *first,* further basic courses of instruction were needed. *Second,* the line managers must be persuaded to take a direct part in the training of their subordinates. *Third,* a program for the preparation of qualified employees for first-level managers' jobs should be undertaken. *Fourth,* many management coordination problems needed attention. *Fifth,* a greater effort should be made to raise the prestige level of those who filled the managers' jobs.

Largely because of the earlier personal acquaintance established in the review and lecture series, Hobe was able to get this total program accepted, one part at a time. He acquired a secretary, a stenographer, a writer, and a possible conference leader. With the approval of the total program, he was able to get Jig to agree to a preliminary budget for additional writers, instructors, typist, plus needed floor space, facilities, and training equipment. When the finance department okayed the budget, Hobe was in position to go ahead.

The education-type courses were organized and supervisors scheduled to attend classes. The subjects offered were, in the main, how to do such things as: a better job of communications, a more effective job of motivational direction, writing clearer and more meaningful business correspondence. The second part of the training program required some selling, since managers generally are much more agreeable to someone else doing the educating of their subordinates rather than participating directly themselves. It was finally concluded that fourth-level managers, the superintendent classification, would conduct regular monthly meetings for all managers reporting to them. Hobe pointed out that he and his staff people would prepare material and help the superintendents get ready for these monthly meetings.

All the members of the management council were insistent that present employees should be considered first, and those qualified should be given training to fill the first-level management jobs made available by expanding employment. It was concluded that, in order to be entirely fair, all interested employees might apply for consideration in this program. The application was simply a statement of "why I feel I would make a good supervisor."

After a general announcement, 1,350 applications were received. A five-man board selected from the management council with the training manager was set up to screen the applicants. Personnel records were checked and the supervisors of those who had applied were consulted. These actions, with a consideration of the application, resulted in eliminating all but 350 from the first group of those to be selected. In further reducing the nominees to a manageable number, the 350 were given an I.Q. test in addition to reading and writing quizzes. Their immediate supervisor was interviewed and, after a personal discussion with the selection board, each candidate was rated. From this data, the board chose 125 for admission to a thirty-two hour intensive training course. Training was designed to acquaint the selectees with some of the situations and problems that they would encounter, together with suggested possible solutions.

The number four feature of the program, that of resolving coordination problems, was attacked by means of several relatively large, general meetings conducted by the manufacturing manager with all other departments and service groups in attendance. The training staff members acted as secretaries, taking careful notes of problems and who was to handle each. Information gleaned from these notes was compiled, prepared, and circulated to all those concerned with the problems; and, in follow-up sessions, a check was made of progress or reasons given why the difficulty had not been handled. This proved to be a very effective way of tracking down and getting action on knotty problems.

Raising the prestige of a manager's job was approached from several angles, using such actions as:

1. higher pay rates
2. organizing a management club
3. starting a management newsletter
4. sponsoring special management speech and investment clubs
5. reserved parking area
6. special identification buttons.

Hobe, Jig, and the management council were interested in the results obtained from these programs. Everyone recognized that, because of the intangible nature of education, some of the evaluations would be the subjective type. For instance, in the basic education series, those managers participating in the foundation courses gave their approval of the value of these studies in written form after the completion of each subject. Also, members of higher operating management not only attended the classes themselves but urged their subordinates to participate. From several sources, numerous reports of greater job interest could be traced back to new ideas stimulated because of attendance in these courses.

In the line-conducted management program, there was a built-in evaluator because, if the communications failed to penetrate the entire organizational unit, it was immediately evident and could be corrected.

The great majority of employees selected and trained in the pre-management course were appointed to a first-level management job which they handled successfully. Approximately twenty-five percent were promoted above the first level within the first two years after the program was initiated.

Coordination meetings with follow-up sessions spotlighted the trouble spots and quickly proved to be self-liquidating as problems were resolved.

The actions taken to improve a manager's prestige should be largely credited with a sharp decline in resignation of managers to take jobs with other companies. In addition, observations of on-the-job performance seemed to reflect more attention to details as a result of the special treatment.

Being a Good Manager in the Functional Area

This actual case of a specific job assignment is described in considerable detail because it illustrates the principles which you must apply on your own management job if you are to become a better manager.

The first problem facing Hobe was the establishment of a basis for planning. The second step was the determination of what needed to be and could be done. The third step involved proposing and getting approval for a specific program. The fourth step was planning, hiring, building an organization, and preparing material to meet the program requirements. All of these details are a part of the planning which the training director was required to handle as part of his job assignment.

The second broad division of a manager's functional responsibility is that of action, or carrying out his duties. In our example, Hobe arranged and conducted special courses, set up a satisfactory line-conducted conference program, put into operation a pre-management selection and training series, carried out needed management coordination meetings, and helped in raising the prestige of managers generally.

The third division of functional duties is a check-up or measure of results. The training director was able to get some worthwhile evaluations of the special courses program. The line-conducted conferences and pre-management and coordination meetings each required some thought in arranging a check-up procedure; but, methods were found in each instance. In the management prestige-building endeavor, some objective standards were noted in the decline in terminations of supervisors and the increased attention they gave to the details of their job duties.

The effectiveness with which you handle the three functional divisions of your current job, as illustrated in our training management situation, will either make or break your future as a professional manager. This functional area is, in fact, the place where you put all your knowledge and skill on display.

The remainder of this chapter and the next one will be directed to your management planning function. Chapters Eight and Nine will discuss functional actions. The last chapter of this section will be concerned with functional check-up or review of results.

Getting Ready to Plan

You are not in a position to perform the first step of your functional duties until you have laid some groundwork.

The maker of a patented aluminum sign established a small production operation in a low-rent building. Let's call this entrepreneur "Del." The product caught on with roadside farmers, nurserymen, small shop owners, and large open-air markets to the point that Del's facilities would not supply the demand. For some time past, Russ, a manufacturer of aluminum storm doors and windows, had tried to get Del interested in making his signs in some unused factory space on machines which were standing idle in his (Russ') plant.

Before engaging in any definite planning, Del had to consider: 1. Could he count on a continued rising demand or was this a seasonal situation? 2. Would his quality deteriorate if the signs were made in Russ' factory? 3. What kind of a deal could be worked out with Russ? 4. Would it be better for Del to expand his own capacity? These preparatory questions illustrate the kind of judgment decisions you as the top manager would make before you began formulating a definite plan.

It is also true that as a first-level manager on a production line, before you can recommend additional facilities to your superior, you must assure yourself that the present crew and equipment are operating at their maximum, added output is needed, and simply increasing the work force is not the answer. You also want to ponder the efficiency of quality output which may result from the acceptance of your proposal and the costs of your suggestion if you should finally decide to submit it as a plan for action.

Meet the Unpredictable Future with Planning

The failure of the Edsel automobile into which the Ford Motor Company poured so much money; the stock market crash which began September 3, 1929, and signaled the start of the great economic tragedy of the 30's decade; and the difficulties which most of you have in meeting your own personal budget, all testify to the uncertainty of foreseeing the future.

However difficult the problem of predicting what will be needed "down the road" to be competitive, as a manager you must plan ahead. Of interest are these observations by noted people. George Santayana, poet and philosopher, said, *Those who cannot remember the past are condemned to repeat it.* Edmund Burke, statesman, said, *You can never plan the future by the past.* The great, early patriot, Patrick Henry, said, *I know of no way of judging the future but by the past.*

Then how are you to do this job of planning? *First,* by applying as many facts as possible. *Second,* by relating the present to what you perceive as the future trend. *Third,* by injecting a measure of optimism. *Fourth,* by convincing yourself that the target can be reached.

You are planning when you say to your secretary: 1. "Our selections for the managers to attend university training courses next year must go to headquarters today." 2. "I want to write a letter requesting information from the fellow who talked to us about programmed learning. It may help us in communication during the projected employment build up." 3. "Oh, yes, I want to call Shifty, of the computer outfit. He offered to run a course for managers on how to make decisions." 4. "Keep in mind that our quarterly and annual reports are due by the end of the month. Let's remind the other sections of this requirement."

Likewise, as a first-line production supervisor on a manufacturing operation, the first thing in the morning you get your facts from the projected schedule. Then you decide how many workmen should be assigned to each operation and about how long they should require to finish each step before going to the next. You anticipate requirements such as tools, materials, and look forward to reaching the goal set at the end of the day.

Company-wide planning frequently takes place on an annual basis. Most organizations project what they expect to accomplish in increased profits, reduced costs, added investments in research and development, beating competition, and introducing new products. Often an annual plan must be restudied and adjusted during the year because of new developments.

Dangers in Planning Uncertainties

As a realistic KNOW-and-DO manager, you should not put all your hopes in a long-range look ahead. For instance, your intention to gain a promotion to the next level of authority in your organization within a year can be as remote as the expectations of the blissful couple leaving the church after their wedding, with visions of years of quiet happiness ahead. Uncertainties working against such a thing coming to pass are the drafting of married men, one out of four marriages ending in divorce, interfering "in-laws," and just the problem of getting used to each other. While a manager must make his own long-range plans as a sort of guiding star, you, as well as the company, will find it helpful and practical to take a quarterly or a monthly look at your progress. As an improving manager, you should frequently restudy your personal goals.

Too Much Conservatism—A Danger in Planning

One of the great merchandising organizations is reported to have been so convinced that a depression would follow World War II that their top management decided to carefully husband every possible resource. Thus, when this economic decline came about, prices would fall and store rights and inventories of goods could be purchased cheaply with the liquid capital which had been accumulated.

A competitor, Sears Roebuck and Co., took the bolder planned approach and actively expanded their retail outlets, hired additional superior people with attractive working policies, good pay scales, retirement plans and freedom of decision-making by local managers. The evidence of Sears Roebuck and Co. successes can be seen in the size and number of new stores which are to be found in every booming community.

While planning goals should not be so difficult as to cause frustration, you should have to stretch to reach your established objectives. As Robert Browning said, *Ah, but a man's reach should exceed his grasp, or what's a heaven for?*

Inflexible Planning Rules Are Dangerous

To improve as a manager, you must be ready, willing, and able to change your plans if good judgment indicates such a course. Stick-to-itiveness is a laudable quality for a manager, but the buggy whip manufacturer who persisted in turning out that product after automobiles became the accepted mode of transportation, and the blacksmith who continued to make horseshoes, soon found themselves without a market.

A cartoon from World War I shows something of the followers' reaction to a leader's insistence in adhering to a plan which to them doesn't make sense. This dialogue is between two privates of the American Expeditionary Forces: The first says, "I hear the general says we are going to capture that hill if it requires a hundred thousand men." The second replies, "Gee, ain't he generous?"

Another example of staying with a plan with questionable results was General U.S. Grant's determination as expressed in a dispatch to Washington when the Union Army was before Spottsylvania court house May 11, 1864, in which he said, "I propose to fight it out on this line if it takes all summer." Total Union casualties, killed, wounded, and missing, in this campaign were reported 26,441 compared to Confederate losses of 9,000, and the war dragged on for eleven more months before General Lee was forced to surrender at Appomattox court house April 9, 1865.

As is true with everything else which the manager does, his planning time, effort, and cost must pay off in actual on-the-job results. If the production plan or step-by-step detailed operational procedure puts individual initiative in a "strait jacket," it is probably too rigid. As a responsible manager, you must have the right, authority, and opportunity to make judgments in accordance with your demonstrated job proficiency; otherwise, the company is wasting money on your salary.

Plan Your Personal Future to Get Ahead

"Slow down. Here comes the time study man" is a whispered admonition which gets passed around among production employees who are suspicious of a possible job rate cut when an efficiency man appears in a shop. Some managers also are leery that planning may cause changes which they will not like. However, as a manager on the move, you need to do a lot of thinking about what is best for you; and this is not as easy as a consultant would seem to have it when he was quoted by Vance Packard as saying:

> That if he were a young man starting out he would, among other skills, learn dancing and charm because many of the smaller companies are now dominated by widows. "On your way up," he said "you must dance with these old gals. Many companies in Manhattan," he stated, "are controlled—sometimes through foundations—by widows who stay at such hotels as the Gotham and St. Regis and in some ways run the companies from the hotel lounges. By threatening to sell or buy ten percent of their stock, they can rattle hell out of a corporation" he said.[1]

The "among other skills" which the consultant mentioned are much more important than the "dancing and charm," because your superior is primarily interested in results which make him and his unit look good. It seems that more and more companies pay year-end bonuses to managers for superior performance.

This is a case in point at the operating level: Gene was the supervisor in charge of a second-shift crew of ten men. The job involved a complex series of machine operations extending through five floors of a large plant. Worn-out, scrapped tires were ground up, pulverized, and cooked under three hundred pounds of steam pressure with a caustic solution. Then the material was thoroughly washed and conducted by conveyers through huge rotating dryers with gas flame heat assisted by fans. From the drying operation, the recovered rubber was conveyed mechanically to mills and refiners for a finishing operation.

Gene was responsible for the entire preparation section on his shift and reported to a department head responsible for all shifts who, in turn, reported to a plant superintendent in charge of the entire manufacturing plant. Gene drove himself hard on the job: a young fellow who spent all his regular shift time checking the machinery; encouraging the operators; listening to their ideas; and seeing that mechanics, pipe fitters, and other specialists were speedily alerted when repairs were required. The operators were paid on a pool, piecework basis, so they directly benefited from Gene's special support. In his spare time, Gene visited other manufacturing plants to get new ideas which he talked over with his department head.

Another of Gene's outside activities was a plant softball team. All the players were members of Gene's crew. It was notable that the sports association directly carried over as a benefit to on-the-job cooperation. The second-shift crew, naturally, was the high producer of the plant, with no friction, absenteeism, or accidents. The operators would quickly pitch in and help whether the bottleneck happened to be on the fifth or first floor. After proving himself on this management job for a couple of years, Gene was the obvious choice for a plant manager's appointment when the company started a new factory in another town.

How Gene Did It

First, he learned all about the operation he supervised. *Second,* he made a special effort to know as much as possible about the people under his direction.

[1] Packard, *The Pyramid Climbers,* p. 206

Third, he helped the people reporting to him. *Fourth,* he treated subordinates with respect and dignity. *Fifth,* he searched for new improvement ideas both on and off the job. *Sixth,* he was able to transfer the sports teamwork from the ball field to the job. In this example, Gene acted sincerely and honestly, even though it was a planned endeavor to promote his own interests. However, in accomplishing his purpose, Gene also benefited his crew and the total organization for which he worked.

On your job you will not have exactly the same situation or opportunities as Gene, but the illustration may suggest a possible practical application of the means and value of planning as an aid to furthering your managerial ambitions.

Cy's Experience

Here is another real-life, leadership planning, success series of incidents. Cy, the teacher of a Sunday school class of high-school aged young people, was having class attendance difficulties. He worked to make the Sunday morning lesson more interesting, but this didn't solve the problem. Finally, one day, Cy drove by the home of one of the young fellows who had been to class a couple of times. In the driveway were seven or eight boys in their teens shooting basketball goals. Cy stopped to watch and noticed that most of the group were extremely expert in faking, running, and hitting the basket. Sitting there thinking, Cy mentally reviewed a plan which he thought might help solve his problem. Getting out and walking over to the boys, he said, "If you fellows would all come to Sunday school, we could win the city church league without any trouble." The next Sunday, four of the group attended the class, and Cy announced that he was coaching a basketball practice in the church gym on Tuesday night. At this first practice, a dozen boys showed up, including the four who had attended the Sunday class. Cy allowed them all to practice but warned them that everyone who played on the team must attend Sunday school. Ten of the twelve became regular attenders and, of course, they won the church league for the next four years, until Cy was transferred out of town.

What helpful ideas can you get from this experience of Cy's? *First,* some imagination and planning can assist you in solving your management problems. *Second,* discipline of both yourself and others is important. *Third,* some reward encourages others to work for your leadership goals.

Internal Planning Aids

First, know your company policy and practice. This is not with the thought that these rules must necessarily be followed exactly, but you should know what planned actions need special approval.

Second, know the established line of authority in every section of the company or companies in which you plan to do some business. You will find such knowledge of the structure especially valuable for communications.

Third, develop your sensitivity for separating facts from opinions. Watch for a distortion of facts by people attempting to sell a special point of view. Save yourself trouble by identifying personality conflicts and incompetence.

Fourth, keep yourself thoroughly informed on the details which have gone into making up a planned decision. This will aid you in looking for flaws in the plan after it is in operation. Such information will be useful to you if a change of course is desirable.

Fifth, keep yourself alert to planning needs by talking with subordinates. As you listen, ask yourself: Is there an idea here which suggests good results? Is his proposal clear? Is this a new thought?

Sixth, use your total purpose as a guide. Don't hesitate to change if your judgment directs such a course.

External Planning Aids

First, surveys—such things as labor reports of employment and unemployment, opinion questionnaires. *Second,* trade journals, business reports of new products, and equipment. *Third,* stock market and commodity trends, production indexes, and consumer price indexes.

In the final analysis when the time for decision comes, you put all the internal aids, external aids, and your best experienced judgment into a common mental pot, mix together, and conclude a plan for action.

People Planning

In your management functional planning assignment, you must give attention to equipment, processes, and materials. These factors have a direct effect upon your success. Machines, particularly, are becoming much more costly as shown by the fact that capital investment per production worker in manufacturing industries has increased more than four times during the past twenty-five years.[1] However, the essential planning component which represents the major operating cost for the greatest majority of business enterprises is its employees. People are also the most difficult entity and require the greatest management know-how to properly plan for and direct for profitable company operation. This problem is increasing rather than diminishing, as indicated in the study of a recent twenty-five year period showing that, while the total labor force was increasing only 33%, the total number of people employed increased by 50%.

Lay Out a Work Plan

Recently, while discussing the importance of physical exercise, an attorney friend remarked, "I walk for forty-five minutes every morning, but I don't waste my time because that is where I lay out my plan for the day's work."

[1] *Economic Almanac,* 1964, p. 273

Whether you choose to do it on a morning walk, at home, or at your desk, you'll find things go better if you go through the mental exercise of reviewing and making written notes of your job duties with a time schedule. Such a written guide 1. relieves your mind for important thinking jobs, 2. allows a convenient check of what you have accomplished, 3. reminds you of items to be handled, 4. as a systematic plan permits review and study for future improvement, 5. is an excellent means to stimulate self-discipline.

Action Ideas for Better Planning

To improve yourself in the manager's pay-off functional area:

1. *Prepare for and plan what you intend to do.*
2. *Recognize the uncertain future, but plan by:*
   a. *finding and applying facts*
   b. *relating the present to what you think the future will be*
   c. *being positive*
   d. *convincing yourself the objective can be reached.*
3. *Establish long- and short-range goals for yourself.*
4. *Your plans should stretch your capacity.*
5. *Don't be too "hard nosed" to change your plans.*
6. *Put yourself in your plan to win.*
7. *Use all the planning information help you can get, both inside and outside.*
8. *Direct your plans toward people, not things.*
9. *Organize your work.*

Chapter 7: Pattern-Thinking Ahead for Profit

"I don't see why businessmen are always harping on profits. Why can't you do your job the way we do and not be always gouging the people who buy your goods?" This was the comment of a clergyman in a state-wide meeting of some thirty-five ministers of all faiths, a scattering of business managers, farm organizations, and labor leaders.

How would you answer this question from a man of the cloth? For too long managers have been on the defensive, assuming that just making a greater amount of better goods and services available to more people would convince everyone that they were doing a good job as stewards of the nation's vital manpower and capital resources.

The remark of this well-meaning cleric carries the innuendo that managers are permeated with a miserly selfishness. In relation to this thought is columnist David Lawrence's review of the statistics for a non-profit organization which collects data on philanthropy. This middle 1960's check showed that individuals, business firms, and foundations gave away annually $10.6 billions to religious, educational, hospital, health, welfare, recreation, character-building and cultural programs.[1] These monies given to charitable purposes come directly from profits taken from the American business system of which you as a management representative are the guiding hand. As Mr. Lawrence points out, such unselfish giving is without parallel anywhere else in the world.

Even though our people are altruistic, without profits to spark your personal initiative there would not be the added money that can then be invested

[1] *The Wichita Eagle*, 12-4-65, David Lawrence's View

in better machines, tools, and equipment. These facilities, your know-how, and the workman's skills enable the capitalistic system to pay higher wages for the greater production resulting from each person's working hour.

Thus, the good preacher could not have his freedom of worship, thought, and speech without *profit,* an essential ingredient in the American system. Of direct importance to you as an improving professional manager, profitable operation is an important yardstick by which your on-the-job proficiency is measured.

A Critical Step in Profitable Management

As discussed in the previous chapter, organizing the details and operating a plan is necessary to build your future as an improving manager. However, your thinking must go further than just making sure all those people reporting to you are busily engaged in an organized fashion, working toward a pre-selected goal.

As an example: In a manufacturing plant which extracted nylon and cotton fibers from scrap automobile tires, a key machine was the pulverizing mill. The mill was the initial machine in the process unit which received the ground material and by conveyer passed it over a series of covered shaker screens. Ground rubber dropped through the screen, and the fluffy fiber was blown by a fan to the next screen and finally discharged for baling, free of rubber. The recovery operation was located on the plant's top floor because of the efficiency in discharging the fiber for baling on the floor immediately below. Storage space was also provided near the baler. Since the operation was largely mechanical, only four workmen were needed on each of three shifts; but the market price for the fibers, particularly the nylon, made the process highly profitable. Stu was considered one of the plant's better young managers and was assigned to supervise the 7:00 A.M. to 3:00 P.M. shift. He studied his job, fully aware that to get ahead he needed to find ways to do more than just keep things going smoothly.

In examining all the facets of his work, Stu detected some ill feeling between the workman in charge of operating the first processing step, the attrition mill on the shift which preceded his own, and Jim, the mill man on his shift. Stu talked with the manager on the night shift preceding him about his observations, but his counterpart passed it off by saying, "Jim is probably beating my man's time with the barmaid down on First Avenue that they are both trying to make." This didn't satisfy Stu; but not wishing to get into the personal life of a good employee, he concluded that, being forewarned, special watchfulness on his part should prevent real trouble. It was a good thing that he was on guard because one morning, soon after the start-up, while checking the unit, Stu saw smoke start boiling out of the discharge separator screen. Stu quickly signalled Jim to shut down the fans and power units, pointing out the fire while he rushed to the floor below.

Through the dense smoke, Stu saw several stored bales of fiber burning. The operators had appeared by this time, and the supervisor helped them truck the nylon bales to safety first and then the cotton. In the meantime, Jim had extinguished the upstairs screen separator fire. Stu and the other workmen put out the burning fiber on the floor below.

In carefully checking back through the unit, Stu was just about to direct a restarting of the equipment because everything seemed in order when Jim called him. What the mill operator had discovered was that the plate showing the setting of the attrition blades in the pulverizing mill had been misaligned to show a false reading. Thus the incorrect gauge had caused the blades to be set so closely together that in striking against each other sparks from the metal disks were drawn into the fiber unit system, starting the fire.

Once the trouble was discovered, it could be quickly corrected. Jim stoutly maintained that the tampering with the gauge had to be deliberate. He vowed that he could not make that kind of a mistake. With what Stu knew about the strained relationship between the mill men, he felt strongly inclined to agree with Jim.

However, in the absence of absolute proof of deliberate intent by the night shift mill man, it was decided to warn him of the very serious consequences which could have resulted from this incident and transfer him to another job. Maybe the barmaid got a new job, too.

Reasons for the Manager's Success

First, he learned very thoroughly the details of the job he supervised. *Second,* Stu found out the most valuable commodity he was producing. *Third,* he studied the relationships of the people important to his management success. *Fourth,* Stu was ready to meet the emergency when it arose, and he acted promptly. *Fifth,* he had gained the confidence of the workmen under his direction. *Sixth,* Stu was not vindictive but acted with good judgment in the disciplinary action which was imposed upon the night shift mill man.

Specific Savings in the Manager's Actions

First, Stu saved the expensive machinery from extensive damage. *Second,* the first product he saved was the more valuable nylon fiber. *Third,* the unit was able to get back into production without prolonged delay. *Fourth,* the crew produced better because of greater respect for Stu's ability to manage.

Failure and Success in Looking Ahead

As a manager at whatever level you may be in your organization, you have an obligation to think ahead and plan to meet emergencies.

An example of a failure to successfully comply with this requirement is the business history of the Packard automobile. In the late 1920's and early 30's, Packard was a luxury car doing well as a strong competitor of Cadillac. Shortly after the middle thirties, a decision was made to change from a high priced auto to a middle range price. Packard was not a successful competitor in this market, and the company finally merged with Studebaker. In the early 1960's, the South Bend, Indiana plant, headquarters of that company, closed down, moving all assembly operations to Canada; and the Packard motor car company ceased to exist.

For an illustration of successfully meeting a serious challenge, you can look to the railroads. Trucks and buses have chiseled away at the government-controlled rail carriers for years until the managers of these important transportation systems determined to start an aggressively competitive counter policy. This included: 1. Contesting work "feather bedding" rules, keeping on the payroll unneeded workmen, 2. Mergers to strengthen financial and competitive power, 3. Several innovations such as diesel-powered locomotives, eliminating unprofitable rail routes, the carrying of auto transport trailers on flat cars, so called "piggyback" service for added revenue. Railroad profits have been improving since the managements started a program of more positive planning ahead.

Forward Planning for Better Total Job Performance

In 1910, the eastern railroads were applying for an increase in freight rates. They had to, they said, because they had just given their workers a raise. At this time, the later distinguished Supreme Court Justice Louis D. Brandeis was a practicing attorney. Through one of his clients, Mr. Brandeis heard about a system of scientific management which an engineer named Fredrick Winslow Taylor had been working on since 1880. Mr. Taylor defined his planned system as:

1. Science, not rule of thumb.
2. Harmony, not discord.
3. Cooperation, not individualism.
4. Maximum output, in place of restricted output.
5. The development of each man to his greatest efficiency and prosperity.

With the acumen that carried Mr. Brandeis to the Supreme Court, he saw Mr. Taylor's plan as a means for greater profit for the railroads which would permit them to pay the wage increase and still not raise freight rates. After long discussion, lawyer Brandeis found the name he needed. Taylor's new philosophy would be called *scientific management*. The popular press picked up this title, as experts argued that by the use of scientific management the railroads could save $1 million a day. Mr. Brandeis' brief, submitted in January, 1911, had at least half of the included material devoted to promoting Taylor's ideas of scientific management.

This kind of advertising stirred nation-wide educators, consultants, and businessmen so much that 300 attended the World's first conference on scientific management at Dartmouth College. Mr. Taylor's *Principles of Scientific Management* was published that same year. It was a best seller on modern management and was translated into twelve languages.

Labor in the United States objected to Taylor's incentive wage system with its penalty for sub-standard performance. They also objected to the discipline of time-and-motion study on the job. Fredrick W. Taylor died in 1915 before his ideas were really fully accepted and widely used.[1] But he must be recognized for an original and important contribution to "thinking ahead for profit."

The Value of People in Your Forward Thinking

With a greater and greater need for more proficient managers who can serve as stimulating leaders, the competition for people with your potential is so keen that it is no longer practical to select, assign, and direct a manager to get on the job and see that a crew or unit puts out a desired amount of production without specific training as to how this is to be accomplished. More and more higher managers are beginning to recognize that mistakes in directing people are tremendously expensive. One reason that it has taken so long to discover this fact is because such wastes are intangible, and the loss does not stand out sharp and clear. By contrast, it is not difficult to recognize the cost of an engineering error. For instance, if a bridge across a stream fails to hit a surveyed and predetermined spot, or if an airplane fails to perform according to the contract requirements, there is no question of the mistake and its costs. When this sort of thing happens, a great hue and cry goes up; key people lose their jobs. In contrast, even today many valuable employees are unnecessarily squelched, hampered, and sometimes lost to their companies through mismanagement, and this mismanagement and cost goes unnoticed. Because of many variable factors, estimates of the hiring costs of new employees vary; but, if you include the lost production due to untrained people, a very minimum amount for the replacement of an ordinary employee in a normal job is about a thousand dollars. And the greater the skill, the greater the cost. If you compute such cost to instances that you know about in which lack of know-how by a supervisor has resulted in unnecessarily handicapping productive employees—in frustration or termination—such waste adds up to a sizeable sum.

You should be careful that you are not among the many managers who fail to appreciate the impact of their decisions in their current jobs on their future. This is a part of the reason why Peter Drucker, an accepted authoritative writer on management, has said, "Despite its crucial importance, its high visibility and

[1] cf. "Revolutionary Then, Orthodox Now," *Business Week*, April 20, 1963, pp. 94 ff.

its spectacular rise, management is the least known and the least understood of our basic institutions." [1]

Vance Packard substantiates your importance in our business system when he wrote, "There appears to be a growing conviction that corporate profits in the future will depend relatively less on materials, money and labor, and relatively more on 'management' than in the past." [2]

If you do your part to fulfill these hopes and expectations, you'll be spending more time and energy looking for improvement opportunities and planning for your functional growth as a professional manager.

Beating the Break-Even Point

A team of managers—let's call the plant superintendent "A," the manufacturing supervisor "B," the cost-accountant department head "C," the sales manager "D"—were holding a meeting to discuss a typical business problem. A collapsible patio table which had been in their factory production line for six months was not showing a profit. Originally, it was thought that one of the best sales features of the table was that it would fit in a rack attachment under the charcoal broiler units in use by thousands of outdoor eating addicts. To appeal to this market, the sales department developed the slogan, "You'll never have to eat off your knees with a KYC (keep you civilized) table."

After the opening of the meeting, Manager C reviewed the statistics. He showed a fixed monthly cost of $2,000. This included expenses if nothing was produced plus developmental charges spread over an eighteen-month period. The variable cost, manufacturing and sales expenses, was $10 per unit. Their company price to the retailer was $20. The average deliveries for the past six months had been 150 units with the highest month 170 (the first) and the lowest 130. Since the break-even point was 200 units per month, a management decision was required.

Manager D wanted to abandon the KYC as a market dog. Manager B was unhappy because the extra fold in the KYC table added an awkward operation to the production line which only the most skilled operator could handle. The top Manager A was doing some thinking ahead as he listened to these comments. "A" speculated, "Everybody has card tables, TV tables in clothes closets, stuck out of sight inside the house; so why don't we cut out the extra fold that is bothering you, 'B?' Then we could change our sales approach with the idea of giving it wider appeal."

The group "perked up" as "A" continued, "Let's get some thoughts together along these lines and meet again Thursday."

"B" reported to the group on Thursday that eliminating the extra fold in the table would permit a truly amazing cut in variable costs. This savings

[1] Drucker, *The Practice of Management*, p. 6
[2] Packard, *The Pyramid Climbers*, p. 6

"C" had calculated, with the additional promotion costs incorporated, would cut the previous cost in half to only $5 per unit. "D" said that in checking with his field force he found some resentment against the KYC name plus little use of the tables by those who had purchased them. "D" proposed that a new name EBNO (everybody needs one) be given the table. He further suggested that, because of the cost saving, their price to retailers be reduced to $18. With the profit break-even number of 154 now only slightly more than the average monthly sales of the KYC, "D" said he could get real enthusiastic about their new product. The management council agreed that these proposals looked good, so the "go-ahead" was given. The first month, the EBNO sold 200, the second 250, and Manager D was exuberant as he reported that bingo parlors were finding their new table ideally suited to their business requirements. "C" predicted that annual profits would set a record.

The management planning evidenced in the EBNO table success situation is not an unusual type of business problem. The lesson is applicable to you, whatever your management position may be, since you can contribute to helping your company reach and exceed the magic break-even point necessary to earn a profit and keep you working. To do your part as a manager, you must continually think ahead and plan for the best way that the people reporting to you can make the most of their abilities.

Encouraging Employees to Change for Profitable Operation

Dr. Louis Miller carried out a very enlightening study of employee behavior at General Electric's appliance park in Louisville, Kentucky. This study was directed to the attitude and performance of workmen in regard to quality. And while the subject is limited to quality, it does carry real significance which you as a thinking manager can use to help your subordinates improve their total job performance.

In Dr. Miller's carefully controlled experiment, twenty-five well-matched work groups (over 1,000 employees in total) took part in the study. Six of the groups were subjected to an intensive, quality promotional-type communications program. All normal techniques were used, such as weekly newsletters, technical displays, informational meetings. Seven groups were individually coached by their foreman with respect to the quality aspects of their work. Four groups received both the communications and the teaching by the foreman at the same time. Eight groups were given neither treatment.

This experiment was carried on for an eleven-week period. In checking quality attitudes, a questionnaire was given to a random sample of the selected groups the week before the start of their programs and, again, to a different random sample selected from the same group during the final week of the program. For performance, the value of the scrapped parts was used as the test measure. As might be expected, the results showed that those who had received neither the communications nor the instructions did not change in attitude or performance. The groups receiving the communications program showed little change in attitude and a negative change in performance. The groups receiving the instructional procedure only showed a negative change in attitude and no change in performance. The groups which received the combined communications and instructional programs showed a strong positive change in both attitude and performance.

Dr. Miller suggests that: 1. The communications alone were largely ignored and even ridiculed. In the doctor's judgment, this occurred because the advertising was not backed up by a positive action program that told each individual how he should actually carry out his part of the program. 2. Instruction by the foreman was probably seen as a threat by the employee and resented as implying he didn't know his job. 3. The two combined, communications and teaching, were likely still seen as a threat; but together, one reinforcing the other, they gave positive evidence of management's intent to make an all-out effort to improve quality.[1]

Helps Toward More Profitable Operations

You should remember these tips as you plan ahead for better total job performance. *First,* just telling a subordinate what he should do is usually not enough. The people reporting to you must see some evidence that you mean what you are saying. *Second,* in helping subordinates improve, use care to avoid arousing resentment by appearing to be too critical. *Third,* on-the-job improvement by employees is worthy of special effort and careful planning.

Be Creative in Your Planning

"I've enjoyed my work. I've liked the people I worked with, and I am leaving with only a single regret: that is the thought of just how much more of a contribution I could have made in my management career if I had learned early in my business experience, say anytime within the first fifteen years, that one of the most satisfying rewards of a manager's work is to discover and put into practice on-the-job improvements." These are the comments of a successful, third-level manager at a party held in his honor upon his retirement from his company at age sixty-five.

As you look around at improvements which have been made in machines, methods, tools and organization, either on your own job or those closely related, ask yourself, "How many of these ideas did I suggest or put into practice?" If you are not proposing your share, there is not much question: you need to take a close look at your work habits to see that you are allowing sufficient time for thinking ahead.

[1] Miller, Dr. Louis, et al.: *An Evaluation of Two Procedures Designed to Improve Employee Attitudes and Performance,* 1964, General Electric, Crotonville, N.Y.

Creativity Is Not Just for Higher Management

Lav had built up a thriving manufacturing business in molding specialty statuettes made from fine-textured but rather rare clay. Material was his most expensive cost item, and his supplier had just notified Lav that his next shipment would have to be imported from South America at a further $5,000 per ton cost. The manufacturer had quoted prices for delivery of miniature angels, shepherds, wise men and camels for the Christmas trade. Now Lav's committed price would not only fail to allow him a profit but actually would not even cover his manufacturing and sales costs.

Lav's plant manager, a man in his mid-forties named Lee, had been with him for many years and had on numerous occasions demonstrated his forward thinking. In this non-profit dilemma, the manufacturer called Lee and explained his problem.

It so happened that Lee had been hunting recently with a friend named Jay who was in the petroleum chemical manufacturing business. Jay was moaning about having ruined some five tons of finely granulated plastics by dumping it from one storage hopper to another in the bottom of which there was a substantial quantity of steel filings. Competition in Jay's business was severe, and his regular customer wasn't interested in this batch of plastic at any price. Lee suggested that he obtain some of Jay's contaminated plastics, soften it on a heated mixing mill, bleach it with a caustic solution, strain it through a fine screen in an extruding machine, and mold it to see what kind of a figurine resulted.

When the plant manager brought his experimental image, made of the new material, into Lav's office, it was identical with the samples the manufacturer had on his desk which had been made of the fine clay.

The boss was delighted: he quickly called Jay, made a deal—and a good one—for all the contaminated plastic. He promised Lee a substantial bonus for working out the material problem.

All was not well, however. When Lee started to operate on the schedule which he needed to follow to meet the required Christmas delivery dates, the steel filings were causing unexpected delays. To obtain the required smooth texture, it was essential that all these foreign particles be removed; and the fine screen used for this purpose in the extruding machine head quickly became clogged, making it necessary to stop, open the machine, and change the screen. To make matters worse, the fine screen was forced into the extruding machine's outlet holes; and, in spite of especially designed knives and bars, often as much as forty-five minutes to an hour was used in removing the screen.

After thinking deeply, Lee decided to reinforce the fine screen with heavier supporting screens to keep the feather-fine wires of the screen out of the extruding machine holes. This cut the loss time on screen changes down to about a third of what it was before, but the manager was still concerned about missing the schedule unless the straining operation could be further speeded up.

Following more thought, Lee came up with another idea. He devised a conveyer belt which would carry a light layer of the plastic granules. Directly over this conveyer, he fixed a strong magnet with a small, loosely woven belt which ran continuously under the magnet and swept off the steel filings into a scrap container as they were picked out of the plastic on the conveyer. This solved the strainer down-time problem and allowed Lee to move ahead on his schedule to meet the Christmas trade requirement. When Lav learned of all his plant manager's troubles, he doubled the amount he had intended to give Lee as a bonus.

Only Individual Managers Are Creative

As William H. Whyte, Jr., described his term, "social ethic," he lists its three major propositions as, "A belief in the group as the source of creativity; a belief in 'belongingness' as the ultimate need of the individual; and a belief in the application of science to achieve the belongingness." Mr. Whyte further says, "Man exists as a unit of society. Of himself, he is isolated, meaningless; only as he collaborates with others does he become worthwhile, for by sublimating himself in the group, he helps produce a whole that is greater than the sum of its parts. There should be, then, no conflict between man and society. What we think are conflicts are misunderstandings, breakdowns in communications." [1]

These statements about the social ethic provide material for stimulating your thoughts particularly as they relate to coming up with new and better ways of managing. In the plastic figurine molding problem, who was creative? Lav recognized that he had a problem and called on Lee for help. Lee as an independent thinker visualized the possibilities of Jay's granules. It was also Lee who successfully experimented and solved the strainer problem.

You can get ideas in talking with a group. Frequently such exchanges spark new thoughts, but as an individual you must always make these improvements a practical application to the job. One of the penalties you must pay to succeed as a professional manager is that you must be an individualist in your thinking.

Things to Remember in Looking Ahead as a Manager

1. *Profit is a necessary stimulant to our economic system and your personal success.*
2. *You must be ready to handle the unexpected situation by:*
    a. *knowing as much as possible about your job responsibilities*
    b. *determining key values and costs*

[1] Whyte, *The Organization Man,* p. 7

   c. studying the people under your direction
   d. moving to meet any emergency
   e. earning the confidence of those reporting to you
   f. treating subordinates fairly.
3. *Difficulties of the management planning job.*
4. *Fredrick W. Taylor's contribution to scientific management.*
5. *People and their importance to your future.*
6. *Help your company to pass the break-even point.*
7. *To stimulate better job performance:*
   a. meaningful actions must support communications
   b. don't arouse resentment
   c. plan what you intend to do.
8. *A thinking-ahead manager must do things which have not been done before.*
9. *Creativity is an individual action.*

Chapter 8: Togetherness Patterns for Productivity

A straight-laced and virtuous woman, after a long life of prudishness, died and went up to the pearly gates where she recounted in great detail to the good Saint Peter all the sins she had *avoided.* As the excessively modest petitioner waxed eloquent about all the many things she had *not* done, the patient gatekeeper finally interrupted with, "We are not as much interested in what you didn't do as what you did. Tell me, what *did* you do?"

Your job in management is a *doing* job. To succeed, you can't be a "didn't do;" you must *do* many things. As a manager, all your knowledge, information, experience, ability, quality, and skill is without value unless you are able to actually use these attributes with judgment and discrimination on a specific management assignment.

As was mentioned in Chapter Six, your second broad functional responsibility is that of action or carrying out your job duties. In discharging this responsibility, you and your fellow managers have a right to be proud of your contribution to our country's steadily rising standard of living, as illustrated by the fact that, "During the past one hundred years, productivity has increased about 2% a year compounded, and the output per workman has doubled about every forty years. With this increased output, the standard of living of our country has roughly doubled every forty years. All of us as consumers can enjoy a higher standard of living without working harder if productivity gains provide more goods and services to distribute." [1] It becomes more and more important that

[1] Michelon, L. C.: *Basic Economics,* p. 70

you as a manager strive to increase the "output per manhour" of those people whose performance you direct. Your job as a manager becomes more vital because of the greater extent to which business and industry touch everyone as our economy becomes more productive. Wage-payment statistics show that in the middle sixties better than 71% of the total national income of the country came from compensation to employees as compared with only 58% coming from this same category in 1929.[1]

Do Some Advertising

In the important job of guiding the efforts of others, a record of continuously improving productivity is a valuable plus in helping you to grow as a professional manager. However, as Thomas Gray wrote, *Full many a flower is born to blush unseen, and waste its sweetness on the desert air.*

Simply doing is often not enough. You must make sure that your boss knows that you are performing in an outstanding fashion. Your advancement depends to a high degree on what your superiors think of your ability to get results from subordinates. You might also remember that the way this information is relayed to your superior can be either helpful or harmful to your ambitions.

For instance, Marv was the manager of a group of six production illustrators. His boss, Jamie, was getting together a proposal for some new business to be presented to Z company, an important customer. The meeting with Z company was tentatively set for two weeks away until, on a Friday afternoon, Jamie learned that a strong competitor was to outline his bid for the same work on the following Wednesday. Since Jamie had previously worked with Z officials, he was able to set a Tuesday meeting on his proposal by telephone. After this was accomplished, the boss went scurrying to see Marv about charts and slides to lend special punch to his presentation to be given before the competitor had a chance to prejudice their customer.

Jamie wanted twenty-two slides, showing performance figures on similar contracts, quality and time schedules, plus projected costs. He felt that color and special art work would help sell their deal. Marv explained that this would take quite a while; and his boss said, "If you need overtime, go ahead and work it. I'd like to have the slides a day ahead of time to practice the presentation." After Jamie left, Marv worked with his crew. They scheduled both Saturday and Sunday for a full shift; and just before noon on Monday, the slides were delivered to Jamie. Marv read a statement in the local newspaper on Friday morning which quoted Jamie that his company had won the Z contract.

Here is an interesting management puzzler for Marv: first, because it was difficult for him to understand whether or not his boss knew of the special effort which the illustration unit had made in the preparation of slides; and,

[1] *Economic Almanac,* 1964, p. 123

second, Marv also felt that his leadership was weakened when his crew heard nothing about their part in winning the new contract.

Marv decided to talk it over with his boss. Fortunately, Jamie immediately saw his management error and thanked Marv for bringing it to his attention. Jamie then arranged to have Marv and the six illustrators receive a personal thank-you from the plant manager for their special efforts. In the in-plant newspaper story of winning the new business, the contribution of Marv's crew was described along with the work of the other sections and departments who had helped in acquiring the Z contract.

You need to recognize that, while Marv's action paid off in this particular case, there is an element of risk in taking such an approach. Jamie could have called him a prima donna and told Marv to go back to work because both he and his crew were paid for their extra work. Suppose he had? Or another problem, suppose that Marv suspected that Jamie would take this course. Should Marv then have said anything to his boss? Even though Marv knew that he would be rebuffed, good management required that he guard his leadership prestige with his subordinates and attempt to establish better communications between himself and his boss.

A Good Manager Takes Some Bruising

Yours is a risky job because you are condemned by the nature of your work to get hurt. As a manager capable of making improvements, you must be both tough and sensitive. A good professional manager must be rugged enough to back his judgments, in spite of opposition, in the give and take with strong-minded, aggressive, competitive men who are thinking first of their own personal interests. You will often come out second best. While you must take this buffeting, you can't allow it to harden you to the extent that you fail to have a concern for the feelings of those people essential to your winning teamwork effort.

It is not possible to keep your ego safely locked inside a hard shell like a coconut and, at the same time, have it as exposed as a ripe peach. The greatest teacher, when He sent out his twelve disciples, said, *Be wise as serpents and innocent as doves.* You must try your best to meet both requirements. But, remember, getting hurt is part of the price you pay for success as a manager.

Don't Be a "Can't-Take-It"

King Jehosophat, after a five-year training period under his father, King Asa of Judah, succeeded to the throne of the southern kingdom of the Hebrews in 873 B.C. The new king united the people, established a system of public education, strengthened the army and national defenses, financed the government by incentive-type taxation, and set up a system of courts with appeals from the lower to higher courts to insure justice for all citizens. Jehosophat, as is true of all good leaders, had a central objective. His goal was to unite the divided Hebrew kingdoms, north and south. He formed a cooperative trade venture with King Ahaziah of the northern kingdom. The two rulers agreed to recreate the shipping fleet originally built at Ezion-geber by King Solomon. Three ships were almost ready for launching when an anarchist set them on fire, thus destroying hope for unity.

A short time later, Ahaziah died from a fall, and his brother Jehoram succeeded him as king of Israel. The armies of Jehosophat joined with the forces of Jehoram for a successful campaign against the Moabites, but the expected economic gains failed to materialize; and the northern king blamed Jehosophat.

This seemed the final straw to the good King Jehosophat, even though he could claim an enviable leadership record and had contributed immensely to the unity of the people of the southern kingdom. However, his goal of rejoining the two parts of the divided kingdom eluded him; so, at the age of sixty, he quit. He allotted his considerable personal fortune among his six sons; designated his eldest as his successor; and shortly afterward, having no aim in life, died in the year 849 B.C. King Jehosophat couldn't take it.

In the early 14th Century, by contrast, history and legends record that Robert I (the Bruce), King of Scotland, was a comeback leader. Bruce was crowned king at Scone, March 27, 1306. Shortly afterward, the English army defeated the Scots in two costly engagements which scattered the new king's soldiers, forcing him to go into hiding on the island of Rathlin. At this time Bruce's cause seemed lost. He was alone, proclaimed an outlaw, excommunicated by the Pope, his wife and daughter in the hands of the English and his brother executed.

Even on the island, Bruce was in danger of capture because of the English price on his head; so he frequently moved from place to place. One of these hide-outs was a barn loft where the king lay in some straw, thinking of giving up. As he reviewed his trouble, he chanced to see a spider swinging on a strand of his web. It became evident that the spider wanted to attach the strand to a beam in the barn roof. The height and distance seemed more than the insect could manage because, in swinging back and forth, he often failed to touch his objective; and, when he did, his grasp failed to hold, and he fell back.

Bruce became fascinated in watching to see if the spider would grow discouraged. The insect's contest with his tough problem continued throughout the morning. Sometimes he rested, but always the spider came back until finally he hit the beam and stuck tight. Within a few minutes, the spider triumphantly crawled down the strand to construct his web.

The king, reflecting upon what he had just seen, was somewhat ashamed of his own self-pity and resolutely returned to the mainland, rallied his soldiers, and in successive battles routed the English, and freed Scotland. He convened his first parliament at St. Andrews, March, 1309. For the remaining twenty years of Bruce's life, his homeland continued to be a free nation.

Identify Yourself as a Leader

Don was a plant manager who liked to get out of his office and visit the manufacturing shops whenever possible. This was a big operation, employing several thousands of people, and frequently Don was able to spend considerable time in an area before the sectional managers learned that he was around.

On one occasion, Don stopped to talk with a lathe operator who had just finished an order of small bracket fittings. The plant manager identified himself and learned that the operator was called Toe. Don asked how long he had worked there, and Toe replied about three months. Then the two talked of Toe's experiences at other plants and what he liked about this job. The plant manager inquired, "Who is your supervisor?" Toe replied that he wasn't sure, but Tom over on a nearby lathe had started him out and showed him how to handle his stock orders. Toe quickly added, "Of course, I have worked on machines of this type for years. Don't need much help."

Don told Toe to keep up the good work and casually strolled over to Tom's machine. The two were friends of long standing. The plant manager asked about the shop's workload, and Tom told him they had been very busy. He added, "Toe, over there, is a good man. He can go ahead on his own."

After a further tour of the area, Don returned to his office for some thinking. Next, he called the management training director, a fellow named Sal, and, without telling him where, related that he had found a workman on the plant payroll for three months who had never met nor did he even know the name of his immediate manager. Don then directed Sal to suggest some actions which could be taken to avoid this kind of thing happening in the future. He said Sal could have a couple of days to think about the problem.

The plant used a central employment department under the personnel manager, so Sal discussed this assignment with the personnel people. It was agreed that the immediate supervisor of a new employee could interview the prospective new hire before he was actually employed.

This feature became a part of Sal's recommendation to the plant manager. He further suggested a line-conducted conference series of sessions titled, "Every Manager, The Leader Within His Section." The program would stress the requirement that: *First,* a supervisor must become well acquainted with all the people under his direction. *Second,* each manager should upgrade every subordinate's skill as much as possible. *Third,* some incentive to develop should be offered. *Fourth,* a reminder should be given to each manager of his obligation to further his subordinate's knowledge of the significant features of our competitive enterprise system. Don approved the program and asked that it be started as soon as possible.

Advantages of the "Every Manager, The Leader" Program

First, involving you as the immediate superior in the hiring of the employee has these pluses: a. The subordinate knows where he should go when he needs help and assistance. b. You will feel a direct responsibility in the success of the employee. c. It enables you to better match jobs and men. d. It increases your importance in the eyes of the employee.

Second, a better acquaintance with the subordinate is essential for you to determine and use present skills and potential abilities.

Third, training and upgrading the subordinate's skills has a two-fold value: *a. to you, the manager, because:* 1. It enables you to feel more confident of the employee on his present job. 2. Puts at your disposal added valuable skills which will undoubtedly be needed in the future. It also enables you to get more productivity out of the capital investment. *b. to the subordinate because:* 1. It gives him more satisfaction in handling his present job because of his greater skill. 2. It enables him to earn a higher rate through greater productivity. 3. It increases the employee's job security.

Fourth, some of the ways you can provide an incentive for the subordinate to improve are: a. Encourage the employee to follow a planned schedule of self-improvement. b. Set target dates for accomplishing the different portions of the program. c. Keep records of the subordinate's achievements. d. Promote your better employees as often as possible.

Fifth, instilling in all employees a better understanding of the values of our competitive system helps them: a. to recognize the value of more productivity, b. to practice healthy competition themselves, c. to make better use of valuable personal talents, d. to see the need for greater teamwork.

An Outgiving, Personal, Working Atmosphere Stimulates Productivity

"Think for a moment of the way that you behave in a committee meeting. In your capacity as group member you feel a strong impulse to seek common ground with the others. Not just out of timidity but out of respect for the sense of the meeting you tend to soft-pedal that which would go against the grain." [1]

To increase the productivity of those who report to you, this same spirit should be evident in your working group. Here is an example which shows how a manager was able to create this kind of a climate: The product was the very earliest attempts at the production of usable sponge rubber mattresses, auto seats and backs, and furniture items. The department manager was named Red. He had specially picked a crew of ten young fellows, all ambitious to get ahead in

[1] Whyte, Op.cit., p. 52

the company. Such a group had probably more immediate disadvantages than advantages, since all were inexperienced not only on this job but in just working, as well. They were full of real personal competitiveness, over-eager, and a little wild. Another disadvantage was that this was a night shift with no scientific help available. Being in the developmental stage, no specialized equipment was in use. For instance, dough mixers designed for bakeries provided the method used to compound the latex (rubber liquid) with the coagulant. The mixture was visually measured into a hodge-podge of different curing molds carried by a belt conveyor to the curing ovens. One of the bottlenecks was cleaning and loading the equipment. Another was sub-standard quality of the products. The cause of poor quality could not easily be traced to its source because often it was some fault in the mixture or a specific part of the handling or production process.

At the beginning of the project, Red called his crew together and explained that they were all in a fortunate position since no step-by-step flow of processing had been firmed up. As a tentative method of operating, employees No. 1 and No. 2 would start mixing, No. 3 and No. 4 loading and unloading the conveyor, No. 5 and No. 6 on the dryer, No. 7 and No. 8 cleaning equipment, No. 9 weighing, and No. 10 as a swing man to help where needed. The manager further told the crew that he was committed for 5,000 pounds of automobile cushioning and 2,000 pounds of furniture material, all of first quality, to be delivered to customers during the fourteen remaining working days of the month. Red admitted that this sounded like a lot and urged anyone with an idea on how to improve efficiency to suggest it and they would certainly give it a try.

One of the first things which appeared evident was that No. 10, the swing man, should spend most of his time preparing the mixture so that the latex would not congeal before it could be placed in the mold. No. 4 was taken off the conveyor, but a jam-up occurred. No. 5 was taken off the dryer for cleaning equipment, and a batch was ruined because of over-heating. No. 9, the weigh man, could move around but needed to be watchful to see that the products were not too heavy or too light. The first working shift for Red's crew was a mess. The ten men went home worn out with 200 pounds of auto goods and 50 pounds of furniture cushioning accepted. The second night it was more of the same and the record was relatively comparable.

The workmen all decided to have breakfast together and talk over their production problem. Each of the ten felt somewhat guilty about their failure on the job. The conclusion they reached was that everyone would have to work hard on his job and keep an eye out for opportunities to help other crew members. In effect, all agreed to learn as rapidly as possible all the operations so that wherever difficulties developed enough of them could shift to that problem to resolve it.

When they reported for work that night, Red was a little bit skeptical of trying to operate a production line on which every operator was a specialist in everything. He finally shrugged and agreed that, anyway, he had nothing to lose.

That night you could feel the change in the atmosphere. There was much good-humored ribbing about first one and then another not being able to keep up; and a great deal of jumping about from the mixer to the scales, to the dryer, to the clean-up area. No. 6 had brought along some ammonia, and the equipment clean-up job time was immediately reduced. Molds were arranged in a balanced order: big ones together, odd sizes segregated, smaller molds in another place along the conveyor. Each workman learned from his partner; every one of the ten accepted his personal responsibility to meet their agreed upon goal. The results could only be termed dedicated service to an ideal which the crew set for themselves; the facing of a personal challenge.

As was clear from the third night on, the production of Red's crew began to climb; and before the fourteen days were up, they were well over Red's promised weight of quality production of sponge rubber.

Specific Gains When Employees Make a Personal Job Commitment

As a manager: You can improve your reputation as a professional leader. You will have fewer problems. You will get better total job performance. *Advantages to the workmen:* fewer personality conflicts, more pleasant working conditions, and a better chance to obtain personal satisfaction on the job. *The total organization also gains because:* There are fewer interruptions of production; there is greater output of better quality, on time, at lower costs; the more productive employees want to work for your organization.

How to Build an Outgiving, Personal, Working Atmosphere

Some managers like to use the word "motivation" as a catch-all for the key to establishing a productive team. Other supervisors call it guiding, directing, enticing, or driving. All authorities agree that a manager must in some fashion convince his followers to strive for a common, predetermined objective. The differences in opinion and action come about when the supervisor tries to figure out just how this is to be accomplished.

You have, no doubt, many times observed the evidence of some undefined force which causes employees, workmen, and managers alike to make a personal commitment to a job. Further, you have noted that what inspires one person or group can't even hold the attention of another. In analyzing the sponge-rubber production problem situation, it is striking that the manager Red set the tone which appealed to the crew members under his direction. Then, in effect, he stepped aside as the supervisor and allowed the ten men to carry through the project to a successful conclusion.

If you want to work in a real pay-off area toward becoming a better manager, find your subordinates' hidden cooperator; but, remember that what appeals to one person or group may have exactly the opposite effect on another.

Finding a Subordinate's Spark Plug

In a small, twelve-man training department serving a large manufacturer, there was a heavy schedule of shop skills, tooling, management, and quality control improvement programs to be carried on. They did not all occur at the same time. For instance, pattern-making and welding could be carried on and then the emphasis was shifted to drilling and riveting. The reading of blueprints and micrometers was almost continuous, as was management training. The varied schedule suggested to the director, Val, that greater efficiency could be obtained from his small staff of eight coordinators and instructors if each individual used some of the initiative he was trying to develop in employees to qualify himself to handle teaching in all of the required subject areas. When Val announced his idea as a working practice, resistance arose at once.

All the staff men were mature with specialized experiences and strongly developed likes and dislikes. One person had always been a shop man. He felt he knew manufacturing processes and that was where he wanted his associations to remain. Another was an expert in getting over to others the fundamentals of management theory. Yet another had an academic background, and he felt most comfortable in a classroom situation. Thus it went throughout the training staff. Some were capable of making the adjustment; but even in these instances it did not appear that the results would be very satisfactory. A good trainer, like a good manager, must want to do a job, and his favorable effect upon others is governed by a strong inner urge to succeed—which, like murder, will out.

Val had cultivated a problem for himself, which should point out a couple of lessons in management for you. *First,* don't start a revolutionary practice without weighing the pros and cons. *Second,* if you see you have made an error, don't hesitate to do what you can to correct it as rapidly as possible.

The training manager re-studied his whole situation by first determining the individuals best fitted for specific services and, second, looking for reasons why they were in the work of their choice. *Val was searching for individual spark plugs.* When his study project was completed, the training manager made some special assignments, hired some part-time instructors, and even found it necessary to reclassify some people. When he moved the second time, Val was on solid ground and could enumerate reasons for all his actions. The result was a better satisfied staff of people and a better job of training. Instead of losing stature with his subordinates, Val proved himself big enough to admit a mistake and correct it, and you can bet that he exercised more responsible leadership after this experience.

Why an Organization

In discussing the unified effort of employees for greater productivity, considerable emphasis has been directed toward the value of allowing all the individual freedom possible to gain benefits from added personal motivations and valuable creative talents. You must not overlook, however, that there has to be a togetherness, a unity of effort and purpose toward a common goal. For this reason, all businesses have an organization.

Colonel Lyndall F. Urwick, management consultant, has said, *Lack of organization is illogical, cruel, wasteful, and inefficient.*[1] Any economic endeavor must have a top decision-maker with a parceling out of authority and accountability among lower-level managers, dependent upon the size and complexity of the organization. This necessity gives a logical reason for the familiar triangle or pyramid used to show the normal reporting relationship of managers progressively from the base or regular employees to the peak.

A primary purpose of the authoritarian structure is to give a priority command order and remind all employees of the need for unity. Second, a lack of organization is cruel because the real sufferers from this lack of direction are the individuals forced to guess at policy, acceptable practices, and who's the boss. Third, it is wasteful because without an organization jobs cannot be arranged in accordance with functional specialization so that productivity can be promoted, and there will not be the opportunity for an orderly development and succession of key personnel as trained replacements. Fourth, operating without an organization is inefficient because trying to use management control without the functional structure as a yardstick encourages promotions based on personalities, which smacks of favoritism and stimulates cliques rather than productivity.

An organizational structure might be compared to the architectural plan of a building because in each we have a central design for accomplishing a specific purpose. Without such a guide, either a building or production tends to be haphazard.

Suppose, for example, we imagine a company named "Tension Release, Inc.," which was incorporated to produce toys, novelties, and amusement items for young and old alike. The board of directors was set up by the stockholders of Tension Release, Inc. They, in turn, hired a president with authority to select, produce, and sell products falling within their business charter definition in what it was hoped would be a profitable venture. This, however, was not the case. Electric trains, banging cannons, and strangling cords ran into too much competition and, after two years with no dividends, at the stockholders' insistence, the president was fired. A new president was hired. His first action, after getting settled, was to talk to the vice presidents of engineering, sales, manufacturing, finance, employee relations, and public relations.

[1] Koontz and O'Donnell, *Principles of Management,* p. 279

An Application of Organization

Each of these officials had an answer, explaining why Tension Release, Inc., was not making money. As the new president listened, he noticed that each vice president tended to try to build up his own position and tear down some other section of the company. The engineering vice president stoutly maintained that Tension Release, Inc. trains ran on time, the toy cannon never missed a bang, and the strangling cord had the best hand grip east of the Himalayas. In each case, this was because of superior engineering. The reason they failed to sell in the market was because of poor salesmanship.

In like manner, the sales vice president blamed poor design, lack of quality, and failure of advertising (a part of public relations) to support the products.

Manufacturing felt that the items in their production line were too tough to make. Finance pointed the finger at a lack of budgetary controls and improperly trained employees on production operations. Employee relations complained that none of the divisions paid any attention to the terms of the union contract and thus made negotiations unnecessarily difficult.

The president then posed a question, "What kind of product would each of you like to see us produce?" The engineering vice president was first to answer with, "Something unique to test our capabilities." Sales suggested, "Something with an appeal to a broad cross-section of the public." Manufacturing wanted to find a product which would enable them to use their present machinery and some of the surplus inventory items. Finance wanted to manufacture something which didn't cost too much but carried a nice profit mark-up. Employee relations wanted to see them make an item which didn't require skilled help. Public relations wanted a different kind of product with some special twists that they might play up for public acceptance.

The new president told each of the vice presidents to work with their different organizations and be prepared in two days to engage in a round-table discussion of what such an item as they had been discussing might be. When the group came back together, many of the proposals were a little wild, but all tended to clear the air. As the meeting adjourned, a suppressed enthusiasm was evident which hadn't been there before. Two days later, they met again and, in a long session, agreed upon a central product which best met the wishes of all.

The item was to be a duck whistle. However, it was a very special type of whistle. A toy, metal duck, two inches high with a bill that opened and shut, was mounted on a wooden stem. This stem extended horizontally to a mouthpiece which the duck faced. A person using the whistle found the duck looking him squarely in the eyes. Pressure of the lips on the mouthpiece set in motion a flapping of the duck's bill with three distinct "quacks." After the third sounded, a cloud of stale tobacco smoke enveloped the whistler. To meet the desires of all the Tension Release, Inc., officials, the capsule delivering the smoke could be removed or left in, thus appealing to the Russian Roulette fans. It was felt that some wives and all do-gooders would go for the stale-smoke idea as a way to urge adults to stop smoking and a deterrent to young folks thinking of taking up the habit. To appeal to the drinking segment of the public, the wooden mouthpiece was flavored with rum, cognac, martini, bourbon, and scotch. For the young people, the flavors of cinnamon, lemon, lime, and orange were used.

The public-relations vice president thought the title of the product, "3 quacks, you're out" would catch the public's fancy. The finance vice president liked the cheap material idea which was simply bottling the air from jet transport cabins because competition had forced the airlines to permit cigar, pipe, and cigarette smoking. Manufacturing liked the simplicity of the product—the fact that present equipment, machines, and materials could be used. Employee relations was assured that no hard-to-hire skills would be required. Public relations liked the many advertising gimmicks they could use on "3 quacks, you're out;" and sales was enthusiastic about the broad appeal their new product would have.

Organization Principles in the Tension Release, Inc. Example

The new president demonstrated how you can *define lines of authority and spell out relationships;* for without such a clear-cut delineation, you or your subordinates spend most of your time duplicating effort, trying to determine just what to do, stewing over decisions, passing the buck, and debating with yourself about the personal advantage of cooperating or playing hard to get. Not only are such actions inefficient, but they wear you out with frustration.

A *second* important principle the president illustrated was the value you can get from *organization flexibility*. He brought all skills, strengths, talents and weaknesses into a critical product choice effort. Yet, at the same time, he maintained sufficient rigidity so that all efforts were directed toward a common goal.

A *third* principle is illustrated as Tension Release, Inc. demonstrates that your *management judgment* should be the most valuable element in your use of an organization. Where the greatest gains can be made, you can stress purely functional duties. However, where it is an advantage, you should make use of special, individual, technical abilities; persuasiveness; salesmanship; and combine the total talents of your group toward the common objective.

Policy Principles in the Tension Release, Inc. Example

"Policies are relatively permanent, general plans of action laid down by management to guide the activities of the enterprise. These rules give a degree of permanence and make for consistency in relationships and avoid the costs of repeated investigations to solve a series of similar problems." [1]

[1] Goetz, *Management Planning and Control,* p. 27

First, a clear understanding was established so you can see that essential consistency, efficiency, and cooperation will be a practice of the Tension Release, Inc., organization. *Second, each division was urged to set up its own operating policies* directed by responsible authority in accordance with the central purpose. Thus, whatever your management position, you have decision-making freedom, but you do not get away from accountability to your superior for performance. *Third, each division was invited to suggest ideas* for the new product to meet their own special interest advantages. However, once a decision was made, in order to avoid administrative confusion, all divisions coordinated their efforts. You are expected to conduct your job on the same principle.

If you think there is a need for a correction in organization policy, you have an obligation to suggest the possible improvement. In most cases, the best procedure for you to follow is to write, as briefly as possible, a clear explanation of the difficulty caused by the policy rules. As an alert manager, you will also have given the situation enough thought to be able to make some suggested corrective changes. Your complete report should then be turned over to your immediate superior.

Many times policies are sufficiently flexible to permit you some interpretation. In such cases, your judgment is often tested. If you decide to make a policy exception, it should only be done after careful thought and thorough investigation has given you full assurance that this specific case warrants special treatment. Frequently, it may be wise for you to talk over such a problem with your superior before making a commitment.

Before you make an exception to policy, be perfectly clear on all the circumstances, realize the full import of the case, consider the people involved, and do not be rushed into giving an answer. Remember that you have to live with your decisions, and unwise exceptions to policy will have a way of returning to plague you.

Unity for More and Better Production

1. *Your importance as a manager is growing with our rising standards of living plus increases in the working population.*
2. *Be sure to do your job and also see that your boss is advised of your performance.*
3. *You must be both tough and sensitive.*
   a. *Take your bruises and come back for more.*
   b. *Keep the ability to feel the need for consideration of others.*
4. *Be proud of the fact and let your subordinates know that you are the leader.*
5. *Establish a working climate which personally involves all your group members—for your own, the subordinates', and your organization's benefit.*

6. *You can get your subordinate's personal commitment to the job by finding and using his hidden cooperator. Everyone has one or more personal spark plugs.*
7. *You must have an organization to keep your group unified and on course.*
8. *An organization:*
   a. *defines lines of authority and relationships*
   b. *brings together varied talents and abilities*
   c. *enables you to use your management judgment in selecting a specific action course.*
9. *Good organization policies:*
   a. *help you operate with over-all consistency*
   b. *allow you to "run your own shop," but do not relieve you of accountability to your superior*
   c. *insist upon compliance but also encourage suggested changes for better productivity.*

Chapter 9: Examining the Evidence Patterns

Alfred P. Sloan, Jr., in his book *My Years With General Motors* tells a fascinating story of superior management actions. From the verge of bankruptcy in 1921—with eight models for sale, but only 12% of the market—this enterpriser brought the General Motors Company to success before the 20's decade was out. The front-running winner in the early 1920's was the Ford Motor Company with the famous Model T and 60% of the total market.

In meeting the competition, Mr. Sloan didn't attempt to gear his business strategy to a confrontation with Ford but, instead, ventured into new fields. His grand plan for General Motors was to concentrate upon the production of quality automobiles in five price classes, progressively from the top price Cadillac, Buick, Oldsmobile, Pontiac, and Chevrolet. New models were designed and built each year. Competition among the different automobiles within the General Motors line was encouraged to gain the best efforts of each organization. The most significant feature of Mr. Sloan's strategy, however, was the opening up of a market for good used or second-hand automobiles which had not existed as a profitable business before this time. When a year-old, quality, General-Motors automobile could be had for less money, Ford's new single model had difficulty in selling customers.

In time, all major manufacturers switched to Mr. Sloan's concept of a product for different price ranges and inter-company competition, although none have been as successful as General Motors which consistently sells 50% and better of the total automobile market.

Before arriving at his unique management action strategy which made

General Motors such an outstanding success, Mr. Sloan had to ask himself some basic questions: What caused the company to come to the brink of disaster in 1921? What must be done to bring it back to business health? What are the actions which should be taken to insure prosperity twenty to thirty years in the future?

Just as the answers and actions which followed were the open sesame for building one of the nation's greatest corporations, so you can further your career as a professional manager by asking yourself: How have I arrived where I am today? What needs to be done to improve my performance efficiency now? What should I do to be a better professional manager in the future?

Because you are now a manager, undoubtedly you have performed many of the basic fundamental functions of your job in an acceptable fashion. However, most supervisors can improve to their current and future advantage in some of these areas which are to be discussed.

How to Take a Better Look at Discipline

Discipline is a bugaboo to many managers, largely because they view their duties as drivers of employees and enforcers of rules, as the old-time boss with a whip. All of these authoritarian actions disturb the modern enlightened manager. He wants others to accept him as an understanding personality worthy of respect because of himself and not because of a position in an organization structure. The better supervisors have learned by experience that "the-do-it-my-way-or-else," command-type leadership doesn't get the best results from employees who are becoming progressively better educated.

You can avoid the Simon-Legree onus if you can create and maintain a positive atmosphere which encourages subordinates to work toward higher standards of performance. If this is accomplished, then correction becomes a minor problem. You must realize that one of your first duties is to make sure that the employees under you understand what constitutes acceptable application of personal effort to the job, proper attention to details, considerate relationships with associates, and other practices which are generally classified as employee discipline requirements.

Generating an appreciation of the values of self-discipline helps you avoid the necessity of "after the fact" punishment for infraction of rules. You can often help subordinates see that personal control can lead to higher earnings, promotion and greater respect from associates, as well as the right of personal independence in decision making. You, of course, must determine what has the greatest appeal to your subordinates. *For as long as the employee can foresee new, better and achievable means to the satisfaction of his needs, he will be ready to change his behavior in the direction of those better means.*[1]

Whether openly admitted or not, subordinates look to the boss first to

[1] Leavitt, *Managerial Psychology*, p. 164

satisfy these needs. Your actions are the real counters if you expect to make progress toward positive discipline; what you do must reflect your own confidence that the organization rules are intended to protect all employees, either physically or in their job security.

How to Use Education for Good Discipline

In furthering the principle of self-discipline, you have an obligation to examine the company rules periodically to determine that these conduct guides are serving the intended purpose of supporting and helping the employee do a better job. After satisfying yourself on this score, you are in a better position to follow a constructive approach which will relieve the normal work tensions. You must strive for a sensible understanding between yourself and those employees reporting to you as to what constitutes acceptable conduct. Then, back up your subordinates 100%; play no favorites; don't close your eyes to violations of understood improper conduct; and make the punishment as nearly uniform as possible for all when the same rule is broken.

In Wichita, Kansas, a city approaching 300,000 population, out of town visitors for years never failed to comment as they were driven around the city about the perfect observance by local citizens of the fifteen-mile-per-hour speed limit in school zones. Many times a visitor's words were, "They surely have you people educated." Certainly a true statement.

How was it accomplished? "Safety Sal" signs, the metal form of a young, school-aged girl set in a weighted base was placed in the middle of the streets at the beginning and end of the school zone area. The police traffic department and city judges showed no mercy in plastering heavy fines on violators for even one mile in excess of the fifteen-mile limit. Most people got educated in a hurry; some of the more stubborn took a little longer; but, over a span of just a few years, even the most hard-headed yielded.

An interesting sequel is that during 1965 the city commission approved the removal of the "Safety Sals" from the streets, largely as an economy measure. Keeping them in repair, and placing and removing the signs throughout the city cost a sizable sum. Instead of the "Safety Sals" which motorists had learned to respect, signs on power poles were installed to mark the zones and the hours during which the fifteen-mile speed limit would be enforced. Motorists immediately started ignoring the new signs, and numerous observers now remark that drivers speed thirty to thirty-five miles per hour through these zones with impunity and seeming open contempt. It appears obvious that a re-education of motorists is needed.

You as a manager should remember: First, that good discipline is not an on-and-off campaign but must be a continuous program; second, that earned cooperation is better for you as well as for employees.

How to Practice "*We*-Can-Do-a-Better-Job-Than-*I*" Management

" 'I've had a few dreams in my life, not realized until this year. At least these two objectives of mine have been reached. One was to have a large airline customer call me up and, instead of giving me hell, tell me he was really delighted with an outstanding airplane, better than the one he bargained for. That has happened with the 727. *We* have done an outstanding job on that airplane.' " These are remarks of President Bill Allen, March 27, 1964, to some 250 members of The Boeing Company top management as quoted in Harold Mansfield's dramatic book *Billion Dollar Battle.* The President continued, " 'The other objective was to see The Boeing Company end up with a profit on a commercial program during my presidency. Well, it has been a long, hard pull, but by God, *we've* done it.' A good many of the *'we'* who had done it were in the room, and throat-full of emotion.

" 'It took two billion dollars and over twelve years, but you've seen the chart on the 707's and 720's. *We* have an unrealized asset as a result of this twelve-year period of effort—a program with substantial earning potential for a number of years. Looking back to the time of the prototype, with all the blood, sweat, and tears, it has been a good investment, a good thing for The Boeing Company. I think the same is true of the 727.'

"Jack (Steiner) could feel the response of men devoted to a leader. The organization wasn't going to let Allen down. Those men were going to reach the goal of business success on the 727, as on other programs of the company." [1]

Mansfield's book traces back through the years to 1958 when veteran engineer Steiner was given the original assignment to study the feasibility of the 727 program. The review details the hundreds of managers and men taking actions, making decisions, both before and after the 1960 day when The Boeing Company board of directors authorized Allen to move on the program if management concluded the prospects warranted. This statement by the board characterizes the "*we*-can-do-a-better-job-than-*I*" concept of good management under which President Allen repeatedly consulted with subordinate managers at all levels before he and John Yeasting, Vice President and General Manager of the Transport Division, said "Go" on the 727 program November 30, 1960.

The direct involvement of the many echelons of managers insured a widespread attention and effort which only comes about when individuals look upon a teamwork program as "my" project.

As another example of "*we*-can-do-a-better-job-than-*I*" management, imagine yourself as the management development director of a large, essentially autonomous manufacturing division of a nation-wide corporation. You have just read a headquarter's policy statement which directs that a corporate-wide train-

[1] Mansfield, *Billion Dollar Battle*, pp. 171-172

ing program be established to identify and develop outstanding young managers and non-managers with potential for future high-level management responsibilities. Your position in the organization is that of reporting to the vice president in charge of the division. You have an advisory relationship with the headquarter's management development director.

How do you proceed? *First, discuss the policy statement with your boss.* Find out any thoughts he may have on how he wants it implemented. You may have some preliminary ideas to propose, but be careful that you don't go too far with commitments before you have thoroughly studied the situation. *Second,* after the "go-ahead" from your immediate superior, *get ideas and help from your own organization.* The results of the study should be a specific proposal, flexible enough to include new ideas which may develop. *Third, clear your suggested program with your boss,* incorporating any ideas he may have. *Fourth, discuss your proposals in detail* with each level of management which has any stake in the program. *Fifth, get as many of your line-management people as is possible to actually conduct portions of the program.* You'll have better results if you can get them to accept this training as their program.

Benefits of "*We*-Can-Do-a-Better-Job-Than-*I*" Management

Like most people, you place a very special value on things which belong to you. It is human nature to take pride in *my* family, *my* home, *my* car, *my* hobby. You must strive to get some of this possessiveness into the assignments of your subordinates because a person will go all out to promote those things in which he has a vital personal interest.

One of your most important managerial requirements is to give subordinates an opportunity for real participation in the challenging part of their work so that you benefit from "*we*-can-do-a-better-job-than-*I*."

> Reducing a job to a simple repetitive level so that an alert twelve-year-old with a capacity for withstanding boredom could handle it . . . reduces the social prestige attached to the job and reduces the employee's job satisfaction and self-esteem; (workmen on such jobs) live for the pleasure their paychecks can buy. If you ask them what they do for a living they say, "Oh, I work for Standard." It wouldn't occur to them to explain what they do there. It is too boring, and not a source of pride.[1]

When you practice "*we*-can-do-a-better-job-than-*I*," *your subordinate benefits because:* first, he has a feeling of proprietorship in the work he is doing. However, be sure you don't try to make him a second-hand partner. Give him all the information, and pay full attention to his ideas. If his proposals are not accepted, be sure you explain why they are not used. Second, be sure he is not frustrated by being forced to accept your decision as the court of final recourse. Your interplay of relationships must be such that, if the two of you can't resolve

[1] Packard, Vance: *The Status Seekers,* pp. 28, 42, 43

a problem to the subordinate's satisfaction, he is free to go over your head in the organization without fear or penalty. Third, the people reporting to you are able to grow in their jobs. Most individuals take pride in service and personal progress. They welcome an opportunity for a "say" in their own futures.

Your total organization benefits when you get all your subordinates into the act because: First, profits are made by people so the more widespread you can encourage thinking about company interests the greater the benefits for everyone. Remember, most of the day-to-day *actions* which you take are directed toward motivating the individuals in your crew or unit; thus, this purpose should require most of your energy and skill. If you are successful, you must put to practical use the knowledge that, while individuals differ markedly, most people have a strong desire to contribute to the carrying out of those decisions and actions which directly affect them. Reliable test surveys show that productivity is encouraged when the producers consider you a real leader, and efficiency is hindered when a manager tries to personally control all phases of the operation. You must by your actions express confidence in the people reporting to you.

Better production will result, as well as improved morale, if an individual's highest abilities and skills are being put to use. It is not essential that some unrealistic promotion take place for this requirement to be fulfilled. A well-adjusted person gets special satisfaction if he has an opportunity to use what he knows are his own personal talents. One of the most important parts of your job is to determine and to develop the productive talents of all employees reporting to you.

Second, you uncover, arouse, and develop latent leadership qualities. Crawford Greenewalt, chairman of the board of E. I. du Pont de Nemours and Company, Inc., has said, "Management has the prime responsibility of filling its own shoes." [1] Continuity of strong leadership is an essential if a company is to grow and even survive in today's competitive business climate. An opportunity to "try their wings" brings to light unknown skills which, if not immediately usable, could prove vital for future needs.

Third, this is one of the few practical methods of getting built-in self-criticism which a healthy, growing company must have. It is insurance against functional blindness, or glossing-over bad policies or practices because those who should just will not see them or they tend to justify a faulty operation as necessary or good because it has "always been done that way."

You as the manager benefit from this type of enlightened management because: First, your personal success is based upon the performance of the people reporting to you. Just the same old way of doing things is not good enough for stand-out management. You must put gems of individuality to proper use. Employees who are treated like clods, act like clods.

Second, such a policy gives you the occasion to practice the type of

[1] Greenewalt, Crawford H.: "Sensing Who Can Command," *Nation's Business,* October 1965, p. 40

management which the future demands if you intend to meet the tests of today's competition. As you advance to the higher echelons of management in your company, it becomes more important that the people reporting to you produce and further new ideas, not resist them.

Third, all truly effective techniques of a supervisor must be natural; a part of the manager. Thus, the sooner you inject into your daily duties *"we-can-do-a-better-job-than-I,"* the greater usefulness you personally will develop as you grow in the profession of management.

How to Handle the Dissatisfied Subordinate

In spite of your best efforts as a manager, you will have some unhappy people reporting to you. Let's look at an example: Suppose you have three subordinates, all too fond of gambling. In a recent high-stakes poker game at a local hotel, X employee walked out a winner, and Y and Z became disgruntled because he refused to give them an opportunity to get their money back. Bad feeling was carried back to the job and reflected in reduced productivity. Can you do something about this? A second example: You have an employee with twenty years of company service reporting to you. He has always reflected a pleasant smile, willingness to cooperate, and evidently enjoys his work. Let's call him "Joe." Because of recent added responsibilities, you have found it necessary to reorganize, promoting another subordinate named "Whit," with only ten years' service, to a higher level. Joe now reports to an employee who was formerly on his level. You notice that Joe has suddenly developed a sullen attitude and there is obvious friction between Joe and Whit, his new supervisor. What should you do? A third example: John is a subordinate who always has a complaint. His desk is not right; he needs a new one. The heat is too high or too low. His machine constantly needs repairs. He ought to be making more money. How about a raise? He thinks he could do better in some other department. His full talents are not being used. What do you do with such a subordinate?

Each of these examples could be viewed as typical of the normal personnel problems which confront an average manager on his job. And each is a situation in which he must take leadership action. In number one: You should be careful that your attitude is not influenced by a feeling that the gambling employees are probably wasting money which properly belongs to their families. This is not your concern as a manager. You are interested in the X-Y-Z grievance because of its effect upon production for which you are accountable. Your first action is to make sure that the performance of X, Y, and Z is responsible for the lower production. It should be fairly simple to check past records, and examine machines, material, or any change in process or method. While it is necessary to take direct action, don't be too hasty. Make sure you are on firm ground before you talk with the disgruntled three. When you are ready, lay it on the line by telling X, Y, and Z together that these are the facts, and asking,

"Now, are you going to cooperate and bring your output back up to where it has been?" If you get anything short of firm assurance that the problem is solved, set a deadline for compliance. In the final analysis, you may have to transfer one or more of this trio, even termination might be necessary as a last resort. You must meet the problem squarely with the facts in hand and your best objective judgment working.

In number two, the Joe and Whit problem: You have a very difficult and fundamental management problem. You have appointed an intermediate manager whom you must support. It appears that Joe is unhappy because Whit, the shorter-serviced employee, was promoted over him. But notice this may not be entirely true because: 1. Joe may have suddenly developed bad health; 2. he may have some home or family worries; 3. the new boss, Whit, may be taking advantage of his position to rub-it-in to Joe; 4. you may not have handled the reorganization in the proper fashion.

First talk with Whit and tell him what you have observed. Should he confirm that he does have a problem with Joe, offer to help if needed. If your choice of Whit has been a good one, he'll want to take care of this problem himself. It is then your move to ask him how he proposes to approach a solution. If what Whit indicates he intends to do is hasty or ill-advised, correct him quickly because he must get his own facts, stand on his own feet, and treat this situation with the importance which it deserves. Your newly promoted manager must not be permitted to destroy an employee who has presumably been a proficient performer for twenty years. In fairness to Whit, you must be sure that he understands your concern if you leave the Joe problem for him to solve.

In the number three, or John, problem: It appears that we have a typical griper. John possibly doesn't really want anything done about his imagined grievances, but he does want to talk about them. It may be his way of getting some feeling of importance; attracting attention. You will find that this can be checked by correcting a few of his minor complaints, and then see what happens. If he still cries, "wolf, wolf," check further; but most likely you have a chronic complainer. You must listen to him, first, because of the possibility that some correction is really needed and, second, so that John has an outlet and will not blow up. Caution: Usually it has to be the boss who listens. He'll not be satisfied with less.

At times you may be inclined to agree with a harassed supervisor who said, "People associated in groups have almost unlimited facilities for becoming unhappy." The manager is frequently faced with employee complaints which may or may not be justified; but, as a growing supervisor, you must not allow such a feeling to be reflected in your judgment since, *Much misunderstanding arises because employees react unfavorably to a supervisor's attitude rather than to his actual deeds.*[1] If you have a poor attitude toward the company, your own position, or people in general, any one or all of these can likewise influence your

[1] Hoslett, *Human Factors in Management,* p. 109

interpretation of an employee's behavior. Distortion often comes about because of an individual's natural inclination to equate actions with preconceived ideas. Don't forget that an improper management attitude can assume real importance. A grievance which adversely affects an employee's performance on the job is a problem for the manager whether the real or imagined condition is unfair to the disgruntled employee or not. Many situations on the job just naturally contribute to the employee's dissatisfaction; for instance, normal work discipline restricts freedom, and the pressure to meet standards of performance can easily convince the workman that his supervisor is not treating him properly.

You must stay alert for evidences of developing employee dissatisfaction. Make every effort to see that rules are clear and understandable and that your full support behind all announced policies is apparent. If your organization has an established grievance procedure, it should be clearly understood and fully accepted as a usable appeal method which specifies the immediate supervisor as the first step available to the complaining employee.

When the inevitable complaints arise, some good rules to follow are: *First,* accumulate as many of the facts and circumstances as possible. *Second,* make an evaluation of individual actions and their effect upon your group's objectives. *Third,* make a judgment on what is to be done, who is to do what, and when the action will be taken. *Fourth,* follow-up to determine the attitudes of those directly involved and the group as a whole, plus the possible effects upon your production.

How to Handle Reprimands Without an Explosion

Since people are human, the very best manager cannot always anticipate disagreements or satisfy all employees; nor can he maintain discipline without some penalties for the violation of rules.

While unethical conduct or infractions of accepted standards is usually an individual action, from your viewpoint as a manager, you must think of the group-wide implications. Such activities do not take place in a vacuum.

Let's consider this example. In a large insurance company department of typing and reproductions, there were approximately twenty-six girls employed with two men working part time who had duties in other departments of the company. One of these in-and-out male employees was named Puck. The supervisor over the typing and reproduction department was named Silas, and he reported to a sectional supervisor named Marner, a second-level manager with accountability for the performance of two other supervisors directly over billing, filing, and underwriters.

One day Puck slipped quietly into Marner's office and closed the door. When the supervisor looked up and saw who it was, he said, "Have a seat. What can I do for you?" It was evident that the employee was perturbed, and now that he was in the office, he wasn't sure he wanted to stay. However, after a deep breath, he blurted out, "You know that Silas just put the bug on me for fifty cents to buy one of the girls in his office a wedding present, and I've been paying my twenty-five cents per week just as if I worked there full time." It was evident by Marner's expression that he was completely mystified. So he asked, "Now, what is all this again?" Puck was somewhat more composed after his original outburst, so in a calmer, more detailed explanation he related that for at least the past two years Silas had collected twenty-five cents per week from each of the girls. The money was used to purchase flowers for employees when they were sick, buy gifts when there was a marriage, or a going-away present in case someone terminated from the company. The touch that triggered Puck's ire was a special assessment which he said Silas made at times when he said the fund was depleted.

Marner told the complaining employee to control himself and not to say anything about their conversation as he promised to look into the problem.

After Puck left, Marner thought awhile, jotted down some figures on a scratch pad, and considered some more before he called Silas into the office.

The typing and reproductions supervisor readily admitted collecting the funds. He vowed it was at the urging of the employees themselves that he had started the system because they didn't like to be bothered by repeated collections for these purposes which seemed to continuously arise.

Marner asked to see Silas' records of receipts and pay-outs. His subordinate said he didn't keep any records, "I just put the money in the desk drawer as I get it, buy what is needed, and at odd times find it necessary to pick up a little special sweetener." Silas further commented, "Nobody has ever complained. They all seemed satisfied for a little over two years."

Marner braced himself as he said, "Silas, I can't imagine you involving yourself in a situation so loaded with dynamite for a manager." Then he continued in a positive tone, "Cut out your collections at once and count up the money you have on hand. Then I want you to go back to the beginning of this fiasco and from our records, your memory, and whatever other sources you can find, draw up a complete statement of income and out-go." After pausing for a breath, Marner said, "I want to see this report within a week, and any shortage will come out of your pocket."

Silas left the office, but the next day he was back, saying that he couldn't check the past two years. Marner was adamant as he said, "You'll have to. The money you have on hand and whatever difference you can't account for is to be returned to the employees. If they want to operate such a fund, it is their responsibility; and any collections made will have to be done outside regular working hours." As a parting warning, Marner told Silas, "You be sure you give me an honest accounting, because you know that I have ways to double check."

Silas, by dint of hard work, was able to account for all but $78.50 which Marner insisted he distribute evenly with the on-hand cash to the employees.

The now thoroughly discredited Silas notified Marner that he was leaving the company at the end of the month. Marner started training a replacement.

Hopefully, not many of your reprimands will be as pressure laden as Marner's was, but it is worthwhile to check this action formula.

How to Reach a Decision Involving Discipline

First, you must avoid arbitrary or rash action. *Second,* control your own biases. *Third,* maintain a calm appraisal of the facts. *Fourth,* examine the violation from the offender's viewpoint, his working associates'. *Fifth,* talk with the employee in private about the problem. *Sixth,* remember that proper conduct is best accomplished through education. *Seventh,* tailor the penalty to the seriousness of the violation.

How to Build a Foundation for More Result-Getting Directions

"Why is this stock coming out of your machine .003 over gauge?" the big boss sternly questioned Jim, the mill operator. The workman's immediate manager, Rye, quickly replied, "This is on my instructions. The right rear bearing on his machine is running hot, and we have a small order for this heavier weight material." The explanation satisfied the boss, and the two supervisors moved on. Later Jim told Rye, "I surely appreciate you taking me off the hook on that heavy stock. With all the quality emphasis we have had recently, I could have been in hot water."

The little Jewish workman, Level, was proud of the fact that he filled a key spot in the total plant operation. But Level was also a devout believer in his religion; so with Rosh Hashanah coming soon, he was worried about whether he could get off from work. Production schedules were tight, and all the machines were in full use. With evident earnest concern, Level explained to Rye why he would lose face with his people if he worked on their very special day. The supervisor quickly assured Level that he could plan to be off on both days if necessary. The operator gratefully assured him that one day would be sufficient.

In a management meeting on Saturday, it was decided to operate the manufacturing plant on Monday, contrary to an earlier announcement to employees that this would be an idle day. Most of the men had telephones, and the managers of the several crews quickly notified these operators. However, Rye had a good workman named Matt who lived in the country twenty miles from the plant. Matt had a large family. He had experienced some expensive sickness and was having difficulty making ends meet. He saved a little money by not having a telephone. Rye knew that Matt needed all the wages he could get, so Rye drove out to the employee's house, informed him of the new schedule, and received an enthusiastic "thank you" from Matt.

These brief examples tell a story of a good manager building a basis for respectful trust by the employees reporting to him. By demonstrating his interest and willingness to help them with their problems, Rye encouraged his subordinates to have confidence in his guidance. "Belief is an extremely powerful force. It wins acceptance and produces great willingness to abide by the wishes of the leader." [1] In such an atmosphere, one of your most important management tools, *orders,* produce the best results.

After Jim had witnessed how quickly Rye came to his defense in the over-specifications stock example—when Level was able to see that Rye appreciated the spot he was in to get a day off from work—and Matt benefited from the special effort which Rye made to see that he didn't miss a day's work—certainly any one of these subordinates would be strongly inclined to follow Rye's instructions, requests, suggestions, directions, or orders.

Benefits of a Confidence-Sharing Relationship

Every good manager hopes that his directions will be clearly understood and carried out with enthusiasm. In reality, there are several shades of gray between this ideal and outright refusal to follow instructions. For example, a subordinate may give outward approval but use little effort or spirit to implement your request. Again, there may be bland acceptance, but the employee waits for step-by-step direction. Still another reaction is sullen disapproval, often evidenced by deliberate mistakes.

You will have difficulty surviving a direct revolt against your orders, and it is a shattering experience to be forced to cope with the gray areas mentioned. Fortunately, if you express the attitude and follow the practices illustrated by Rye, you can, in most instances, avoid these hazards.

In giving instructions, requests, suggestions, directions, and orders, the only thing you need to be concerned about is to follow the cardinal principles of good communications—detail *who-what-where-when-how* and *why.* In some situations, the "how" and "why" might be omitted; as in the carrying out of a routine assignment by an experienced workman, "how" might not be necessary. The "why" would be superfluousness in an obvious emergency.

One of your greatest helps in directing others is a knowledge of the employees reporting to you. For a veteran workman who knows his job, brief, verbal orders may get proper results while the less experienced person will require more explanation. When there is mutual understanding between yourself and those reporting to you, directions can be expressed in positive style with consideration for the capacity and possible limitations of each employee.

In following good communication practices, the timing of the order-giving can be important. In the normal course of the day's work, routine type of directions should be given as close to the time of execution as is practical. If

[1] Terry, *Principles of Management,* p. 413

your instructions mean a change from the workman's regular method or style of operation, gauge your discussion so as to obtain the most favorable reception to the orders. When you are reasonably sure that the employee will either like or dislike his new directions, time your instruction so that production is benefited because delays can be caused by an unplanned and disturbing announcement.

Most orders are given verbally. At times, however, written orders should be considered; such as 1. if they are lengthy and complex, 2. if the action is to be taken at some future time, 3. if the action specified must be followed in an exact sequence, 4. if the supervisor lacks confidence in the person receiving the order, 5. if the manager thinks he might fail to pass on some important instructions at the proper time.

Getting Better Results from Your Actions as a Manager

1. *Review:*
   a. *how I arrived where I am today*
   b. *what needs to be done to improve my performance efficiency now*
   c. *what should I do to be a better professional manager in the future?*
2. *Try enlightened management rather than force to get better discipline. Use education to accomplish this purpose.*
3. *Get everybody into the act. Practice* "we-*can-do-a-better-job-than*-I" *management.*
4. *Get the benefits of productive employees who express pride in* my *job, which means that:*
   a. *subordinates get returns*
   b. *the total organization benefits*
   c. *you add to your reputation as a professional manager.*
5. *You must squarely face the dissatisfied employee with facts, judgment, understanding, and action decisions.*
6. *There must be penalties for violations of rules, and you must enforce them. Do these things:*
   a. *take your time*
   b. *watch your biases*
   c. *look at the facts*
   d. *examine different viewpoints*
   e. *discuss in private with the offender*
   f. *try education*
   g. *make the penalty fit the violation.*
7. *Build an atmosphere of mutual respect between yourself and your subordinates—by interest, consideration, and helpfulness. Then, benefit through following the rules of good communications.*

Chapter 10: Target-Patterns

"In order to survive in the competitive climate in which our company operates, we have found that it's just good business to help you—who have shown that you are among our most intelligent and energetic employees—develop and qualify to become better managers," was the opening statement of XYZ Corporation President Henry as he addressed a meeting of supervisors in an educational session. He continued, "What you are doing here supplements your on-the-job experiences, and I am convinced that such a program should continue; however, you must set some specific, personal targets of your own. I hope that each of you have your eye on a better position with the company within the next few years." After pausing momentarily, Henry went on, "As you are able to raise the level of your total job performance, not only will you gain, but the organization benefits because of our mutual interests."

After the president concluded his speech, Slim, a management training conference leader conducting the meeting with a group of young supervisors, referred to these remarks to illustrate a way in which their organization had arrived at one of its over-all objectives. Also, he suggested that their meeting was a good way to pass on this information to the staff. Another point which Slim stressed was that each of the managers should have some personal goals; and, as growing members of a demanding profession, these objectives should be in accord with the company aims, one supplementing the other.

How You Can Test Whether You and Your Organization Have Compatible Goals

Charlie, one of the young supervisors who had been in the meeting, stopped to talk with Slim. The newly appointed manager appeared to be about half angry as he complained, "What do you mean by such terms as 'fit your goals to the objectives of the enterprise'? How do I know what the company objectives are? Furthermore, I'm not even sure what I am working for except that I like my regular paycheck."

The conference leader realized that his session had accomplished one of its purposes because here was a supervisor who had been stirred to do some thinking. Slim told Charlie to have a seat while they discussed his question about goals. The young man listened as Slim related that many top managers were unwilling if not unable to formalize the basic aims of their companies in an understandable fashion. This likewise made it impossible to pass down an authoritative set of goals through the organization.

However, Slim continued, even when another manager fails to do his job the way you feel he should, this is no alibi for you. To be a better manager, you must set your own objectives. Talk with your immediate superior. Find out what he expects in performance from you. Then decide whether your job holds more pluses than minuses.

Slim advised that the only way you will fulfill your potential in an assignment as difficult as that of a manager is to be sure you are doing what you want to do. He quoted for Charlie from the poet Gibran:

> Work is love made visible. And if you cannot work with love but only with distaste, it is better that you should leave your work and sit at the gate of the temple and take alms of those who work with joy.
>
> For if you bake bread with indifference, you bake a bitter bread that feeds but half man's hunger.
>
> And if you grudge the crushing of the grape, your grudge distils a poison in the wine.[1]

Slim told Charlie that, for purely practical reasons, he should come to some early conclusions about whether he liked his present job prospects because fringe benefits were becoming more important. For instance, he said, in the fifteen years just preceding, up to and including 1962, *employer payments* for such things as social security, private pension, health and welfare funds, compensation for injuries and pay of the military reserve had increased by 90%.[2] In addition, many companies were installing savings plans, stock options, and other incentives to encourage continued long service with the same organization. Slim pointed out, "It is not only more money in your pocket, but greater future security if you make up your mind about the outfit that you want to work with and give it all you have."

The instructor's final words to Charlie were, "Whatever the difficulty, to be a better manager you must have some objectives. Remember that the fundamental difference between a follower and a leader is that the leader knows where he wants to go. So set yourself some targets."

[1] Gibran, Kahlil, *The Prophet*, p. 28
[2] *Economic Almanac*, 1964, p. 77

Build a Road Map for Your Future

As was true in Charlie's thinking, most employees spend too much time worrying about what *"they"* ought to do for *"me";* even veteran managers unduly concern themselves about the lack of good performance by associate supervisors or superiors. What you should do is concentrate on "me," the one place where you can call all the shots and make the greatest improvements.

In our representative form of government, congressmen, senators, assemblymen, councilmen and commissioners are only secondarily concerned with foreign policy or the nation at large. They are first and foremost very sensitive to the opinions, wishes and desires of their own constituents, the people who elect them to office. Likewise, as a manager, you have subordinates and a superior who are your constituents. They should be your primary consideration; satisfy them first. They are the foundation of your success, so common sense dictates that you help them at every opportunity.

A First-Level Manager Sets Helpful Targets for Subordinates

Henry Laurence Gantt in World War I developed a system of management charts which in form at least are used today throughout every segment of industry. These charts record idle machine time, output of individual employees, the planning of research and development work, and, in some instances, control a factory's output.

In Professor Alex W. Rathe's edited volume, *Gantt on Management,*[1] several of his thoughts are pertinent in helping a first-level manager set targets for the people reporting to him. He says that a manager's greatest problem is the economic utilization of labor. The limiting of output by the workman, and the limiting by the employer of the amount that a workman is allowed to earn, are both factors which work against harmonious cooperation between employer and employee, which is essential to their highest common good. In the long run, both parties must regard their arrangements with each other as beneficial. The employer who insists on more service than he pays for, and the employee who demands excessive wages for his work, both lose. The former is plagued with labor troubles, dissatisfaction, and strikes; and the latter can well put his employer out of business because in our competitive society high wages and high efficiency must go together.

Benefits of a Fair Method of Wage Payments

You should recognize that the only two methods of paying for work are: 1. The amount of time a man spends on a job, and 2. the amount of work that he does. The first method is day work and the second is piece work. All pay-

[1] Rathe, *Gantt on Management,* pp. 113-115

ment systems are variations of these two. As a realistic supervisor, you know that it's to your advantage to get as much production for the wages paid as you can. Likewise, the workman wants as much money for his time as he can get. Your key duty as an improving manager is to harmonize these conflicting viewpoints to the greatest advantage of both parties.

In the payment of day work in which no record of individual performance is kept, everyone in the group receives the same amount of wages regardless of the amount of work he does. Under this system, you are forced to pay a rate which is determined by supply, demand, and union pressure. Your hardest working and efficient workmen are discouraged because of the lack of recognition and tend to slow down to the "get by" speed of production. This method of operation is similar to buying an electric iron at the store just because that is what a product is called without regard to quality of article.

When a workman being paid on a day-work basis has his output evaluated on an impartial and objective basis, and his wage rate is determined by this measurement, efficiency begins to increase and the more deserving employee gets the earnings to which he is entitled.

The very best type of payment for any individual's service is piece work, that is payment for results where such accomplishments can be fairly determined. For an example, on an automobile tire building operation, an experienced individual could produce a tire every ten minutes, and the established piece work rate, set by a study of the motions and time required, was forty cents per tire. This rate was understood and well established, thus most of the operators exerted themselves to a little above what was considered a normal pace and built 7½ tires per hour. As a consequence, they earned three dollars per hour instead of only $2.40. Sometimes, on occasions, when a workman needed extra money, he would step up to 8½ tires per hour, adding an extra dollar to his income over the standard norm.

Through piece work wage payments: *the workman gains:*

1. a feeling of fair return for his work
2. an opportunity to set his own pace
3. helps keep his company competitive.

As a manager, you gain:

1. work discipline is not a problem
2. you can spend more time helping to improve production
3. feedback of information from workmen is better because of their personal interest in production.

The total organization gains:

1. greater returns on the capital investment
2. better continuous production
3. labor costs per unit of output can be determined more accurately.

When you are in a first-level management assignment, if possible, you should have a piece-work incentive target for your subordinates. A second-best method is day work with a fair means of evaluation so that individual merit can be recognized. Avoid the non-competitive step toward mediocrity which results when all workmen are paid the same rate regardless of effort or skill. Seniority, which most labor unions would like to use as the determining factor for rate increases and promotions, has all the disadvantages of a flat, day-work rate because length of time on a job does not give any assurance that the holder is any more efficient; in fact, security and tenure has the reverse effect since it eliminates the stimulant of competition, causes the individual to relax, take it easy and "not rock the boat" by searching for new and better ways to do the job while he waits for retirement and a pension.

Using Objectives to Develop Subordinates

To illustrate the application of objectives as a means of improving managers, let's apply some sound operating principles to a management development department. This organization had a director named Zee with over-all administrative guidance of the department and selected specific duties such as personally handling the management objectives program, universities' relationships, restricted seminars and conferences. Reporting to the director was a supervisor, Wel, who had reporting to him three coordinators, five instructors, a technician, and a stenographer to complete the operating department staff personnel.

Wel's coordinators were veterans of long experience and knew the people to see on problems throughout the plant. They could lead meetings, conferences, and teach classes. The supervisor's principal problem with the coordinators was to keep abreast of what they were doing.

The five department instructors were specialists in selected fields: business law, economics, speech, communications, human relations, organization, and management techniques.

The technician's chief activities were to serve as an information source for company-encouraged, college and university manager improvement-type programs. A part of the job duties included enrolling managers in general education courses plus keeping records. The written reports issued from time to time for the entire department were also a requirement of his job assignment.

The stenographer's work was largely routine: typing, filing, letter writing.

Zee had talked about personal targets and goals for managers but, because it was a newly established program, had not gone into detail on the fine points with his supervisor. It sounded like a good idea to Wel, so the climate was favorable when Zee called Wel and told him that he should give some thought to establishing targets for the next six months. The boss further said that he would like to drop up to Wel's office and discuss these objectives on the following Tuesday at 9:00 A.M.

How to Set Your Specific Job-Improvement, Performance Targets

Promptly on the day set for their meeting, the director and supervisor got together. Zee asked, "What have you concluded that you should accomplish in the next six months?" Wel was used to this abrupt launching into the job at hand so he replied, "I'd like to prepare a new course in rapid reading for managers, and rearrange classroom number four to seat thirty-seven people instead of the present twenty-six. We need a new slide projector and a renewed subscription to the *Harvard Business Review.*" At this point, Zee interrupted, "Just a minute. Remember we are talking about objectives to be accomplished in the next six months. Wouldn't you agree that most of these problems you have mentioned are everyday, routine administrative duties?"

Zee continued, "Let me give you a little more background. *First* we want to limit the selection to not more than four items. *Second,* two of these should be job-oriented improvement, and two designed for your own personal growth. *Third,* these targets should require you to stretch but still not be out of reach. *Fourth,* we need to make them specific, not general." The director then went over to Wel's office blackboard and briefly listed the four points he had just made. Then, when he sat down, Zee took a pad of paper from the supervisor's desk, turned it horizontally, and drew four vertical lines from top to bottom of the sheet. As he did so, he said, "This form will also be helpful." At the top of each column across the page he listed, "Objectives-Results Expected," "Specific Actions to be Taken and Key Approaches," "Methods of Measuring Progress—Follow-up Controls," and "Review of Results and Disposition."

The director said, "Just as a starter for job objectives, how about extending the line-conducted conference program, oh, say by between 10% to 30%?" Wel, getting into the spirit of the exchange, replied, "Tell you what I would rather do. Let's increase our total service activities in this percentage range without increasing our costs." Zee agreed, "That's a deal. Under our first job-improvement heading, let's make that note."

Next, the director asked, "How about the second column? How do you propose to attack this goal of extending your services?" Wel answered thoughtfully, "I'll want to review this with our staff, but, basically, we'll need to find new ways of encouraging line managers to involve themselves in specific training efforts. Let's note that in the second column; and, under the follow-up, third column, I would like to talk with you about our progress midway in the six months' period, say about March 23."

Zee said, "Fine. I'll make those notes, and you do the same. We'll leave the last column open for final results. Now, what about a second job objective?"

The supervisor answered, "Our reproduction and printing costs have been rising. I would like to bring it down, say between 15% and 25%." This was agreed to and noted. Wel thought he might approach a solution by studying the cost and effects of a new kind of copying machine. He also thought it might be well to discuss progress on this item at their March 23 meeting.

How to Set Targets for Your General Improvement as a Manager

Zee asked, "What about your objectives for personal management improvement?" Wel enthusiastically replied, "The first one is going to be to see that each of the coordinators sets four specific goals just as we are doing." Notes on the four column sheet were made by each, leaving the follow-up open to be reviewed by either if it seemed appropriate. When this was completed, the director remarked, "You know our rate ranges have always seemed something of a mystery to me. Are you up on them, Wel?" The supervisor answered, "I feel pretty confident, but I'll tell you what I would like to make my fourth objective." When Zee nodded his approval, Wel said, "To better use salary increases as an incentive for improving on-the-job performance."

After the two managers agreed that here was a tough objective, they discussed the specific actions to be taken. Included were Wel's careful study of their present salary payment scale, the current rates, a means of evaluating the subordinate's present performance, and how improvements might be determined. The director and the supervisor felt that the column marked "Methods of Measuring Progress—Follow-up Controls" should be left open until they could get back together on February 1.

In concluding their conference, both Zee and Wel commented that they had spent a lot of time on setting these six-months' targets, but each felt that their efforts would pay off in better over-all good management results.

Alternatives to the Objective System and Their Disadvantages

It is generally agreed that one of the essential functional duties of any management job is that of follow-up—a determination of how things are going. You can plan; other executives can determine broad policy; as a manager, you can issue directives; but to insure that proper action results, someone with authority must check up and evaluate what is being accomplished.

> The efficient development and utilization of the management team entails a periodic examination of the capabilities and weaknesses of individual managers and their assignments as members of the management team. The techniques of management appraisal and inventory are intended to provide this periodic assessment . . . and are the basis of much of the management development of any organization.[1]

[1] Mahoney, *Building the Executive Team,* p. 125

No doubt in the course of your experience you have observed possibly all of the subsequently listed attempts to improve the performance of managers. The *first* method can be titled *Survive or Perish.* Practitioners usually have an attitude similar to that expressed by a line-management department director when he remarked, "Good managers have to be tested under fire. I like to keep the pressure on them to make sure they perform. Right now I have a subordinate supervisor who just can't take it. Gets sick about once a week. But he'll make it himself or else." Such an approach should make most students of management wonder just how many potentially effective managers have been lost by being assigned a job with no more assistance than the hope that they'll come through. The extent of loss will, of course, never be known, but undoubtedly such waste is tremendous. Even after a course of instructions, if the new manager is left on his own, losses come about as the result of a lot of unnecessary fumbling.

A *second* frequently used method could be called *The Partnership Co-operative.* Here the new supervisor is assigned to work with a trainer manager, a supervisor who knows the job details. One of the special disadvantages is that the learner acquires all the bad habits of his tutor. Another liability is that the assisting manager usually has no special incentive to encourage the new manager. Yet another handicap is that the break-in manager is seldom trained to teach.

A *third* device used to develop managers is *Progressive Advancement.* This method has had its greatest use in the past when the only standard for judging management potential was to view the superior technical performer, the man who could best do the physical job, as a future director of others assigned to the same kind of work. When an operator showed a special ability to produce on a lathe, it was considered logical to assume that he could tell and see that others did the same thing which, of course, doesn't necessarily follow. However, even today, being an outstanding performer on his present job is the best means for an employee to attract attention if he has ambitions to become a manager. A young, inexperienced employee, almost without exception, must prove himself as a workman before he will be considered for supervision.

A *fourth* developmental method used in attempting to improve managers is *Appraisal and Coaching.* Still carrying some of its original "fad glow," the idea can be described in a fashion which makes sense to some of the most practical-minded business managers. The reason for the long-term popularity of "appraisal and coaching" is because it is based upon such sound human desires as: 1. You and I want to know what the boss expects us to do on our jobs. 2. Particularly as a manager you want to improve yourself. 3. You also want to get rid of any gnawing uncertainty about what your superior may think about your job performance. 4. You would like to know where you can go if you need help. 5. You and all of us like to be recognized for a good job performance.

While all these principles are sound, as usually applied, "appraisal and coaching" breaks down because it fails to work for most managers on the job.

In looking for reasons, here are some of the answers: 1. No matter how much you "sugar coat it," both you and your subordinate recognize this kind of an evaluation is a personal criticism, and you both naturally resent it. 2. If you can, you dodge the appraisal and coaching session or get it over with as a distasteful chore as quickly as possible. 3. You can use an annual appraisal and coaching requirement as a means to avoid the essential daily, weekly, and/or monthly corrections and improvement helps for subordinates. 4. The method concentrates on past happenings. Even while the intent is to assist in improving future performance, most of you would rightly prefer to forget the mistakes of the past and look to the future. 5. Appraisal and coaching confines itself to job practices, and, as was noted in the use of objectives for helping managers to improve, your personal ability as a superior performing manager is of at least equal importance as technical job duties.

How to Secure the Benefits of Using Objectives for Improving Managers

A first essential is that a session such as that held by Zee and Wel should not be hampered by any consideration of salary or rate of pay distractions. (a) How much you or your subordinate should be paid must be entirely divorced from a conference held to encourage the personal performance of you or managers reporting to you. (b) A second reason why Zee did not discuss money with Wel was because setting objective standards for the judgment of a manager's performance is difficult. (c) Zee recognized that the complete and willing cooperation of managers is essential to the success of the organization. Care must be exercised to secure the effective improvement which can have such a wide and beneficial impact. He likewise did not want to risk upsetting these key people who can have an equally detrimental reverse effect.

A second essential in the use of the objective method to help managers improve is in the way you apply it. (a) You must center attention on the job to be done, thus taking personal criticism away from the individual. (b) Take full advantage of the forward look; soften emphasis on past errors. (c) Keep it practical. In the example of Zee and Wel, note: 1. The simplicity of explanation and its understandable application. 2. He required only the barest minimum of paperwork. 3. The obvious flexibility. The objective method can be adjusted to meet the best judgment of the superior and subordinate.

A third essential is to encourage the subordinate manager to set his own targets because: (a) He is the most knowledgeable of what needs to be done. (b) He will strive harder to reach an objective which he has established. (c) Such a practice improves superior-subordinate communication and makes you better able to benefit, in whichever position you may be, to either give or receive help.

A fourth essential is to make sure that both parties to the discussion understand that the intent of the objective-setting program is one of mutual self help because: (a) Both the superior and the subordinate have a stake in getting good results. (b) Realistically, managers know that improvement requires personal discipline and hard work. (c) The purpose is not intended to concentrate on correcting problems. The most outstanding manager may improve more than the poorest supervisor, so the entire management line should be involved.

The fifth essential is to use the built-in follow-up because: (a) A target-setting session is recommended for each six-months' period. When one of these time periods is completed, the forward look is extended for an additional half year. (b) Each conference is individualized for maximum returns to the managers who participate. (c) It forces special attention to the important duties of subordinate correction and improvement coaching by the manager in the best position to help, that is your immediate superior. (d) In a superior position, it helps you prepare for your own promotion by developing a follow-up manager to take your place. (e) As a subordinate, it is most beneficial in furthering your personal ambitions for advancement in your profession.

The Written Position Description Aids Your Objective Improvement Plan

On the fields of Runnymede June 15, 1215, beside the Thames, the English barons forced King John to approve an early written position description. The document limited the supreme power of the king. It spelled out what the monarch's performance would be as related to such specific areas as: 1. Requiring feudal tenure of serfs. 2. The king's ownership of the nation's forests. The Magna Charta, the name by which this position description became known, also included these general sections: 1. No levy of taxes without representative consent, 2. forbid arbitrary imprisonment and punishment without lawful trial, 3. established the rights of habeas corpus, trial by jury, 4. defense under law to be prompt and equally available to all, 5. set up a supreme civil court separate from the power of the king.

In your job as a modern professional manager, better results can be obtained if neither party to the superior-subordinate association is forced to accept the dictates of the other. A cooperative understanding will do more to help achieve both individual and organization goals.

The written position description can best fill its purpose as a helpful tool in the objective improvement program if you participate in its preparation with your superior or subordinate and make sure that it states the subordinate's: 1. *list of duties,* 2. *authorities,* 3. *relationships,* to which the two of you have agreed.

The Magna Charta met only a few of these criteria. In a general way, it limited the king's authority and specified his relationships with the English barons. However, when you give more detailed attention to a written position description, it will serve as: 1. An excellent starting place for a superior-subordinate discussion of objectives. 2. A reminder and guide to avoid overlooking job duties. 3. A standard to check progress toward an established target. 4. A way to avoid the "fencing in" of a good manager. Remember to make your write-up general enough to permit the manager to improve with some "running room." 5. An invaluable aid in discussing a new management job assignment with a supervisor unfamiliar with that particular work.

The written position description is most helpful when it spells out and is understood by both the superior and the subordinate as to "just who is going to do what."

A Replacement Table Review Helps in Setting and Meeting Targets

Many forward-looking management organizations annually list first and second replacement choices for each key management position. If you, for example, are the supervisor in charge of a department with, say, three levels of management—in order, X, Y, Z—between yourself and the workman, to build or review the replacement table, you would say to yourself, "If something should happen to X, who would take his place?"

To make such a practice valuable, it must be formalized to the extent that you answer this question in writing. List a first and second choice for the important jobs. State the ages of incumbents and proposed replacements and how much time will be required for both one and two to be ready to fully discharge the duties of X's job.

If you go through this replacement table exercise with thoughtfulness and carefully apply your best judgment, it will suggest some improvement needs of the better performing managers reporting to you. Logically, the next step of an ambitious manager is to discuss these areas with your key subordinates and show them how they can make use of special developmental opportunities. And if you have made a proper selection of really superior employees, there should be a special incentive to work for personally established objectives.

Management Inventory as an Assistance to Goal-Setting

Most large companies try to identify—in terms of experience, performance, skill, and education—the more valuable members of their management team. A quickly available review of the organization's most important human resources is their basic purpose.

Such a list offers still another opportunity to encourage your better supervisors to become interested and to work toward the target of improving their personal performance. If you have some of these outstanding managers reporting to you, here is the place to get some pay-off results. Spend some of your special attention and efforts in helping to target their improvement efforts.

Wage Payments as a Peak Performance Incentive

As noted earlier, you will obtain much better results in the objectives program if it is divorced as much as possible from the wage-and-salary setting function. Realistically, these judgments do have a bearing upon the money paid to managers, but in using objectives as a development medium, goals should be set and reviewed at a different time of year than when salaries are discussed.

While job evaluation rates should be kept separate from the objectives program, you do use money to help in carrying out your measure of results function. *The supreme challenge in salary administration . . . is to get every ounce of motivation from every salary dollar spent by the company.*[1]

It is worthwhile to review some of the numerous methods used to determine wage rates for supervisors. The more common are: 1. Simple ranking based upon the subjective judgment of someone supposedly qualified; 2. classification based upon comparable jobs; 3. point system with the job details assigned a total score; 4. setting the value on the related factors in key jobs. It appears that very few companies use any of these methods exclusively; rather, most are a combination of several.

In each salary payment method, the intent is to provide equal pay for comparable value received by the company. Your wage plan should be: 1. sufficiently flexible to meet the changes in supply and demand, 2. appropriate to the individual growth of the manager, 3. freely administered to permit the exercise of management judgment in timing and in the amount of merit or incentive to be paid. Such standards give you a difficult assignment which requires a continuous review of people and their performance, but it is essential if money is to be equitably used as a reward for achievement.

Cost Saving Targets Improve Your Professional Performance

To be effective, such an approach means job improvement. It suggests the elimination, combining, or possible rearrangement of processes, job duties, and assignments. This requires an evaluation of time, materials, and manpower. In any cost control effort, the best results are obtained through teamwork by the entire organization. A single section becomes discouraged in its cost-reduction efforts if another department ignores obvious cost-saving devices. Company-wide control of minor items, such as fringe benefits, travel, advertising, long distance telephone calls, postage excesses and secretarial costs, represent a sizeable saving.

[1] Merrill, *Management News,* April, 1965, p. 5

Quality and Volume Values in Target-Setting

Quality production is closely related to your measure of results responsibility. While every conscientious workman agrees on the importance of a good product, actual results require your continuous attention. Poor workmanship can easily develop from the human desire to relax. You must devise some means of sampling and establish an early warning system to spot approaching trouble. Be particularly alert during pressure periods when mistakes are most likely to occur.

As an improving supervisor you have learned that in most management situations there is an optimum balance of production and quality requirements. You cannot, for instance, devote complete staff or crew time to eliminating every possible error and still get creditable production if such an operation requires repeated checking and rechecking while output is halted. Absolutely perfect quality often means too few pieces, pounds, gallons, or whatever other measure of production is used. This becomes an area where you must apply management judgment.

To fulfill your specific job duties, set up some targets for accomplishment. Such goals establish a standard to use in measuring results. The study of your own and the jobs under your supervision is a continuing obligation.

Gains from Working Toward Agreed-Upon Targets

You are able to: 1. make better forward plans, 2. improve your skill in human judgments, 3. adapt to changing conditions, 4. think, work toward, and encourage real improvements.

Your subordinate can: 1. give maximum attention to worthwhile goals, 2. think and work regularly on his own improvement plan, 3. prepare for advancement, 4. apply self-discipline to specific and easily understood goals.

Shooting for Specific Targets—A Review

1. *You should have your own goals and know those of your organization.*
2. *Build your future by concentrating on the features of your job which are important to you.*
3. *As a first-level manager, your job is primarily to see that both the workman and management get a fair shake.*
4. *Use payment for results as the best method of determining wage rates.*
5. *How to set objectives to help managers improve:*
    a. *importance to technical job operations*
    b. *general importance as a manager.*

6. *Alternatives to the objective method and their disadvantages:*
   a. *Survive or Perish. Waste of talent.*
   b. *Partnership Cooperative. Bad habits, helpers not qualified as trainers, lack of incentive.*
   c. *Progressive Advancement. Good managers are not always good workmen.*
   d. *Appraisal and Coaching. Good in theory, lacking in practice.*
7. *To get the best improvement results from objectives:*
   a. *Separate the consideration of goals from wage rates.*
   b. *Use careful consideration in application.*
   c. *Encounter subordinate to set his own goals.*
   d. *See that accomplishment is mutually beneficial.*
   e. *Make it a continuous improvement program.*
8. *Use the written position description as a guide in objective-setting.*
9. *The value of the replacement table as a reminder of the need to plan, set, and work toward established targets.*
10. *Using management inventory as an incentive to self-improvement.*
11. *The benefits of wage payments as a means to obtain peak performance.*
12. *Places to look for cost savings in your management target-setting.*
13. *Consider balancing your quality and quantity goals for best results.*
14. *Both you and your subordinate gain from working toward agreed-upon targets.*

Chapter 11: How to Work Smart

"I've been asked to list the qualities of a good executive, and I just can't. What the questioners want is a list of words such as decisiveness, judgment, ambition. You can set them down but they don't mean much. A man can be really high in every category you list, but he may not be a good executive. Or he might be low in a number of these items and be a good one. What you have to do is perform a sort of mental integration of everything you know about a person and come up with a good conclusion. . . . I remember the first time I met General Eisenhower. He came in the room and leadership stuck out all over him. You could tell it in a glance. There he was." [1]

In these comments Mr. Crawford Greenewalt, president of the E. I. du Pont de Nemours and Company for fourteen years, and later chairman of the board, raises some questions which continually challenge thoughtful students of professional management.

Most such puzzlers take this form: "What is it about a person that enables him to become a good manager?" Almost everyone holding a job in business or industry sooner or later is intrigued with the obvious fact that one manager can effectively plan, direct, win the respect of others, and control a complex operation, while another person who seems equally competent fails as he endeavors to accomplish similar results.

Many people have from time to time tried to list the success traits that mark a good manager. William E. Henry states,

> From research it became clear that the "successful" business executives studied had many personality characteristics in common. It was equally clear that

[1] Greenewalt, "Sensing Who Can Command," *Nation's Business,* October 1965, p. 110

> the absence of the characteristics was coincident with failure within the organization. This personality constellation might be thought of as a minimal requirement for "success" within our present business system.[1]
>
> Clearly, the principles of leadership can be discovered by research, but the application of them to a specific situation is another matter. It seems unlikely that leadership skills will ever be simplified to the point where they can be taught in "ten easy lessons." [2]

These authoritative references indicate some of the work done in this area. However, to my knowledge, there has only been one really practical study which "makes sense" on the specific question, "What is it about a person that enables him to become a good manager?" This intensive study was made in a large manufacturing organization.

How to Find the Essential Personal Qualities of a Successful Manager

You will undoubtedly agree that if you want to determine the reasons for management success you can get your best answers from people who have, at least to a degree, succeeded.

Our studied group consisted of 517 successful, on-the-job managers representing all echelons of the organization from top to first level. The numbers in each level of authority were weighted according to the total number in that echelon; however, the actual supervisors were selected at random. The 517 number was 25% of the management organization—large enough to insure that the results could be considered representative of the entire organization.

This group of managers voluntarily took an intensive battery of written tests, such as personality, special interests, depth perception, manual dexterity, intelligence and language. They were personally interviewed, their superiors in the management line were interviewed, personnel records were checked, and salary progressions were noted. After all the information was compiled, each individual manager who wished had a private discussion with a competent staff person about his own results. An interesting by-product of the analysis was that only in very rare cases did any manager disagree with his personal profile when it was explained to him.

You can imagine how exciting the study became as our realization grew that here was practical data which could provide answers to, "What is it about a person that enables him to become a successful manager?"

Values from the Successful Manager Studies

With great expectations, all information was carefully studied from many angles. For instance, we determined that if there was such a thing as an average

[1] Dubin, Robert: *Human Relations in Administration,* p. 167
[2] Likert and Hayes, *Some Applications of Behavioural Research,* p. 62

manager in our organization, he would be thirty-eight years old. He would have been with the company eight and one-half years; three and one-half of these years below the first level of supervision. Two years had been spent in the job he left to come to our organization.

Our average supervisor was found to be a member of two and one-half organizations; including churches, civic clubs, YMCA, American Legion, and the like. He owned $10,000 worth of life insurance, exclusive of gifts from the company. He was 5′ 9½″ tall, weighed 175; he was married and had two children. He was driving 10.5 miles to work each day and grew up in a town within 200 miles of the plant. During the past five years, he had averaged two days absence a year due to illness. In the armed services, he reached the rank of corporal. His formal education equalled one year in college, and he had an I.Q. of 113.

Our experience in determining information about an average supervisor was interesting, but of more value are several useful facts which were discovered by tests, interviews, questionnaires, discussions with superiors, and records. *First,* the skills, qualities and abilities which made the managers successful are developed and acquired methods of operating as contrasted with inherited talents.

Second, these outstanding qualities were evidenced by actions. This number two fact should have special significance for you because it means that, in the personal leadership category, the door is wide open for you to be as good a manager as you really want to be.

You can set your own pace and make your own judgments, which is not true in the general and functional divisions of management job requirements where company policies, practices, and organizational restrictions sometimes prohibit freedom of operation. Remember, it can't be too strongly emphasized, that your success stems from something you do, and not from latent or dormant aptitudes. Here is an actual case illustrating the importance of action. Some years back, a fellow—not too old, not too young; just about right in age—wanted a job in our department. He had some time to spare and was willing to spend it taking a series of tests. We used him as something of a guinea pig; gave him all sorts of standard tests—interest, aptitude, personality, perception, skill, I.Q., the whole gamut. He scored exceptionally well on all of them. The applicant had a nice appearance, was neat, talked well and seemed like a good risk, so we gave him a job. It was not a particularly tough assignment; it required some initiative, not really rush-rush compelling, but from the very first our new hire had trouble. Several of us—at least four supervisors—had been in on the decision to hire the man. All of us had a stake in seeing him succeed, therefore, we took a hand in trying to help him perform satisfactorily at this job. After a time we had to give up and conclude the new man just would not do in that position. After leaving our department, the man drifted around in the organization at first one job and then another before he finally left the company entirely. The point of the example is that undoubtedly the man had the ability to do the assigned work, but did not use what he had. To be a better manager, you must *do* something, not just *be* something. As a successful manager, you must use your skills and abilities; not just hold them in reserve.

A *third* important fact our study uncovered was that a good supervisor tends to be an individualist. At one extreme you may have a manager called "A" who does a good job. He looks different, acts different, has a different philosophy and a different way of going about getting his results from a manager at the other extreme, whom we might call "B." However, "A" and "B" do an equally good job. Such a situation is the rule rather than the exception and is the reason why it is so difficult to answer the question, "What, if any, are the personal qualities of an individual which enable him to become a good supervisor?"

The Real Break-Through on Your Personal Power Sources

While our study of successful managers contrasted the non-conformist features of one good manager with that of another equally good manager, the most important discovery made in this analysis was that every successful supervisor demonstrated definite, distinctly identifiable strength dimensions of qualities, skills, and abilities. These strength areas, not necessarily in order of importance, because all are needed, are: 1. Demonstrated intelligence, judgment, decision-making, problem solving, 2. self-motivation, energy, drive, 3. administrative skill, planning, directing, controlling, 4. broad knowledge, wide interests, experience, 5. motivating others, influencing, guiding, encouraging, attraction for others. Admittedly these qualifications are general in nature, but they can be valuable to you as guidelines for your own self-improvement as well as to suggest possibilities for helping your subordinates' growth.

Awareness and knowledge of personal leadership principles is only a part of your job as a manager. The people, situation, and circumstances under which the rules apply are of at least equal importance with the principles themselves. Thus, you must know when and how to apply the knowledge you have acquired.

As you seek to benefit from the application of attention to these power sources, it is well to note that, "Character, intelligence, and intuition are often classified as innate while experience, adaptability, and special skills are acquirable." [1]

Unquestionably, individuals vary widely in intellectual capacity, physical make-up, and the opportunities offered by environmental advantages. These are facts of life, but disadvantages in any of the three categories have not deterred innumerable successful managers in the past who were willing to apply themselves and more fully exploit their total capacities. "The wisest man who ever lived came nowhere near using the full capability of his wonderful mental store-

[1] Newman, *Administrative Action,* pp. 326-327

house. Quite possibly people in general employ only 10% to 15% of the brain's capabilities." [1]

Demonstrated Intelligence as an Important Power Source

You will remember that in our analysis of the 517 successful managers it was mentioned that the average supervisor in the study survey had an I.Q. of 113. The score is based on a scale of 100 for the average adult member of the population, with 133 the top of the scale. Therefore, 113 is a good showing, but notice this is not the kind of quality, skill, or ability we are talking about here. It is important to keep in mind that we are discussing an action function. I.Q. is a dormant quality unless it is used. Intelligence, judgment and decision-making ability must be apparent in the supervisor's performance.

Let's look at a situation in which this power source could be used to advantage. You are in charge of purchasing materials for a large manufacturing company. One of your receiving supervisors, let's call him "M," has just called to notify you that the ABC Company has not delivered some special steel due in your warehouse two weeks ago. Slamming down the telephone after M's call, you are not only upset about the late schedule, but steel prices have gone up within the past week. You dictate a blistering wire to your secretary to be sent to the ABC Company sales manager. Then, with some of your ire relieved, you decide to talk with Mr. D, the responsible buyer for the steel coming into your plant. Mr. D changes the picture considerably since he informs you that ABC had notified him in plenty of time that they would be unable to deliver on the committed schedule. The buyer said that the supplier had put him in touch with the XYZ Company and he was able to purchase the needed steel at the lower price; and, further, it was in the factory on the production line at that time.

With a very red face, you hurriedly get hold of your secretary to see if you can stop the telegram. This is an ordinary run of mill, manager judgment type bit of decision making. But why did you get into trouble?

Beware of the Mercurial Quartet

In every decision there are four changing factors which make the exercise of good judgment difficult. As one employee said of a high-level manager, "With the power and the glory go the headaches and the ulcers. One of my top-level friends died the other day of 'Industrial Suicide.' As for me, I'd rather have a happy, pleasant life. What's the use of killing yourself?" [1]

The four shifty quantities helping to generate the pressures are: 1. you, 2. the individual or the individuals directly involved, 3. the organization, 4. the situation.

[1] Bliven, *Your Brain's Unrealized Powers,* Readers Digest, October 1956
[2] Dubin, op.cit., p. 232

In the case of the supposed late delivery of steel, you thought the shop was almost out of material. You were left "holding the bag" for an up-coming delay in production, so you vented your spite on the ABC sales manager. M, the warehouseman, had not recognized that the XYZ steel filled the need, but Mr. D was on top of his job with all the information. The changed situation which Mr. D reported started you thinking that your company might want to do some future business with ABC, so you turned to your secretary to bail you out.

Then, of course, the whole difficulty could have been avoided if you had taken time to check each member of the variable quartet.

Why Active Intelligence Alone Is Not Enough

"Numerous studies have indicated a positive relationship between measures of intellectual factors and managerial effectiveness . . . while above-average intelligence appears important to managerial effectiveness, there is some doubt about the relationship of highly superior intelligence to effectiveness . . . the intelligence of a leader should be above that of his subordinates but a marked difference of intelligence appears just as destructive of managerial effectiveness as does lowered intelligence. The exact nature of the relationship is not known, however, and further study is required to determine the relationship between markedly superior intelligence and managerial effectiveness." [1] Another related statement from a different source writes, "Many business executives have found that persons of unquestioned high intelligence often turn out to be ineffective when placed in positions of increased responsibility. The reasons for their failure lie in their social relationship." [2]

Supporting this opinion and dealing with the general question of intelligence are some further views which can be titled "Why Executives Fail," and listed in order of importance, "First, poor delegation of responsibility; second, shortage of general knowledge; third, inability to analyze and evaluate; fourth, inability to judge people; fifth, inability to cooperate with others; sixth, inability to make decisions; seventh, lack of knowledge of organization and administration." [3]

How to Make the Ideal Practical

As applied to the manager's job, intelligence is a multi-meaning term having a direct bearing on all sections of the personal leadership category. In applying this performance requirement, the good supervisor must have abstract reasoning ability, that is be able to summarize information, generalize from broad concepts, and make practical application of his thoughts.

[1] Mahoney, op.cit., pp. 189-190
[2] Dubin, op.cit., p. 167
[3] Guadet, Dr. Frederick J.: Excerpted from *Changing Times, the Kiplinger Magazine,* Copyright 1956 by The Kiplinger Washington Editors, Inc.

Let's take the experiences of Sid, a newly appointed first-level manager in a large manufacturing company. Our neophyte supervisor had been taught in his preparatory training courses in management that: 1. People like to be recognized as individuals. 2. Employees will take pride in their work if given an opportunity. 3. Most people want to advance to positions of greater responsibility. 4. Good leadership will overcome a person's natural resentment in having to take directions from another. 5. The majority of employees have untapped skills, abilities, and qualities.

Sid supervised a noisy, dirty, greasy, dangerous automobile wheel production line with fifteen operators on the various machines and service work. As any young, vigorous, ambitious manager, our hero was impatient to apply his newly acquired knowledge. The top production job, the final checking and approving of each wheel, was held by an employee we will call "A." Another operator, "B," interpreted the schedule and selected the stock and its processing —the second highest prestige and money job on this fully integrated production unit. "C" was a workman who had to be very dexterous in handling the wheels going into the squeeze machine for rounding. He was near the center of the line and determined the entire flow of production. "D" ran a rolling machine which started the wheel-making process. The contour angle had to be just right or, otherwise, a bad wheel might go through the whole line. "E's" spot was well down the line but a precision sort of job because his responsibility was to get the bearing cavity smooth within .008 tolerance. These were the five top jobs. Next, in 1-2-3 order, seven crewmen operated punch presses, swedging pneumatic hammers and rollers—"F" through "L." The three lowest level jobs supplied stock and loaded out the finished products. For brevity, we will list them as "M" through "O." Payment for the entire crew was on a pool, piecework basis. The plant was fully unionized.

The new manager, Sid, had come up through the ranks. He knew the technical operations of the wheel-making job thoroughly, but was not personally acquainted with the men under his direction because all his time had been spent in other plants and on different shifts.

Sid spent the full first two weeks talking individually with "A" through "O" in that order. In these conversations, he discussed with each man his work and how he felt about what he was doing. As he carefully interjected his own knowledge, Sid invited each man to suggest any of his own ideas for improvement.

Our new manager got two or three usable ideas on rearranging the flow of production which he installed. Then he personally followed up to see that the individuals who had made the proposals were paid under the plant suggestion system.

After Sid had been on the job for about a month, "B" outlined a plan which would reduce the crew to fourteen men. The manager could see, as he studied the new conveyors which would need to be installed, that "B" was somewhat apprehensive about what the other operators might think about his proposal to put one of the crew out of a job. The manager welcomed the idea as an excellent test case because: 1. The productivity improvement was evident. 2. The timing seemed good, since he had been able to establish a measure of confidence in himself with the crew. 3. "A" was being considered strongly for a full quality control assignment, a promotion. 4. If this change should be successful, his crew could be led on to be the most outstanding teamwork group in the whole plant.

Sid convinced "B" without making any promises that the supervisor should discuss the new arrangement with the other members of the crew. The really sensitive part was to get "B" to agree that he should be given full and open credit for the idea; but, after Sid persisted, the operator finally conceded.

As our new manager quickly learned, several of the operators were suspicious. He heard the term "speed up" from a couple in the "F" to "L" category; and, naturally "M," "N," and "O" talked to their union committeeman because the job of one of them would be eliminated. "A" may or may not have known about his possible promotion, but he was for the change anyway. "C," "D," and "E" were all veterans of many years of production experience. They talked with the other crew members at coffee break and lunchtime, arguing for the change because: 1. The new supervisor would treat them right on a new rate. 2. It was more efficient, and, as they said, you can't hold back progress. 3. The plant was big and whoever lost out in their crew could be transferred to another job, maybe better than the one he had. 4. Under the new plan the stock flow would be more constant and thus easier for everyone along the line.

Sid was alert. Aware that the key men were selling the change to his crew, he insisted to his boss that he (Sid) should give the signal before any move was made to install the improved method. He proposed to do this only after "A" through "E" had completed their salesmanship job, and the promotion for "A" was a certainty and could be announced. At the appropriate time, our new manager gave the word. The maintenance crew started installing the conveyor. "A" was happy with the new job. "B" liked his present assignment as was true with "C" and "D." So "E," actually the logical successor to "A" because of the special nature of his experience, was given that quality-inspection type job. "F" moved up to "E's" job. Finally, the new supervisor was able to convince the efficiency department that the fourteen member crew was actually doing more work than before, and thus the operators were entitled to a higher rate of pay all along the line.

How Applied, Good-Management Principles Made Improvement Possible

First, Sid *made a special effort to get acquainted* with each member of his crew. This is one of the best ways that you can let subordinates know that you look upon them as individuals. You are saying to them in actions, not words, that, "You are worthy of my complete attention."

Second, the new manager *asked each individual for any suggestions* on improving his job. The new and drastic reorganization of the work was also reviewed with each operator. When you take such an action, you are telling the employee that he is doing important work.

Third, Sid *used his judgment* to reach the conclusion that "A" would want the promotion offered. He may have been well enough acquainted with the other key operators to suspect who would and who would not be interested in "A's" job. At any rate, in such a situation you often find that some employees do and others do not want to move into jobs of greater responsibility.

Fourth, the new supervisor *carefully built his leadership prestige* by consideration for his subordinates, using his technical knowledge wisely, protecting his men and going to bat in getting a fair rate for the changed job. You have to work smart all the time as a manager to gain the respect of hard-boiled, realistic, practical factory employees. *Fifth, Sid was able to get minor improvement suggestions from other crew members in addition to a major idea;* indicating some valuable qualities not previously tapped. In giving "B" credit for the superior idea, the manager encouraged others to follow his example. These are some of the important lessons you should learn from the automobile-wheel, production-line case.

Beneficial Ideas You Can Use in Decision-Making

Think of decision-making as the pay-off evidence of action management. To carry through, you have a two-fold duty: 1. arrive at a choice of action, 2. convince others that this is indeed the appropriate action to take.[1] You must maintain the mental flexibility which enables you to recognize and accept new ideas. Further, you must make use of them in purposeful fashion. Strive for mental improvement through bolstering your judgment, which is one of the most important factors in your complex of intellectual requirements. As Dr. Mahoney says: "Judgment appears to be the ability to consider alternative courses of action, draw the proper implications from each, and assign the proper weight to each consideration in making a choice." [2]

How to Get Some Mental Exercise

Your decision-making ability comes from your mental capacity, and, like any other part of our body, if you don't use your brain it becomes flabby. As a developing manager, you must give your brain a chance to grow. The best way to start is to "think about the way you think."

[1] Bross, Irwin D. J.: *Design for Decision,* p. 15
[2] Mahoney, op.cit., p. 190

When one manager, let's call him "Super," looked at his schedule chart on Monday morning and saw that his crew must produce three more sub-assemblies than it did the week before when everything seemed to hum right along, he began to do some real "in gear" thinking. He looked over his material carefully, reviewed the available manpower, and considered some of the possible emergencies, such as absentees, scrapped parts or lack of staff support. Then Super braced himself, mentally at least, as to what he might do in each case. He set hourly targets in addition to a daily schedule so that he could keep abreast of just what was happening. Super was getting double value from his efforts because he was improving his self-discipline while he got his mental exercise.

Now, suppose another manager named "Luc" sees the same schedule as Super's. However, the thoughts traveling through Luc's mind go like this: "Say, that is something. . . . This means I've got to get organized. . . . What about manpower? . . . equipment? . . . capacity? . . . That reminds me, I'll have to have someone look at my air conditioner before hot weather. . . . Wonder what the kids will do this summer. . . . Oh, yes, the schedule. . . . May have to move some people around. . . . Wonder if we will have a big crowd at the lodge meeting. . . . Well, back to the salt mines. Just how will I meet this increase in schedule?" Of course, some decisions are reached in this fashion, and possibly for an experienced manager, routine questions can be resolved by the "free-wheeling" method. Obviously the same mental stretching exercise quality is not present as when you really put your thoughts "in gear."

Let's look at still a third type of manager. Call him "Flot." He sees by his schedule chart the same increase which stirred Super and Luc to activity, but it doesn't bother him. He is very relaxed about what some of the difficulties may be and the hope floats through his mind that some breaks will come along enabling him to get out the necessary production. Flot feels no particular urge to think. He is drifting along in neutral. His past performance has been satisfactory—doesn't need to get stirred up about a little schedule increase. "I'll take the mental way of least resistance and maybe we'll get what they want. No need to get excited."

Actually the type of thinking exhibited by both Luc and Flot has greater danger for the manager than just the lack of mental exercise. Each supervisor is condoning lax self-discipline.

Another Reason Why You Must Think About Your Decisions

When you make a decision, there is pressure generated which you cannot escape. As the leader you are unable to get away from the judgments you must make. In your out-front position, a decision made on what appears to be a minor problem at the time can very quickly become a front-burner item. As you improve in your management job, you become more and more aware of this and know you can never really relax when making a choice.

By way of contrast, the philosopher in the quiet of his ivory tower develops a very logical theory. He has only an academic interest in whether the people involved react as the textbook vows they should. Likewise, the hired management consultant is only a short way closer to the really difficult problem of obtaining measurable results. You, however, must keep as your own personal concerns today, tomorrow, and into the future the people under your direction and the success of the entire organization.

How to Look at Your Management Problems

Your decisions as a manager are problem oriented in the sense that what you decide to do is always: 1. In an effort to "head off" a developing problem. If you see that you will run out of material for production, you use substitutes if possible, or inventory, or switch the type, kind, or style of product. 2. To ease the impact of a problem. If one of your production machines breaks down, you may do the job by hand methods or use older, normally surplus equipment, or change the product schedule. 3. To settle a problem. If an employee isn't doing the job, you try to find out why and get him started in the right direction, transfer him to another assignment, or dismiss him entirely.

How to Solve Your Management Problems

Let's examine this case: In a specialized manufacturing company, "X" is the general manager, "Y" is the manager of finance, and "Z" is the manager of contract determinations and processing. X is a forward-looking executive who realizes the value of a solid organization in depth. He continuously watches for signs of management know-how in the key employees below the top level reporting to him.

On several occasions, he had tested A, the follow-up man for the manager of finance. In discussions on cost and profit trends which A enjoyed and did well, the general manager had interjected some questions on the performance of his subordinate. A always "ran down" those reporting to him while building himself up. X also discovered that A always had a feud going with some other department, often because he said they didn't get their figures to him on time, twisted the results, or had some other handicapping deficiency.

The general manager followed his concern for building the organization by looking into the contract management strength below the top manager. The finance and contract departments were required to cooperate in the exchange of information; for instance, the responsibility of pricing products overlapped. Budgets, payrolls, costs, and profits were all finance responsibilities but were also factors to be considered in entering into product contracts. X found two strong subordinate managers below the top contract-manager level. Let's call them "B" and "C." Both men were in their early thirties, had good formal educations in business, and bachelor's degrees with some advanced study. They were experienced in the finance department fundamentals. Two other factors had a bearing on this illustration: 1. It was not customary to transfer upper level managers from one department to another. Past practice had been for each department to develop and promote their own managers. 2. The manager of contract and the manager of finance did not enjoy a warm, personal relationship. Each tended to be somewhat suspicious of the other's motives.

X's first action on this problem was to talk with Y about A, the man indicated on the replacement table to succeed to the finance manager's position. After a considerable amount of squirming, Y did admit that A was not performing up to his expectations. But Y quickly added that he did not have anyone else as well qualified.

The general manager's next action was to talk with Z about his replacement. The contract manager was rightly proud of B and C. X then asked Z which of the two he would recommend for the key finance job. Some conversation was required as the contract manager felt that Y should develop his own men since he had special plans for all his men. The general manager listened but was still adamant until Z finally recommended C. X told Z to hold everything until he was able to get back with him. Then the general manager had another talk with Y in which he proposed C as a trainee in finance with the ultimate intent of making him the finance manager's replacement. Fortunately, Y had been impressed with C's work and it was not hard to convince him that he was acquiring a good subordinate.

The general manager next brought Y and Z together into his office where, after some discussion, the details were worked out by which the smooth transfer of C to the finance department could be accomplished. X also made it clear to each department manager that, while the purpose of the move was to strengthen the management depth in finance, no promises should be made. He was interested in the management morale in both departments, and C would have to prove himself before being given the choice finance spot. The general manager also said, as the department managers started to leave the office, that he would be personally reviewing the results of their decisions and actions.

Benefits of the Six D's Problem-Solving Formula

The first D is "discover." Over a period of time, X found out that A was not the proper successor for the finance department top job. This was not a hasty conclusion. The general manager considered allowing the problem to slide but felt he couldn't risk such a serious hole in the finance organization to remain open. X convinced himself that he had a problem.

The second D is "distill," which means get rid of the non-essentials, boil down the known quantities and review the facts. The general manager selected the contract department as the logical place to look for a finance department replacement because of their related duties. He had in mind past practices and the special relationships between the two top managers as possible obstacles.

The third D is "dissect," meaning to break the problem apart. Try to solve it piecemeal instead of all at once in its entirety. X talked with Y and Z separately and used persuasion plus firmness as he worked on the problem.

The fourth D is "decide." In this step you balance gains against losses, and ask, "Do the values pay for the effort? How can the possible solution be put into practice?" These are some elements of the mental review which X went through before he concluded that C should be brought into the finance department.

The fifth D is "do," which means put the corrective action to work. The general manager did this by bringing Y and Z together into his office for a clearer understanding of what was to be done. A part of the conference was X's admonition about the special care to be exercised in making the change. Notice that the subordinates were given the responsibility of carrying out the details.

The sixth D is "detect," or follow-up to determine whether the solution is working out. Such a review offers an opportunity to correct any mistaken actions before they have gone too far. It also serves as an educational experience for you to use in future problem-solving. X alerted his two subordinates that the check-up would be a definite part of his concern until he was assured that the problem was really solved.

You will find that a great deal of the pressure which you experience in your management decisions will be lessened if you remember to apply the six D's formula.

How to Overcome Decision Blocks by Understanding

While you are using the six D's problem-solving method, remember that most of your problems on the job must be faced squarely. *The primary principle* to keep in mind as you reach a decision in each situation is: *be sure that all the circumstances of the problem are as clear as time and the information available can make them.* Always analyze any unfamiliar elements and terms. *Second,* before you reach a conclusion, *determine how many people, how much area, and what departments are involved.*

In making such determinations, you are not only selecting a course of action but also preparing the way for the acceptance of your decision by the people reporting to you.

Because making proper decisions is so important to your success, you should give your attention to the elements which disrupt or block these judgments. For instance, you may sense that a certain procedure is the proper action. If questioned after taking this action, you might have difficulty explaining why and how the decision was reached. It is often remarked that you followed your hunch or intuition. While such decisions usually do come from long-forgotten, successful past experiences, it should be noted that following these impressions contains an element of calculated risk.

Factors That Hamper Your Ability to Act

First, when you are being pressured for a quick choice, the very urgency of a demand for action can create indecision, delay, and even block your ability to act.

Second, closely related to your desire to obtain some concrete support before acting is your suspicion of the first choice solution to a problem. If valid support is lacking, you tend to avoid action.

Third, immediately following an important action, the feed-back reactions from people can be over-valued, particularly if it is based upon a limited number. One early violent objection to a new plan can at times cause a correct position to be abandoned; or, directly contrary to this result, an enthusiastic evaluation can over-emphasize the acceptance of the information, changed procedure, or what not. The opinion of others is essential, but you must give it a careful evaluation.

Fourth, your experience is often not as complete and reliable as you may think. Many times it only partially covers the problem situation you face. Thus, your action can frequently be delayed while you vainly search for past experiences to serve as a guide. If needed support can be obtained from former successes, no one can object provided it is really helpful and is not used as an excuse for not reaching a decision. You should often get out of the rut of past practices and "come up" with original decisions.

Fifth, it is becoming more and more the thing to do to hire special consultants for assistance in management problems. Experts and specialists often provide helpful answers which you cannot obtain. However, you must still make your own decisions. Good management is an art, requiring good judgment and actions based on opinions. The experts frequently disagree on which course to follow in the same circumstances, and they are often wrong. The decision must fit the special circumstances of the problem, which you know best from experience on the job. The experts have their place as advisors, but you are the one responsible for actions, which should not be too long delayed in waiting for specialist opinions.

Sixth, the traditional way of doing a job has in its favor the placid course of a time-tested procedure. You can be misled into following the easy road just because it is the way things have been done in the past, overlooking the fact that circumstances have changed as they always do. New methods are often painful but necessary if you are to be successful.

These examples of the difficulties common to management decision-making indicate that this part of your job should not be over-simplified. The ability to use judgment with consistency, overcome obstacles, and move the enterprise toward established goals is the chief commodity which you as a manager have to sell. As such, it should not be expected to be a simple task.

The Benefits of Working Smart As Well As Hard

If hard work was the only factor needed for success, then the diligent beaver, the persevering ant and the busy bee would rule the animal and insect kingdoms. To succeed as a manager, you must *do* many things. Among these are:

1. Pick your spot to make decisions and act.
2. Be sure you are following sound principles.
3. Expect to lose one now and then.
4. Encourage subordinates to take responsibility.
5. Give full value yourself and get your money's worth.

Some *don'ts* to remember:

1. Don't try to imitate another successful manager.
2. Don't assume that one favorable success experience insures the same results in all future instances.
3. Don't neglect the application of creative imagination to your job.
4. Don't fail to be ready with a second and third choice if the first does not succeed.
5. Don't overlook the importance of getting willing acceptance in your leadership.

Work Smart by Using Demonstrated Intelligence

1. *"What is it about a person which enables him to become a successful manager?" It is a difficult question; but there are some personal power sources on which the ambitious manager can draw.*
2. *Demonstrated intelligence, judgment, decision-making, problem-solving are your strength areas. Improve these attributes by applying sound principles.*
3. *Recognize that there are four changing factors which limit a decision's usefulness. This moving quartet consists of:*
   a. *you*
   b. *the other person or persons*
   c. *your organization*
   d. *the situation*
4. *Ideals are only good if you give them practical application.*
5. *Give your brain some mental exercise by doing some "in gear" thinking. Limit your use of "free wheeling" and eliminate "neutral" thinking on the job.*

6. *Solving your management problems by the six D's trail:*
   a. *discover*
   b. *distill*
   c. *dissect*
   d. *decide*
   e. *do*
   f. *detect.*
7. *Defeat your decision blocks by:*
   a. *avoiding pressure decisions*
   b. *accepting a first-choice solution if it is a good one*
   c. *watching the reactions of others more carefully*
   d. *not delaying a decision too long while you look for a past experience that fits that particular situation*
   e. *accepting good advice but remembering that it is your decision to live with*
   f. *trying something new when it looks like a good idea.*
8. *Work smart as well as hard. Do the things which further your career as a professional manager. Don't do anything to handicap your improvement as a* KNOW*-and-*DO *leader.*

Chapter 12: How to Fire Up and Go Ahead

"The American standard of living is a resultant much less of natural resources than of the increase in the capacity to produce and this was the result, directly, of human endeavor—the ventures and struggles of the pioneer, the exertions of the workman, the ingenuity of the inventor, the drive of the enterpriser, and the economic efficiency of all kinds of Americans, *who shared a notorious addiction to hard work.*" [1]

All the statistical history of the development of the United States supports the basic contention that the initiative, energy, and drive of individuals in stations both high and low have built a system in which the material rewards are such that with, "roughly six per cent of the world's population, our economy produces some forty per cent of the world's goods and services." [2] This is a truly fantastic accomplishment never equalled by any other peoples in all history.

How to Determine What Makes You Run

To make your contribution, you must develop and use more than your average share of "the urge to accomplish" as a personal power source so that you can exercise leadership in becoming a better manager. Remember that your company is in constant need of new ideas, improved ways of producing goods and services which have proven useful in the past, plus new thinking about articles and practices as yet only a dream in your own or some other good supervisor's mind.

1 Potter, *People of Plenty,* p. 89
2 Spence, *The Sinews of American Capitalism,* p. 1

In working toward improving the success-drive, it is helpful to you to know something about your own self-motivation.

Let's look at an expressive episode involving a manager at the section-head level, fourth echelon, in a large manufacturing company. The section manager, call him "Adroit," had approximately eighty managers reporting to him. To insure good communications, Adroit divided these subordinates into groups of about twenty, thus helping to get more effective individual participation through discussion. Meetings were held in a sizable room convenient to the section manager's office. The room was also used daily for numerous management purposes, such as discussion of cost controls, budgets, quality, scheduling, and innumerable problem-solving meetings by staff and line employees.

Adroit wanted to brighten up the conference room by buying new, comfortable chairs, some tables and draperies. He also wanted to improve the lighting, and install visual-aid facilities such as a movie screen and chart boards. When the section manager proposed these improvements to his superintendent, a veteran, old school manager named "Tufnut," his superior slapped him down hard with a growling refusal, "You coddle your men too much. That room is good enough for them. They are well paid. Tell them not to spend so much time talking and more time on the floor getting production."

Nevertheless, our section manager still thought he had a good idea. He did some checking with the purchasing department and plant maintenance. As a result, by cutting some corners, he found that the grimy conference room could be transformed into an inviting, attractive, more useful management work area for twelve hundred dollars.

After a particularly good production month, Adroit again requested Tufnut's approval for redecorating the conference room. The superintendent was even more hostile as Adroit detailed the items to be secured or improved. When the twelve-hundred-dollars cost was mentioned, Tufnut really hit the ceiling. It was evident he wasn't even listening when the section manager pointed out that, considering only the supervisors using the room, not to mention staff and support people, this added up to only fifteen dollars per man. Adroit patiently forged ahead with his sales talk which included the fact that the improvement was an addition to the capital assets, gave the managers recognition, and tended to invite them to plan for and accomplish better communications and to exercise more careful use of the company's equipment. The section manager confidently stated, "It'll do a lot to encourage our managers to work as a team." All this conversation failed to even dent Tufnut's conviction that dressing up the conference room was an unnecessary expense. He still said, "No." The cause seemed lost.

However, Adroit was a confident manager, willing to back his judgment with chance-taking when in his opinion and good judgment it was warranted. Of course, there is no way to prove that the series of special training meetings for managers, which Adroit initiated soon after Tufnut's last refusal, was in any way connected with the renovation of the management conference room, because the section manager continually gave his subordinates opportunities to improve.

The current program which Adroit started consisted of a weekly meeting with all the supervisors reporting to him. The twenty-men groups met in the conference room for a total elapsed time of one hour where Adroit discussed a planned subject followed by questions and suggested specific applications. The section manager invited the superintendent Tufnut to talk with these groups. He accepted, and his ideas seemed to ring a bell with the attendees. A lively discussion followed. The superintendent left the meeting feeling good and commended Adroit for having such a live-wire group of managers.

The section manager suggested that it might be mutually beneficial if the vice president and general manager could be persuaded to talk with his supervisors. Tufnut, thinking of his own experience, volunteered to ask their top man, a fellow named "Mityhi," but added that Adroit should arrange to bring his entire group into a single meeting because Tufnut thought that they couldn't ask the vice president to give more than one talk.

Mityhi agreed, and the group met in the crowded, smoky, dingy conference room. In spite of the disagreeable physical conditions, the vice president was impressed with the alertness of the managers in attendance. They asked thought-provoking questions, followed carefully all the discussion, and expressed a genuine regret when the meeting time ran out.

After the supervisors had gone, the vice president stayed over for a few words with Tufnut and Adroit. Mityhi commended them on their program and suggested that something similar should be carried on continuously. His next remark came as a shock to Tufnut; but Adroit remained impassive as the vice president said, "You'll have to get that conference room dressed up. It is detrimental to efficient management thinking as well as an insult to important people to ask them to meet in such a place." Mityhi continued, "We still have some capital asset funds in the budget, and I can't think of a place where we can get a better return than to use it to make your conference room a proper place for managers to meet."

Professional Thinking Adds Pluses to Your Forward Drive

In the conference room example, one of the first strong mental qualities Adroit evidenced was the ability to "take it." Tufnut gave him a resounding "no" when he requested approval to spend money on the room. For a less determined manager than Adroit, his boss' rough refusal would have been enough to cause him to tuck his tail and run. Our section manager, however, just came back for more. Notice Adroit's reasoned approach. He found out what the suggested improvements would cost and had all the advantages neatly determined, but still did not succeed in selling his superior. Some observers might call the series of management training meetings which Adroit scheduled as just a lucky break—

maybe—but certainly everyone would agree that the section manager didn't let a string of minor defeats dampen his enthusiasm for carrying out his job with zest and vigor.

Former President Harry S. Truman had a snappy rejoinder, which seems appropriate here, when an associate complained that politics was a rough business: *If you can't stand the heat, stay out of the kitchen.* As a growing manager, you have to be able to take it and come back for more without forgetting the need for good judgment.

Values in Practicing These Mental "Do's"

First, develop a fierce personal pride in your ability to control your own mind. We can speculate that Adroit was upset by his superior's refusal to even listen to what he considered the valuable results which could be obtained by redecorating the conference room. However, the section manager held his temper in check, gained a sense of pride in his own personal self-discipline, and added to his feeling of importance in the challenges of the work he was doing. You can do the same by learning to control yourself and by increasing your personal confidence as a professional manager.

Second, insist that others respect your right to think. Prove your good judgment as Adroit did by persisting with his idea in spite of opposition. Although far from an easy road, it is one you must take if you are going to be a better manager. You must avoid timid thinking.

Third, think about the results of success. If you begin figuring out an alibi before your cause is lost, most likely you'll have to use that excuse for failure. Winning is habit-forming, so give the seeds an opportunity to grow by refusing to give up on your ideas until your own best judgment directs such a course.

How to Avoid Diluting Your Mental Go-Ahead as a Power Source

First, you can't afford to indulge in complacency. As Mr. Greenewalt states, "Satisfaction with one's own performance . . . is largely a subjective matter resulting from self-appraisal, and I am not sure that many of us are sufficiently strict judges of our own performance. That inner glow associated with a job well done can all too easily become a resting place for ambition and a safe backwater in which to relax. The question is not whether we are doing an adequate job or even a good job, but whether or not we are using to maximum effect the abilities with which we are endowed." [1]

Second, you must constantly remind yourself of just what it is you want to accomplish. Keep your objective clearly in the forefront of your attention. Such

[1] Greenewalt, *The Uncommon Man*, p. 32

an attitude helps determine the items of primary importance and steers you away from unproducive diversions. Some managers just can't seem to bring themselves mentally up against an assignment. Here's a typical example. Slo's superior was a manager named Move, who liked to lay plans and start action so that his unit could move on to something new, more interesting and challenging. Slo didn't quite approve of this method of operation and, as a result, whether consciously or not, resisted when the boss assigned a project with a "hurry-up" tag on it. Here's what happened when Move asked his subordinate to collect some facts and recommend ideas for a presentation on a new job program for top management approval.

Slo first pointed out the difficulty of the assignment to his boss. When Move had patiently overcome the hurdle and returned to his office, Slo took time out to discuss the football prospects at his alma mater with a crony who frequently dropped by his desk to discuss items of mutual interest. After this interruption had run its course, the delaying manager decided that he ought to take some time to be nice to a stenographer who had done what he considered a good typing job on one of his reports. A number of exchanges were involved, including: "What fine people we are," "How's your family?"—all of course in the cause of good human relations.

Slo finally went back to his desk and started asking himself why the boss had requested the information, and telling himself that he didn't really need it. Slo had a few welcomed interruptions on the telephone. By now it was getting close to his lunch period, and he and several other supervisors always had a jolly time of relaxation, needling each other and swapping cracks. Naturally he had to prepare for that session.

After a full and refreshing lunch break, Slo returned to his desk and mentally poked around the edges of his boss' assignment, never setting a direction to follow by questioning the goal he should shoot for, the quickest way to get there, or any planned procedure. He finally decided to make some phone calls to some people who might know what had been done in the past when a similar job had to be sold "upstairs."

Slo had lots of friends and of course they all liked to talk, so he was in the middle of these pleasant exchanges when Move called to find out about his recommendations.

The subordinate took a lot of time explaining how hard he had been working, mentioning all the different people he had talked to, but ended by saying, "I'll have to have more time. Maybe tomorrow."

You had better be sure that you are not handling your job like Slo, because sooner or later Move is going to take some corrective action; and, I believe, we can be fairly sure that the subordinate will not enjoy the experience.

A third way to avoid a mental handicap to your own self-discipline is to be sure that fears for tomorrow don't take away from today's efforts. You have a natural urge toward security; but as you think realistically about your future, you must recognize that specific job methods—ways of doing things—will change. Your personal drive for security in your chosen profession must be toward improving your skills in working with people, because this is the only unchanging essential in the unstable climate of business enterprise.

How to Develop and Use Action Self-Discipline as a Go-Ahead Force

Discipline, as used here, means "training which corrects, molds, strengthens or perfects." *The first action "do"* is to let it be seen that you are personally working efficiently and hard. John D. Chesterton, writing of their successful world-wide company, said:

> We want aggressive men, determined to succeed in the face of any obstacles, impossible to discourage. We want persistent men, who never coast, who never think they are doing well enough, who don't slacken when things are going smoothly nor quit when they get rough. We aren't interested in genius, but we do seek intelligence, the ability to grasp ideas.... Finally we want an independent man with enough self-confidence to want to run his own show, who is impatient with close supervision.[1]

Set a similar goal for yourself, and don't keep it a secret.

The second action "do" is to think and talk about the values of hard work. Just keeping yourself conscious of the job to be done is a self-discipline stimulant. To be a better manager, you must make it one of your first concerns to check on low volume, quality, or any deficiency in production.

The third action "do" is to direct your efforts toward providing others with the tools they need. Give them judicious help.

The fourth action "do" is to be available to your subordinates. If you lose touch with the people reporting to you, your personal drive tends to decline, because as a manager you are out of the main stream which drives a supervisor in this demanding profession.

Avoid Headaches by Staying Away from Action "Don'ts"

Your progress as an improving manager will be slowed down and possibly stopped if you: 1. excuse subordinate's disruptive conduct, 2. tolerate carelessness and lack of thought, 3. permit willful disregard to the feelings of others, 4. allow difficulty to be the excuse for dropping a project. Here is a series of incidents which were allowed to build up into a difficult management problem.

In a diversified machine shop with from fifty to sixty operators, A, B, and C are first-level supervisors who report to D, a second-level manager. The superintendent of the shop is E. The owner-manager of the company we will call F.

[1] Chesterton, "The Maverick Manager," *Personnel*, Sept.-Oct., 1965, pp. 38-39

A and B are close friends and fishing companions, so A doesn't hesitate to ask B to cover for him when he comes in late. D can't help noticing the situation as it becomes a common practice, occurring two or three days a week. Neither A, B, nor D considers the effect on the workmen in A's crew. Soon, they too are finding feeble excuses for arriving late and quitting early. Finally C goes directly to E, telling him what is happening.

The superintendent reprimands C for not taking the trouble up with D. C is so upset that he takes the whole story to F. The owner is naturally very much disturbed and starts back down the line through E, and so on. The problem becomes a "federal case," and what had been an orderly operating shop now becomes a mess. The line of managers cannot advance as professionals until they resolve the difficulties which grew from willful violation of basic rules of good conduct on the job, carelessness, and lack of thought by all managers, plus a woeful lack of consideration for the personal feelings of D and C. However, even though it was a difficult situation, it had to be settled. How would you start to handle such a headache?

This may not be the most perfect series of actions to take, but here is what E did. He held a round-table meeting with his managers at which all angles of the situation were discussed. A refused to admit any wrongdoing, so he was offered a job running a lathe, which he turned down; therefore, he was discharged. D was reduced to a first-level management position to replace A. E stepped down to the second level. F promised to take a more direct interest in the over-all supervision of the shop. B was warned to do some deeper thinking in the future about the importance of good discipline. F also talked privately with C, pointing out the importance of following the line of organization with future problems.

How to Keep the Initiative

If you are to improve your driving power source and become a better manager, *a first "must"* on your list is to avoid letting a problem such as the machine-shop example develop. B could have prevented it by a frank discussion with his friend A. D could have halted the growth of difficulty by stopping A's delinquency as soon as he noted what was happening. E was too rigid in his organizational thinking; and, if C had possessed some of our section manager Adroit's management persistence, most likely he would have found a better way than he selected to approach and help solve the impending problem in its early stages.

A second "must" is that you have to act—don't wait to react to problems that have already developed. Look ahead and experiment with new ways of doing things. Go into untried situations deliberately relaxed for a possible change of direction. Always have a careful follow-up in mind, and try to accomplish better results. In a controlled situation where damage can be minimized, you can safely gain a great deal of valuable know-how without upsetting any important working relationships. Test some generally-accepted management belief such as *competition.* Not all people are stimulated by a raw "win or lose" confrontation. Certain managers and employees alike freeze up in such a situation. Remember, in developing yourself as a better manager, you need to experiment and find better ways to work with your valuable subordinates.

The way you talk to people: Not all people respond to the same stimulus as some general textbook might lead us to believe. You can banter and kid with some subordinates and get good performance, while with others such levity is disastrous. Often, finding out the best operating practices is a process of trial and discovery. *Do your homework* as you apply your talents to making a success in your chosen field. You'll find that you can't limit your drives to an eight-hour day. As George Odiorne says it, "The manager works 55 to 65 hours a week on the average . . . the well-paid manager who spends evenings at community activity for public relations purposes, who travels 100,000 miles a year, usually (some of it) on his own time, and whose entertainment is a tension laden extension of his office," [1] is doing a part of the full time work of a modern successful manager. You must put forth the special effort necessary to do all the things which must be done, including tasks which people less dedicated than a manager on the move might find a drudgery.

A third "must" is to keep everlastingly at the job of being a better manager. Former President Calvin Coolidge is reported to have said:

> Nothing in the world can take the place of persistence. Talent will not; nothing is more common than unsuccessful men with talent. Genius will not; unrewarded genius is almost a proverb. Education will not; the world is full of educated derelicts. Persistence and determination alone are omnipotent. The slogan "Press On" has solved and always will solve the problems of the human race.

Most of the obstacles which you meet can be successfully overcome if you prepare yourself and work at your job. In the final analysis, *you make your own career.* The skills, abilities, qualities, and actions which determine success are learned or developed. If you choose not to make the most of your opportunities, then as Shakespeare wrote, *The fault, dear Brutus, is not in our stars, but in ourselves, that we are underlings.*

Use your own judgment. By study, observation, and meaningful experiences, you can find out how to do your job better. However, just understanding the principles is not enough. The pay-off comes when recognized good practices are actually applied to your job. This is your real test because, if simply following a list of rules was the total requirement for success in management, the profession would be flooded with followers.

While to succeed as a manager you must know the basic rules governing your job, the success key is how you use your judgment in applying these principles. If you boldly force decision-making on a timid subordinate who wants

[1] Odiorne, "The End of Leisure," *Adult Leadership,* October, 1965, p. 119

only the closest direction, you may not only be using poor judgment but it could completely ruin that subordinate's usefulness.

Since you must bear the responsibility for securing the greatest amount of continuous high quality production on schedule at the lowest costs, you must realize the need for a strong sense of independent judgment. Such a basis for self-confidence is necessary if you are to grow in modern management because your job assignment is unique in its details as compared with all other jobs.

Differences come about because of the exceptional nature of the problems and challenges posed by the degrees of skills, special personalities, and energies of your associates, subordinates, and superiors in every job—all of which you must meet with understanding, adjustments, and management know-how.

How to Be an "Improve-with-Age" Manager

Drive yourself; be a self-motivated manager. With even a moderate amount of effort, most supervisors enhance their value to their companies by accumulating experiences, knowledge, and know-how which can become almost irreplaceable. When you are willing to really work at your job, the resulting broadening, extending, and expanding of your mental tools and performance capabilities will grow as time passes. This is in direct contrast with machines and equipment which wear out after a relatively short life. The point is made again that people are the most valuable asset of any organization. You and most managers recognize the need for self-improvement, but it doesn't mean that you are willing to drive yourselves. As Mahoney says, "It is difficult to suggest any single best motivation for managers, whether it be social prestige, money, family security, authority, power, or merely the thrill of achievement. In fact, the studies of values . . . suggest that the motivations will vary for managers in different fields of endeavor." [1]

Whatever happens to be your self-starter, you should find it and get it fired up. One manager's experience suggests some avenues to explore. Gogo was a middle management supervisor, reporting to the director of employment, employee services and relations, in a large, local division (multi-thousand employment) of a nation-wide corporation. Gogo was fifty-four years of age and had worked his entire twenty-seven years with the company in this same kind of personnel work. He started as a hiring interviewer, then successively served as employment supervisor, grievance checker, personnel supervisor and manager of procedure writers. For the last ten years, he was in charge of all employment with two levels of management reporting to him. Gogo also managed food service with, again, two levels of management reporting to him. He directed the union contract interpretation and was a key member of the negotiation team for management. His activities also included personnel records, exit interviews and

[1] Mahoney, op.cit., p. 195

handling special employee problems. Once more he had two levels of management reporting to him.

In each of his areas of direction, Gogo set stiff targets for accomplishment. The supervisors in employment knew that it was their job not only to hire the needed number of people but to obtain quality as well. During the years that Gogo held his position, the business of the division declined and substantial numbers of skilled people were lost; but, our manager never allowed an employee to be laid off until any complaint which he might have made had been thoroughly checked out. During these lean years, also, Gogo was able to hire the cream of the college graduate crop. However, he didn't neglect his other duties as labor relations were always smoothly handled—no strikes, sit-downs, slow-downs, walkouts.

Our manager supervised all these jobs without any outward display of special effort or strained emotion. He always seemed to have just the right balance and exhibited no evidence of frustration, even when more aggressive managers in other areas snatched the credit to which Gogo was entitled.

In his many faceted responsibility, our manager frequently found that his ideas, instructions and suggestions didn't get through to employees as they should. Gogo didn't explode or lose his temper. He investigated; and the next time, communication went better.

Subordinates made mistakes, but our manager counseled them and their performance improved. Other people were promoted throughout the division to much better jobs. Gogo could have compared his record favorably with those who were given greater opportunities, but he didn't. He calmly went on striving, expanding his goals and reaching them. Gogo's wife had a serious operation. One of his sons made a mistake; almost went to jail. His daughter gave her parents some unpleasant hours by running around with the wrong crowd. These difficulties didn't detract from our manager's efforts on the job.

The division's workload went down to the point where rumors were rampant that the plant would close. Gogo's boss told him that they would be lucky to keep all their employee services in operation. Our manager, however, just kept right on working as before.

It so happened that all the other divisions of the corporation were thriving, and the headquarter's management control had been having considerable difficulty filling the special skills needed for company operations around the country. The present real employee need was for a fair share of college and university graduates. Gogo's performance record was examined. He was asked to attend a general corporate meeting for a discussion of employment problems. As a result of his participation, evident knowledge, past successes, and his generally good impression, he was offered the corporate personnel director's job at three times his current salary with increased fringe benefits such as thicker carpet on the floor, special inside parking, etc. Gogo accepted his promotion with the same calm self-assurance he had exhibited throughout his management career.

Lessons to Learn from the Promotion of the Older Manager

First, set your own goals for your section, department, group, or unit. You don't have to wait for someone else to do it for you. Gogo didn't need any urging to do these things for himself, but he did use the same thoughts expressed by former General Electric's official Harold Smiddy in his advice for his own subordinates, which was, "Each man needs to be aware of his objectives and needs to be aided in learning the values of continuing self-appraisal, self-discipline, self-control, self-motivation, and self-improvement in actually attaining those objectives." [1] Our middle-level manager derived his urge to go ahead from the challenge of the targets which he set with his subordinates in each operation under his direction.

Second, expect high-level performance from subordinates. Gogo found opportunities to display the special abilities of those reporting to him by convincing them to accept goals worthy of their best efforts. He passed along meaningful decision-making opportunities to deserving managers under him.

Third, you should strive to develop sufficient self-confidence so that you can exhibit built-in emotional stability controls when: (a) someone else grabs the glory you should have, (b) late information or lack of it causes you extra work, (c) subordinates' errors cause you embarrassment, (d) you are passed over for promotion.

Fourth, you must be able to rise above: (a) personal worries, (b) the temptation to take it easy when you have your management job under control, (c) the stigma of "you have gone as far up the promotional ladder as you can go."

Inner Strengths Help You Become a Self-Propelled Manager

First, you must accept that good management is truly a profession. The efficient direction of others requires a planned, conscious, organized human approach as contrasted with a hit-or-miss, luck-and-chance system of operation. As practitioners in the art of management, you, just as those people in such professions as medicine, law, and accounting, have special qualifications for your work. You have, through the application of special training, experience, and developed abilities, assumed the responsibility to increase, expand, and add to the profits of the business organization of which you are a part.

An important difference between your own profession and that of the older, more established callings is that management is more directly results-oriented. For instance, a lawyer, a doctor, or a teacher can deal with a problem situation today, dismiss it (they don't always do it), and then direct their attention to a new and entirely different situation tomorrow. However, you as a man-

[1] Smiddy, Harold F.: *Integrating and Motivating for Effective Performance*, p. 22

ager can't get away from your decisions. They had better be right or the things you do and say will haunt you for years. The very pressure of the need to be right should increase your sense of job pride—the feeling of importance in the work you are doing.

Second, you must cultivate thinking flexibility. If you see your job as simply following a check-list of rules, then there is no stimulation of professional pride. Without the excitement of decision-making, your job is dull and unattractive. Develop your inner strengths by releasing your personal enthusiasm as a forthright, decision-making manager.

Third, help your subordinates to grow. If you get the results that success in your profession requires: (a) The stockholders or owners get a fair return for their investment. (b) The consumer gets a better product at a lower over-all cost. (c) The employees generally improve their job positions. As has been mentioned, the only way you can succeed is through the efforts of those reporting to you. Use your inner strengths to search for, determine, and stimulate the use of your subordinates' highest skills.

How Exhibited Actions Help Develop a Manager's Necessary Success Drives

First: By their works you shall know them. Your attitude toward your job is one of the strongly determining factors as to whether you will perform so as to be noticed, commended, and/or promoted. Such a climate which we can call "right attitude" is often designated by the term "good morale." Let's define good morale as a state of mind which causes you to feel that your present position is at least temporarily satisfactory. You are confident in your ability to perform your duties and feel that those reporting to you are loyal and competent in their assigned jobs. You believe that your superior is qualified to be a leader in his position, and that the boss is giving you a fair shake.

The effect of good morale on your performance is difficult to measure, of course, but "Such great military leaders as Napoleon considered it to be vital to success. He stated that, 'In war, morale conditions make up three-quarters of the game: The relative balance of manpower accounts only for the remaining quarter.' "[1] Good morale and good performance go together.

Second: Set the stage. When you do your part to establish the right climate, you are alert to the company policies, rules, and operating procedures. To properly fulfill this duty means more than just a knowledge of what these controls are. It also expects you: (a) to have an understanding of the boundaries of what is considered acceptable action, (b) to have the necessary confidence to act within the limits of established policy, (c) to have earned sufficient personal stature that suggestions for changing current practices receive a thoughtful hear-

[1] Beishline, John R.: *Military Management for National Defense,* p. 42

ing, (d) to have displayed sufficient scientific professionalism in both management and the jobs you supervise to determine and evaluate alternate courses of action within practical limits.

Third: Act. To really make progress as a manager, you must do more than just operate within the rules. You have to exhibit imagination and creativity in your job performance. This is often a difficult assignment even for a well-seasoned manager because a natural question arises as to "Where shall I start?"

Here are some suggested areas where you should look for opportunities to demonstrate management drive: *Cost reduction and control.* Costs of operation are a universally recognized measuring stick for management excellence. In our competitive economy, any organization which produces the best quality product at the least cost stands out as an unquestioned success. Anything you can do which will get your company more dollars returned for the money spent is an area where you should spend some time. You must exercise caution, however, to avoid curtailing essential services which might cause higher future expenditures.

Critically examine any way of doing a job which has not changed for a reasonable period of time. "Managerial initiative in bringing about technological and non-technical progress is to the general advantage of that business organization, capital investments, employee and managerial skills, and community values are thus conserved in a competitive society." [1] We are living in a dynamic age, so you should expect external changes as well as internal. Watch sources of supply and markets to make sure that any advance of knowledge and technical progress doesn't pass you by to the advantage of a more wide-awake organization.

Be suspicious of any trend downward. You may find a warning sign in the quality of the product, production hours required, sales to old and new customers, or in the numbers of employees assigned to a specific activity. Be concerned any time the progress curve fails to show an upward tilt.

"Finding the cause for trouble spots" is somewhat related to "wrong trends." Often the smooth flow of production is interrupted by the failure of people, machines, equipment, and methods. Correcting such difficulties can reflect to your credit.

Look at the way you spend your own time—is one of the most fruitful spots to take some actions in your success drive. Ask yourself these questions: Am I directing my attention to those things which I can best perform or am I doing a job because it is something I like to do which someone else can do as well or better? Will a little training enable an assistant to take over some of my most time-consuming duties? Do I allow enough time to just think about what I am doing or ought to be doing? Attention to one or all of these proposed action-getting areas may stimulate you to greater management self-motivation.

[1] Riegel, John W.: *Management, Labor and Technological Change,* p. 55

Some Benefits to You When You Can't Be Stopped

Health and inborn physical qualities can affect your needed management drive and energy, but such innate qualities comprise only a minor part of what one authoritative survey lists as needed for self-motivation. This study detailed these ideas of value to you:

> Initiative begins with inner drive which less effective managers lack. Initiative means sorting out the vital from the trivial, and driving for the vital goals.
>
> Initiative means that its possessor is tough minded.
>
> The action-getting manager instills a desire to excel in others in the organization, and releases their initiative as well as having it himself.
>
> The result-getter initiates intelligent action—not just random activity.[1]

Notice that even your vigor and natural energy must be trained in the choice of a goal. Its path must be selected with care which requires your considered management judgment.

When you can't be stopped, you are able to withstand personal pressures, drive yourself, and concentrate on a singleness of purpose. "As one executive put it: 'I think people in positions like mine have found a secret weapon which isn't a secret at all.—We don't quit.' "[2]

When You Fire Up to Go Ahead as a Manager:

1. *Have the urge to succeed on your job.*
2. *Be able to take it as well as to dish it out.*
3. *Control your own mind. Insist on your right to think. Think about success.*
4. *Avoid complacency. Keep your objectives in mind. Don't worry about tomorrow.*
5. *Work hard and efficiently. Talk about the values of hard work. Provide work tools for others. Be available to your subordinates.*
6. *Require self-discipline. Avoid carelessness. Have proper regard for the feelings of others. Don't let difficulties stop you.*
7. *Stay on the offensive.*
8. *Use your opportunities to improve your performance through experience.*
9. *Become self-propelled by regarding management as a profession. Be a decision-maker. Assist subordinates to grow.*
10. *Encourage right attitudes. Set the stage. Act.*
11. *Be a better manager because you can't be stopped.*

1 Odiorne, *How Managers Make Things Happen,* p. 50
2 Ibid., p. 53

Chapter 13: How to Use Balance-Patterns in Your Management Work

As you develop and use your personal management power sources for your own and your organization's benefit, it is essential that all the required action areas receive a fair share of your attention.

You may have earned a Phi Beta Kappa key for your intelligence. You may have human drive comparable to that of a diesel locomotive. You may have trained your mind to catalog knowledge like an Encyclopaedia Britannica. You may have exhibited the know-how which attracts multitudes of followers. Yet, even with all these attributes, you can still fail as a growing manager because you have neglected the administrative skills category.

This important strength area which includes your exhibited ability as a planner, a director of others, and a controller of a working group—while it is necessary to your success as a manager—can be and often is overvalued. Overstressing comes about as a holdover from less complex times of the past when most managers were merely drivers of less sophisticated employees than we have today. Some individuals still tend to assume that these duties constitute your total job as a manager. Such a notion gains creditability because these are the most concrete and tangible evidences of the doing chores of a manager. The uninitiated might conclude that performing your administrative functions well should insure your success as a supervisor.

However, as an improving manager, you have to increase and exploit each of your personal power sources and at the same time keep them in balance.

A Trio of Aids to Help You Become a Better Administrator

Mr. A was a veteran manager with some thirty-three years' experience in a wide variety of factory assignments. He had worked on the mills and supervised at all levels of management up to that of factory manager. Mr. A had weathered depressions, recessions, and booms. He had witnessed successful unionizing drives, taken part in strike breaking, and single-handedly met mobs of angry workmen running rampant through a plant, bent on intimidating all employees who wanted to continue working. Mr. A, therefore, had some reservations about idealism in manager-workman relationships.

In the management organization being described, Mr. B was a first-level manager, twenty-eight years old, who reported to Mr. A. Before his present assignment, Mr. B had earned an excellent formal education, had a reputation as a go-getter, had studied management, and applied his knowledge. He spent four years after college graduation in production planning, industrial engineering, and computer programming. Mr. B had always worked in pleasant surroundings for good wages; no disagreement ever marred the even tenor of his experience. The economy was on the upward path and raises in pay were automatic as time passed. He was convinced that management in modern industry was a breeze when he started getting some line, manufacturing-management experience, reporting to Mr. A.

B's job was to direct piece-workers operating machines producing a variety of compounds using natural and synthetic rubber. These special pieces of equipment frequently needed mechanical repairs requiring skilled machinists and pipe fitters. The repairmen were paid day work. The piece-workers naturally wanted the machines to always be in tip-top shape, the scraper knives cutting cleanly, and heat on mills just right. To maintain the equipment required constant attention from the supporting day workers who did not get any more money regardless of how many knives they changed, or pipes they replaced, or bearings they repaired. Frequently the supervisor had to settle disagreements between the operators and repairmen about what needed to be done.

Mr. B liked to get along with everybody, so he tried to keep harmony by balancing his support, going first with the hourly workers and the next time with the piece-workers. This, of course, didn't make anybody happy. Fortunately, Mr. A found out what was going on and directed Mr. B to study his job, learn how to bank on his own judgment, and have repairs made or not made as the need existed from his own determinations.

Shortly after learning his lesson, Mr. B had a second installment on the realities of management-workmen relationships. A new union was interested in extending its influence; and Mr. A, who did have good communications and enjoyed mutual respect with his crew, was assured that whatever came up he could count on their being at work as scheduled. The political contest between the old and new union group aroused sufficient dissatisfaction that a picket line started patroling the plant. Only two of Mr. B's eighteen-man crew showed up for work, but the others all gave him good excuses for their absence when they did return. Mr. A advised the new manager not to be upset because actually two out of eighteen was better than average for such a situation. The older man said, "Leadership is a personal activity which means that you can exercise it best by being on the spot, directly with your followers." He continued, "Frequently, it's impossible to guide others by remote control."

Your first management help as illustrated here must come from your own personal power source. The judgments you use, the way you administer your job, depends upon: (a) the knowledge you have gained from your past experiences, (b) the way you view your present situation, (c) your hopes and ambitions for the future.

In the case of managers A and B, you see contrasting experience backgrounds and substantially different attitudes. A is somewhat cynical; B more trusting. B can learn from A. You should remember to evaluate what happens as a result of your management actions, relate them to future experiences, and make use of the information you have gained.

Your second management help is the predictable and unpredictable reactions of subordinates. Mr. B could quickly understand that the money motivation of the piece-workers and that of the day workers could not be coordinated. He attempted to compromise but found it didn't work; then Mr. A reminded him that he had to be the boss and call the decision according to his own judgment. The failure of the crew members to report for work was no surprise to Mr. A; but it should teach you, if you're ever in B's spot, that the power of group opinion is tremendous and often different from the views held by the individuals making up the group.

Your third management help is found in the situation itself. When B was confronted with unfamiliar circumstances, he made the mistake of putting himself in the middle. Keeping score in an effort to allow each side in a controversy to win an equal number of times is no way to determine whether or not a machine needs to be repaired. Your best management judgment is the only satisfactory way to accomplish a purpose. In the rival union squabble which caused the plant shut-down, B should have learned that a leader must be exceptionally powerful to exert an influence over his followers unless he is in direct contact with them.

You should remember that as you attempt to improve as a manager you can get help in the important administrative skills requirements from: (a) your own personal power sources, (b) understanding those people who report to you, (c) a recognition of the situation with which you are confronted. All these elements will affect the way you size up, handle, analyze, and carry out your duties to direct, coordinate, control, organize, and plan for the individuals, group, or section for which you are responsible.

How to Develop Your Own Administrative Style

Every manager, whether consciously or not, assigns his own value weights to selected segments of the total job responsibility. If you have a special interest in finance, you naturally place more weight on budgets, costs, company profits and money. As a full-fledged planner, you probably look for greater organizational efficiency. A strong quality interest causes you to stress perfection of products, goods or services. To become a better manager, it is essential that you be aware of your own value bias and give it consideration when arriving at an administrative decision.

A second important element in developing your administrative style is the freedom of choice and direct authority which you permit subordinates to exercise. As a manager, you can select any spot in the entire range from being a personal dictator, calling every shot, to the other end of the scale which is cooperative decision-making. While under certain conditions you may vary from your standard pattern, in most cases you will select a recognizable fashion of operating, based upon your subordinates' abilities and your own personal confidence in yourself. Assuming that you feel you have well qualified subordinates and you are on top of your own job, you will normally allow your understudies greater freedom to operate on their own judgments.

Whichever way you choose to go, develop your administrative style as early as practical and be sure that your subordinates understand, fundamentally, how you expect to operate. This is the only fair way you can expect top performance from the people reporting to you.

How You Benefit from Delegation

"In every enterprise of two or more people, there must be delegation of authority and the accompanying obligation to act." [1]

At the turn of the century, Andrew Carnegie, an early wizard in managing the manufacture of steel, said, "When a man realizes he can call others in to help him do a job better than he can do it alone, he has taken a big step in his life." [2]

Even though delegation is the very essence of management, how well you use the talents of others is largely a matter of personal choice. "And thou shall teach them (selected, capable men) . . . the work they must do . . . as rulers of thousands, hundreds, fifties, tens." Thus, some thirty-five centuries ago, did Jethro, the Priest of Midian, tell Moses the proper way to lead and manage a large number of people in working toward a planned objective. Since that ancient day, delegation has been accepted as management's way of life.

[1] Newman, op.cit., p. 203
[2] Terry, op.cit., p. 300

When you give your subordinate freedom to choose and execute his own attack on your problems and make it work, one of your gains is that you are creating an organization flexible enough to expand and adjust to the competitive pressures of the modern business climate. This is possibly the most important single management requirement in our changing society.

How You Can Be a Better Administrator Through Delegation

First: Recognize that you can't escape accountability. When you delegate, you simply transfer your decision-making power from yourself to another person. While the authority to decide and act changes places, the responsibility is not transferred because you as the delegator are still held accountable for the results of your subordinate's actions. For instance, if you borrow your neighbor's lawnmower and later decide to lend it to your son who lives across town, and he allows your grandchildren to run it through a gravel pit, obviously your neighbor's wife is not going to be angry with the cute little children.

Second: Improve your own performance. The more keenly you feel the pressure of accountability, the more hesitant you will be to delegate action authority to a subordinate. However, you will find many times that the manager who complains because his boss withholds authority is either not using all the authority he has been given or has failed to convince his superior of his capability to share responsibility. When you successfully complete an assignment, you attract additional authority to act. Paraphrasing, "For whosoever has performed, to him shall be given, and he shall have more abundance of assignments: but whosoever has not performed, from him shall be taken away even the assignments he has."

Third: Encourage those employees reporting to you. You can improve your directions as you delegate only if the members of your organization, "Come to want to act more on their own; to want to make more of their own decisions; to want to grow as a result of their own educational efforts; to want the added personal freedom which comes with demonstrated ability to discipline themselves; to want to increase their own competence—their very ability to get needed work done and on time." [1]

You will recognize that proper delegation usually becomes a question of improving your superior-subordinate relationships. You can force accountability by fear, using such threats as loss of wages or salary payments, position in the organization, status and prestige extras. However, you will find that this tends to build up frustrations and loses the special advantages to the company which can only be obtained from enthusiastic and dedicated managers.

Since you must delegate action authority but retain responsibility for your subordinate's results, you have a direct interest in encouraging those people reporting to you to use their brains in making better assignment decisions. You

[1] Bittel, *Management by Exception,* pp. 267-68

should, insofar as practical, allow the subordinate to determine his own approach to accomplishing the assignment with you as a helper.

How to Avoid Dangers in Delegation

Probably completely free delegation can only be used in ideal superior-subordinate relationships. Undoubtedly, you would need to apply such a hands-off choice with judgment. Serious problems can arise in a business organization when the completely free-choice, action-decision idea is initiated overnight.

To prevent damage from delegation, you need to recognize several cautions or danger points and either avoid or be prepared to meet them. These are: *First, be sure that you know and frequently remind yourself what it is that you want to accomplish.* You can compound the amount of time wasted if your subordinate fails to clearly understand an assignment which has been delegated to him. Suppose you as an upper-level manager are going to discuss manpower, facilities, and markets with your boss at a luncheon meeting and, in preparation, you ask a subordinate for some employee figures on the number of people assigned to each of these areas. Now, further suppose that your understudy in his zeal to do a "bang-up" job assigns ten people to accumulate not only numbers of people but ages, rates of pay, skills and historical trends. He turns up at your office at 11:30 A.M. with a twenty-page typewritten document plus charts and tables.

What you had in mind was a general, informal, possible fifteen minutes of conversation with your boss. For this your organization has spent hundreds of dollars in wage payment time, taken attention away from more important work, and wasted materials—all because of poor delegation.

Second, study and test the subordinates with whom you are associated. Your personal secretary can be a valuable assistant, but you must know her strong and weak performance qualities. To gain the information you must have, it may be necessary to misspell some words, rearrange a paragraph or so. Deliberately scramble some thoughts in important correspondence. Be concerned about the reaction of important visitors and colleagues to her appearance and poise. You need a great deal of knowledge about a subordinate before you can avoid the hazards and get the total benefits from delegation.

Third, don't try to move too fast. Be patient. The mistake of too much delegation too fast can not only get you into trouble but might well destroy the usefulness of a valuable future helper. Crowding or pressuring a subordinate beyond his capacity may ruin his confidence.

Fourth, be sure that you always retain sufficient control so that you personally know what is going on. For instance, suppose your superior is a manager who likes to personally handle all the public relations and outside contacts for your company. You can, because of an oversight, allow your subordinate to experience some unnecessary embarrassment by allowing him to assume you have given him the go-ahead for company commitments in community affairs. If you are not on top of specifically what is delegated, the same kind of error may occur in the internal operation of your organization. Give your subordinate freedom, but don't let him wreck himself.

Fifth, use reasoned and measured judgment in encouraging and helping your subordinate to grow. If you over-assist those reporting to you, they are weakened rather than strengthened. You can waste the effectiveness of a good management tool by over-praising; too much of this stimulant, just like tobacco, alcohol, or dope, reduces and finally destroys their results-getting benefits. Save your special commendations for real break-throughs in performance. Be available and willing when your subordinate is in real need of help. Notice that here again is the need for balance in your administrative managing. You must use these tools, but they deserve to be handled with care.

How to Help Subordinates Grow

"Personality characteristics are always manifestations of an interaction between the individual and his environment." [1] This observation as it relates to your job situation is a factor you must consider as you endeavor to carry out your administrative duties.

Let's look at the experiences of a department manager in a large industry —call him Wys. Reporting to the upper-level manager was Sertn, a third echelon supervisor with responsibility for controlling allotments of people assigned to indirect labor throughout the entire organization.

Through long experience, extremely hard work, and devotion to his job, Wys had earned a respected position for himself as an administrator. You can learn something from the working exchanges between these two managers. For instance, almost without Sertn realizing it was happening, his superior kept a close check on the activities in which he took part. Wys managed to limit his subordinate's contacts with numerous people with whom Sertn couldn't seem to get along. Although it often took some doing, the administrator felt that Sertn's flair for flawless figures justified special support.

Wys had originally hired Sertn because of his skill in statistics. The subordinate approached the genius category in his ability to mathematically construct the proper ratios and predict output under every conceivable combination of equipment arrangement and numbers of employees. He never made a mistake with figures, and Wys was assured of his complete personal loyalty to him as his superior.

With all his good qualities, Sertn had one bad habit which was his positive attitude: "I'm right, and if you disagree, then you're wrong." Again, Wys understood the situation and made allowances.

When Sertn's management attitudes began to become apparent in his

[1] Wickens and Meyer, *Psychology*, p. 354

subordinates, Wys realized that he had to take some decisive action. A "holier-than-thou" bearing by these managers stifled communications and started causing administrative difficulties. The superior and subordinate got together, and Wys went over Sertn's good points as well as his shortcomings as a manager. You might say it was a brutal thing to do without any warning after having protected Sertn, and you are probably right. This is an actual case, and Sertn didn't accept his superior's changed attitude which resulted in our subordinate being stepped down to the next lower management level. Sertn is now doing the same kind of work as before. He is a valuable employee, doing what he likes, and his exceptional precision continues to be unusual. Do you think that he will go still lower on the management scale?

If you were in Wys' position, how could you have avoided what seems to have been a mistake in administrative judgment? You could have started by asking yourself these questions: Does Sertn really have high-level management potential? Does he even want to be a supervisor? Why can't he take constructive suggestions? Does he like secure surroundings and close supervision? What was my real reason for covering up for him?

Let's consider how Sertn may have been assisted as a manager by the application of some good administrative principles.

In our complex, assembly-line, mass-production-type business, especially designed structures with many different kinds of people are needed in specialized jobs just to keep production moving. To direct these people, machines, equipment, and methods is the primary purpose of an administrative organization. Good management as applied to this directional need should be an extension of the supervisor. The leader, to earn his salt, must be able to multiply the productivity of the group he directs over what they might accomplish without his guidance. It appears obvious that Sertn did not grasp the first good management essential. As you encourage subordinate managers to develop themselves, be sure they understand and accept this first administrative essential.

A second practice which an improving manager must cultivate is that of expanding his usefulness. When you are appointed to a position of authority and accountability for the results of others, either directly or indirectly, outside limits are set upon your area of influence. If you are to grow as a manager, you must find ways to break out of these restraints. An improving administrator must grow and expand or stagnate and decline. Sertn didn't try to apply his talents outside his special interest area, and Wys certainly didn't encourage such practices. As you endeavor to help the managers reporting to you, be sure you instill in them the desire for continued growth.

The number three means for helping subordinates improve as administrators requires you to use a fine balance between the authority you must exercise and the service you must provide. If your personal control is too tight, your subordinate is denied the opportunity to build a sense of confidence and act on his own initiative. On the other hand, while job enthusiasm is healthy and desirable, the administrator must be alert to protect a subordinate from being "carried away" to the extent that he makes an unwise or foolhardy decision. Inspiration and bubbling passion must always be tempered with sound judgment.

It appears that Wys erred more on the side of too tight restraints upon Sertn. To meet the number three requirement for aiding subordinate's growth, you should seek an equitable balance. Adjustment should be between your management responsibility to see that the job gets done and giving your subordinate some "running room" to strengthen his talent tendencies and improve weaknesses.

How to Dispose of Administrative Blocks

Your boss takes a greater personal interest in you and encourages you if your organization is alive, doing things and achieving results.

One of the most deadening obstacles which can handicap and destroy an organization's needed vitality is fear. You can have it because you feel the pressure for results from your superior. An administrator can react to the tension by saying to himself, "This is so important. It must be done correctly. If I do it myself, it'll be done right." If you succumb to such a fear, you are not an administrator or a manager but a doer. A second damaging effect of fear is that you may, even unknowingly, create such tenseness in your subordinates that they are unable to perform at their best.

To get rid of this block: 1. recognize the damage that fears do to your organization, 2. relax yourself; as the boss, those reporting to you respond as they sense your mood. A word of caution, however. This doesn't mean take it easy. Again, as has been repeatedly stressed, good administration requires balance. You can get steadily improving results without the handicap of fear. 3. Be sure that you are conscious of the possibility that some unexplained action on your part, such as the unnecessarily abrupt refusal of a request, a hurried memorandum, even a thoughtless phone call, can hamper the performance of a valued subordinate.

A second administrative block you must avoid is the failure to get idea-support from your organization. One of the greatest helps to you in improving as a manager is a free-flowing, two-way communication between yourself and those reporting to you. You tend to prevent the needed exchange of ideas when you credit your subordinate with all your specific knowledge and experiences. If you take this view, your communications will likely be faulty, your understandings will be warped, and subordinate's efforts may be directed toward getting out product A when you thought the two of you had agreed to stress product B. Or he may think you want to add skilled people to the payroll when you wanted his thoughts on a better method of packaging your finished products. To overcome this block: 1. You must understand each other. You have to "try and test," find out by experience the best way to get your thoughts over to your subordinates. Gear your communications to what you think will get the best results, and then check back to see how well you were able to get across. 2. Have the patience to apply your own best efforts to encouraging subordinates in a teamwork endeavor. 3. Treat every suggestion from a subordinate with respect. Even if that particular idea is not a winner, there may be more where it came from.

The third administrative block which you must guard against is your own preconceived idea as to how a job should be done, a problem handled, or a project carried out. Some of the disadvantages of such an administrative practice are: Your subordinate will tend to refuse to accept any personal responsibility for the results. Also, you may lose the advantage of some broad, record-breaking method of operating which had not even occurred to you. Then, too, spelling out in detail the methods your subordinate is to follow restricts rather than develops him. To overcome this block: 1. Push the decision-making authority as close to the point of action as possible. 2. Be sure that the objective is understood. Then, if at all possible, give your subordinate the freedom to choose the best method for carrying out the assignment. 3. Learn to absorb the mistakes of subordinates without allowing these errors to handicap your own performance as a top-notch administrator. You can encourage the growth of such a personal attitude by appreciating that some mistakes will occur if any improvement is to be made.

How to Fit the Magic Relationships into Your Role as an Administrator

"Managing a business or running a department is more involved today than it was a generation or two ago and requires a correspondingly higher order of executive and administrative skill. Executive development is no longer a semi-automatic process. If development is to take place, if people are to find opportunities, if management is to have qualified executives available when they are needed, management itself must assume responsibility for creating the conditions and providing the leadership that will make these things happen." [1]

As you strive to make personal improvements, remember the need for balance between getting your work done and at the same time developing your subordinates. This is one of the practical tests of a successful administrator. To achieve the two-fold purpose, you will find reference to two of the three magic relationships in the results of an authoritative study in which a majority of top ranking businessmen interviewed by researchers from Michigan State University answered this question, "What is the most important stepping-stone to success in management?" After 116 interviews with executives from 83 firms, the ques-

[1] Worthy, *Manpower Inventory and Planning,* p. 2

tioners concluded the answer was, "being an effective subordinate to the man above you and, at the same time, possessing the capacity to develop capable aides of your own." [1]

To comply with the conclusions of these executives, a growing administrator must improve his own ability to exchange constructive thoughts with both his superior and his subordinate. In addition, he must develop, stimulate, and even expand his personal relationships in a way which furthers the objectives of the entire enterprise.

Pick Your High Potential Managers and Apply the Magic Three

Your organization should have some means of early identification of younger employees with the special attributes for higher management positions. The location of these high potential employees should be followed with carefully prepared opportunities and encouragement to help those chosen to develop themselves. Such an effort can best be carried out if all sections of your management group are interested and cooperating.

Here is a brief general description of how one large company handled its development program. To forestall the jealousy often expressed by the disparaging criticism that you shouldn't have a "Crown Prince Corp," the "Comers" list was made flexible, meaning that individuals would be added and taken away as performance warranted.

After a general maximum age limit had been set, the responsibility for selection of the Comers belonged to their superiors in the management line. When you are in a position to make such a selection, the weight of responsibility will cause you to work at a better understanding with your subordinate and your superior because they are both directly interested in who the choice will be and just how you have arrived at your conclusions.

After the list of selectees had been determined, the objective for each individual was to custom-build a suggested development program to meet each trainee's specific needs. Here, again, is the place where such a program requires improved personal relationships between the members of the management line, that is, superiors and subordinates. If you are an upper-level manager, you must become involved because you have made definite selection commitments. You are also the one who knows the most about your subordinate and can provide him with the greatest help.

As you attempt to establish a better relationship with your subordinate, either in the original selection or in helping him to improve, you need to know: 1. as much as possible about his attitude toward the job of management, 2. his

[1] Jennings, Eugene Emerson: "It Takes Two to Reach the Top," *Nation's Business*, November 1961, p. 202

own opinions of his strong and weak qualities, 3. something of his thoughts on the importance of planning, team membership, and his own ambitions. Some tested questions which will help you gain the needed information are:

In general management philosophy: 1. Do you consider management a profession? 2. Can skill in this field be acquired? 3. What is your basic approach to the job?

In formal education: 1. What were your most important courses? 2. What further courses would you now like? 3. Were your extracurricular activities of special value?

In work experiences: What specific jobs helped you on your way? What further type and kind of work would have been helpful? Has any spare-time activity contributed to your success?

Your personal opinion of your managerial abilities: What are your strong qualities? What are the areas in which you need to improve?

Your future: What do you need to qualify for my job? What type of work best fits your special abilities? What target in management are you shooting for, and how much time do you think it will take to achieve this goal?

As managers at all levels went through the experience of selecting and helping others improve, understanding, communications, and relationships also became better. And as more competent managers were chosen and better prepared for their jobs, the total organization also benefited completing the magic three-way relationship improvement.

You Can Use These Benefits from the Comer Program

First, good management is a skill to be learned. *Second,* your most valuable assets, both actually and potentially, are the people reporting to you. *Third,* challenge your subordinates' capabilities to encourage their growth as top performing supervisors. *Fourth,* your job can best be accomplished by forward planning, setting of goals, and maintaining high performance standards.

A markedly significant point of agreement among the interviewees was their opinion that managers develop best on the job by experiencing the pressure of direct responsibility and by the give and take of association with people in their own organization, outside departments, suppliers, customers, and the public. It was also generally expressed that your subordinate's improvement can be accelerated if you are a strong superior who sets high standards for himself; if you establish goals for both yourself and your subordinate and let it be known that you expect results. Many of the supervisors interviewed stated that managers performed better if the boss allowed them to have a part in setting their own job and personal improvement targets.

Still other essential needs uncovered in the training project included: your subordinate should be given responsibility and authority with guidance and counseling as necessary; you must establish a fund of broad knowledge, experience, and information; you should be alert to developing company operations and have a general technical understanding of the requirements of the jobs you supervise; you should continually strive to familiarize yourself with those things which assist in a better understanding of people, both in groups and as individuals.

Advantages to Improving Your Ability as an Administrator

A better job of administration gives stability and purpose to your organization. As you get on top of your job, you can take more time to do the necessary over-all planning. Your staff has a clearer understanding of what they can expect from the boss, and you have a better knowledge of the individual performance you can anticipate from your team members.

A second value which you gain from good administration is action-centered decision-making. The manager closest to the point of action calls the shots. You gain these values from such a practice: 1. greater speed in decision-making and a more flexible organization; 2. generally better decisions, easier follow-up, and quicker evaluation; 3. helps in building job pride, stimulates enthusiasm, increases the confidence of the supervisor; 4. helps in stretching your abilities by giving you under-pressure decision-making opportunities. It is an essential for on-the-job growth training.

Using Your Personal Power Sources for Better Balance in Managing

1. *Administrative skills, planning, directing and controlling is often given an "out of proportion" value as a personal management quality because practice areas are more easily identified.*
2. *To do a better job of administration, use:*
    a. *your own personality*
    b. *a better understanding of subordinates*
    c. *a more accurate evaluation of the situation.*
3. *Gain benefits by developing your own administrative style and let the people reporting to you know what it is.*
4. *Proper use of delegation makes your job easier and enables you to more smoothly meet the constant changes taking place in modern organizations.*
5. *Avoid the dangers in delegation by:*
    a. *reminding yourself of what you are trying to accomplish*
    b. *studying and testing your subordinates*
    c. *being patient*
    d. *retaining controls*
    e. *using judgment and balance in helping your subordinates to grow.*

6. *Develop those reporting to you by:*
   a. *using your influence to multiply your group's effectiveness*
   b. *helping subordinates expand their accountability*
   c. *carefully balancing your assistance with the freedom you allow the people reporting to you.*
7. *Watch for these administrative blocks:*
   a. *fear*
   b. *lack of idea-support from your organization*
   c. *spelling out a step-by-step method of operating.*
8. *Know and use the magic relationships:*
   a. *with subordinates*
   b. *with superiors*
   c. *with the total organization*
9. *Proven good management facts:*
   a. *Management is a skill to be learned.*
   b. *People are your greatest asset.*
   c. *The best learning takes place on the job.*
   d. *Challenge your subordinates to encourage growth.*
   e. *Cooperative goal-setting is a valuable stimulant to performance.*
10. *Values you can gain by becoming a better administrator:*
    a. *stability and purpose in the organization*
    b. *more planning time*
    c. *your organization knows what to expect of you, and you know what to look for from them*
    d. *more action-centered decisions.*

Chapter 14: *How to Know a Great Deal About a Lot—and Use It*

To become a better manager, you must gain a great deal more knowledge than you now have and put it to work for you.

Just let your imagination roam for a few moments over the different things that you *now* realize you need to know more about to become a better manager; such things as the tremendous implications of computerized decision-making, PERT, and operations research. In the actual physical productive processes, there are tape-controlled machines, new metals and materials, and new fabrication methods. In the broader general areas, there are the great social problems such as securing enough pure water, resolving the problems posed by civil rights, labor relationships, juvenile delinquency, population growth, and small wars all around the world which could explode into bigger ones at any time. And remember, these are just a few of the things that we need additional working information about. Experience has shown that throughout history every new fact, every bit of new knowledge which has been discovered, has always opened up new vistas to be explored.

The acquistition and use of new information is an essential power source to which you must give special priority, because one of the things which the Soviets proved with their first sputnik was that knowledge is an indifferent giant —it cares not whether it helps a freedom-loving economy such as our own or a dictator-dominated state where people are virtually slaves. The contestant who finds the control levers first puts his opponent on the defensive.

As an individual manager, you can help to give our economy the edge and help yourself by staying up to date on the things you need to know to handle your present job, as well as studying projected future needs.

Train Yourself for Future Requirements

Of course, everyone would agree that you could do a better job of preparing yourself to meet management problems fifteen to twenty years down the road if you knew what they were going to be. You don't, however, and neither does anyone else. Don't stew and waste time worrying about an unknown future. It makes much better sense to keep yourself current in handling your job problems and probe for as much future knowledge as is practical.

> "Harry Arthur Hopf landed in America in 1898, a penniless, fatherless, immigrant lad of 16. Six years later, he discovered his vocation—telling company presidents how to run their businesses.
>
> Young Hopf was no more than a foreign language stenographer for the Germania (now Guardian) Life Insurance Co., his experience confined to minor clerical jobs. For years he'd been making only $40 a month. But Horatio Alger never had a better pupil. And New York University's new School of Commerce never had a more ambitious evening student." [1]
>
> As Hopf developed himself as an expert in the art of management by acquiring as much knowledge as he possibly could, *Business Week* says: "He learned habits of observation and analysis that gave him an unparalleled reputation for walking into a company and immediately asking the right questions—the ones that would pinpoint the problem and suggest its solution." [2]
>
> For his services to managers, he earned a great deal of money. "Money counted to Hopf. To the end of his life, he was willing to work nights and Saturdays to earn his fee. Yet even more important was recognition, and for this he worked even harder. Among the results: 69 lines in *Who's Who.*" [3]

Hopf's experiences tell a success story in management know-how about a man who concerned himself with learning about and doing the things he determined a good manager should do in meeting current and reasonable future needs. He didn't worry about "Blue Sky" future "might be's."

How to Make the Most of Your Learning Opportunities

First, recognize that there are only two ways that you can learn. Let's call them *second-hand and first-hand;* and, for the greatest benefit, one must supplement the other. By the second-hand method, you get information from reading, discussions, lectures, seeing movies, slides, and by absorbing knowledge previously uncovered by someone else. Through the first-hand method, you discover usable facts, ways of working for yourself. These can be unplanned happenings analyzed in an after-the-fact review or planned exploration in which you deliberately experiment with original methods and carefully observe what takes place.

Second, be sure you appreciate the values of added learning. A study

[1] "Man Who Asked the Right Questions," *Business Week,* August 31, 1963, p. 74 ff.
[2] Ibid.
[3] Ibid.

of the effects of a better total education for more people in our country reveals a fascinating story of tremendous increases in material well-being as well as cultural satisfactions for the entire population. Consider the statistical facts: (a) the number of men in the age group of twenty-five and older with some high school training in the period from 1940 to 1960 increased by 48%; while those with some college education increased 80%. (b) The lifetime earnings of the average male high school graduate are one-third more than the average elementary school graduates. The college graduates earn two-thirds more than the average high school graduates.[1] You will find that many skeptics in reviewing these facts say, "Yes. But many other factors in addition to education account for increased earnings, because people who finish college tend to have more drive, innate ability, and physical and financial capacity to get through. All of which are qualities contributing to increased earning capacity." In answer to these objections, the Committee for Economic Development has the following researched facts: (a) Brothers—men of the same family background—with college educations earn more than their brothers with only a high school education; likewise, brothers with high school training earn more than brothers with only elementary school training. (b) Earnings of college graduates have been shown to be higher than earnings of those with the same high school class ranking and intelligence test scores. (c) On the average, people with low education suffer much more unemployment than people with higher education.[2] Sylvia Porter in her column said, "Unemployment among those with less than a high school education is four times the national jobless rate." [3]

Third, test your information, facts, and knowledge in your daily work. Notice how often when you are confronted with a management problem on your job, how valuable it is to you to be able to draw on a built up reserve of knowledge, experience, or interest as you try for an answer to the difficulty. Frequently, the solution you finally decide to use is not something which has happened or that you have learned in connection with the current job assignment. For instance, in convincing other people of the value of an idea, an approach or a way of doing something, the technique you apply may well have come from reading a good novel, serving as chairman of a PTA meeting, or another activity unrelated to the immediate job at hand.

Fourth, convert as much of your information as you can to the "for-sure" kind. Samuel Johnson wrote, "Knowledge is of two kinds: We know a subject ourselves, or we know where we can find information upon it." In applying this thought to your job, you must remember that knowledge needs to be translated into practical usefulness if it is to help you improve your job performance. Knowing is necessary, but doing must follow. For example, you know that people generally resent a fault-finding manager, one who fails to recognize

[1] First National City Bank, *Monthly Economic Letter,* August, 1965, pp. 94-95

[2] Committee for Economic Development, *Raising Low Incomes Through Improved Education,* September 1965, p. 16

[3] *The Wichita Eagle,* 2-2-65, Sylvia Porter Column

and commend their good work, yet you continue to delight in "nit-picking," destructive criticism of an employee's efforts and never give your subordinates a word of praise. Consequently, you will probably be the first to complain of the difficulties you are having in developing competent subordinates and of their lack of cooperation.

You can act with more speed and confidence if you know that you have the right knowledge. In the course of studying, experimenting, chance-taking and broadening your activities, you acquire further insight into where to look for valuable information. Add as much of this as possible to your "for-sure" knowledge tank.

Fifth, meet the increased competition for success as a professional manager. Today's top managers throughout the business world are much better educated than those of a generation ago. Dean Joseph McGuire of the University of Kansas writes that, "75% have attended college, 57% are college graduates, 19% of these have received graduate degrees. In 1920, only 30% were college graduates." [1]

The pressure on you as a manager to improve your own education is emphasized by the rapidly increasing formal education of the nation's total labor force. The Committee for Economic Development finds that in the previous thirty-four years ending in 1964, members of the American labor force with only an eighth grade education or less had been reduced from 58% to only 25%.[2]

A Three-Fold Benefit Through Improved Knowledge

One of the opportunities which a full-service management-development-minded company must provide its employees is off-working hours, voluntary, general educational classes. In an on-the-move organization, such a program should include several specific classes for areas, such as *Management Principles:* (a) This is a study of the fundamental job duties; organization, an exploration of specific principles and techniques, plus their application. (b) Company organizations and their functions; the history of the establishment and development of your enterprise; how each part of the business contributes to the whole in working toward company goals. (c) Business Law; an attempt to clarify your rights and responsibilities and the possible legal effects of your actions and decisions upon the company.

Human Relations: (a) Studies directed to helping you develop a greater awareness and understanding of people as individuals (b) Communications; identifying some organizational communication problems and suggesting ways in which you may deal with them.

Financial and Economic: (a) American Economic History; a background look at the foundation and growth of our Free Market System. (b) Business

1 McGuire, Joseph: op.cit., p. 167
2 Committee for Economic Development, op.cit., p. 19

Economics; a factual grounding for you in such fundamentals of our business society as money, jobs, supply and demand, taxes, competition, security and material growth. (c) Understanding the corporation; attempts to develop a working knowledge of the various types of organizations, their structure, financing and profitable service. (d) Financing the corporation; exploring the advantages and disadvantages of using stocks and bonds for working capital and fixed investments as well as a delineation of some common financial difficulties of companies. (e) Business cycles; a study of the exciting phenomenon of the rise and fall of the general level of commercial and industrial activity.

Personal Skills: (a) Business Writing; a course designed to help you improve your written communications by developing a clear, concise, factual style of expression. (b) Business Speaking; a course in which primary attention is directed to developing your oral communications of ideas and thoughts to others. (c) Improved Reading; training designed to help you increase your reading speed and comprehension. (d) Business Statistics; through the use of exercises and problems, you can learn to use statistical methods for the collection, analysis, and interpretation of quantitative data.

Community Services: (a) Your Community Responsibilities; a course of study directed toward the businessman's duties in public relations. (b) Political action; a series of study sessions intended to acquaint you with the mechanics of the political processes.

To determine the real worth of such activities, a two-year study was made of 801 managers promoted and demoted in this time period. The analysis showed that managers attending such classes had a 60% better chance for promotion than managers who did not attend. While those enrolling in such educational courses showed an exceptionally high promotion rate, three-fourths of those supervisors demoted failed to attend any of these classes. It should be mentioned that there is no policy or practice which in any way requires attendance. The evidence verifies that such a program benefits you, your management superiors, and your entire organization.

Another test of value can be found in the selections made of young managers with superior potential, previously described in the Comer Program. Of those finally selected as participants in this special group, 90% had attended general education-type classes. Here we have another positive means for determining the three-fold benefits to be gained from knowledge improvement.

How to Provide Full-Service Self-Improvement Opportunities

First, your total program must be designed to offer development assistance to all categories of your management—top, middle, first and second levels plus a preparation of qualified employees for promotion to the first rank of management. *Second,* the program must be of sufficient interest and apparent value to attract enthusiastic participation by those you seek to help. *Third,* it must have practical and demonstrated on-the-job value to those who make use of your program. *Fourth,* you must use both internal and external organizational agencies and methods to sustain interest, obtain variety, and insure a full, rounded, total program. *Fifth,* self-involvement or personal experience-sharing by participants in the program must be an integral part of your over-all development efforts.

How to Use Consultations as a Self-Improvement Medium

Let's define consultation to be: when you talk with a subordinate about anything which you think will assist him in doing a better job. In its broadest sense, consultations can be of help not only in talking with individuals but also to both small and large groups of subordinates. In every case, remember to use good management judgment in determining the approach and amount of help you should give subordinates in solving their problems.

First, looking at some examples of situations in which you can help individuals reporting to you. (a) Manager X comes to you, his boss, Y, with a letter from a supervisor's professional magazine which requests him to write a short article on how he has been able to reduce the number of "fire-fighting" types of decisions which most managers find so pressure-laden. You should take the time to listen while X explains his planned approach to the subject, and discuss any company policy which is applicable. You may or may not have the time to review X's outline. If you feel you can't spare the time, recommend some possible staff help if it is appropriate. What you are doing by this encouragement is stimulating X's morale, helping him think more logically and concisely about his job, and aiding him in improving his ability to communicate.

(b) X comes to you with a request for suggestions in arriving at budgets and general costs for his department. You can identify meaningful indexes for him and tell him where to find them. You may also want to give him your own interpretation of past experiences.

(c) You can talk with and encourage X to tackle a challenging new assignment which will help his growth as a manager.

(d) You can help X in meeting what may be best defined as the "fear problem" which hampers communications. You often, consciously or unconsciously, scare your subordinates. Signs of such a situation are evident when X hesitates to speak up in meetings or when he refrains from asking questions for fear of being thought stupid. The most destructive product of such fears is that it creates an unsure feeling which handicaps your subordinate's efficiency in acting as a good manager must. A qualified personnel man might be able to give some advice, but largely this is a situation which the individual himself must work out. It is not an unusual problem; most supervisors have similar maturing experiences.

(e) When X has an opportunity to make a presentation to groups of people, urge him to accept. Your organization will benefit from this sharpening of your subordinate's ability to communicate, his increased persuasive skills, and the added self-confidence which such an exercise generates.

(f) You should keep a sharp lookout for study courses, assignments, articles, books, which will benefit X in absorbing information which can be usefully applied to the job.

Second, group consultation-type of activities are appropriate when the need for improvement applies to all the managers in a selected segment of your organization. For instance, let's look at a metal parts forming department using many punch presses, angle formers and shaping machines, operated by fifty to sixty workmen under the direction of three first-level managers who in turn reported to a general foreman. The factory superintendent found in checking the records that accidents were double the working manhour rate of the total plant. While the superintendent knew that the section normally had a higher rate than other shops, the one hundred percent increase had just come about in the past month. He called the general foreman whose explanation was, "Lots of new hires." Not satisfied, the superintendent told his subordinate to call his supervisors into a meeting where they could have a general discussion of the problem.

The first-level managers agreed that their turnover rate was up, but they also complained that the new people sent to them seemed to have no conception of the dangers present in operating the various pieces of equipment. The superintendent asked for suggested solutions to the difficulty. The first level managers made three proposals: (a) that the training department spend more time with new hires on safety education, (b) that they could check out safe practices with the new people better than they had been doing, (c) that they should review the safety rules with all employees in the shop, bringing to their attention the past month's poor record. The superintendent agreed that their ideas sounded like an excellent attack on the problem.

Notice the gains which were obtained from group consultation: (a) The managers at the first level, in the best position to solve the accident-rate problem, made the decision on what was to be done. (b) You can bet that a greater effort will be made to see that the three-way approach is more aggressively followed than if the general foreman or the superintendent had ordered the same thing to be done. (c) These first level managers were given encouragement to develop themselves as supervisors through thinking and making decisions about their job problems.

Third, a type of consultation which can be called department- or division-wide differs from group consultation only in the number of people or area included. The larger size of the total group in most instances means that several meetings should be held rather than a single session. The groups must be limited to relatively small numbers if the exchange of ideas among individuals is to take place. Large groups tend to cause such a meeting to become a lecture instead of a consultation. An example of such consultations might result if the general manager decided that his entire organization of a thousand supervisors should initiate a general campaign for better product quality. The effort would be launched in a consultation meeting with the general manager's top staff. In the general discussion at this level, policy agreements on procedure would be reached.

In the meetings which followed, each top manager would talk with the dozen or so people reporting to him. They, in turn, would, through the medium of small group discussion, carry the information down through the first level of management. At the lowest management echelon, the supervisor would explain to his crew the ideas which have developed as the information progressed to and through the successive levels.

If your job is that of a first-level manager, you should remember to get and use as many ideas as possible from the workmen because they can do more than anyone else to insure the success of the quality program. Such a consultation method tends to encourage teamwork all along the line. This is essentially the same idea suggested by Alfred P. Sloan, Jr., when he wrote:

> Much of my life in General Motors was devoted to the development, organization, and periodic reorganization of these governing groups in central management. This was required because of the paramount importance, in an organization like General Motors, of providing the right framework for decisions. There is a natural tendency to erode that framework unless it is consciously maintained. Group decisions do not always come easily. There is a strong temptation for the leading officers to make decisions themselves without the sometimes onerous process of discussion, which involves selling your ideas to others. The group will not always make a better decision than any particular member would make; there is even the possibility of some averaging down. But in General Motors I think the record shows that we have averaged up. Essentially this means that, through our form of organization, we have been able to adapt to the great changes that have taken place in the automobile market in each of the decades since 1920.[1]

Line-Conducted Conferences Build Your Knowledge Power Source

Line-conducted conferences are a most practical kind of internal broadening education for managers and are somewhat related to problem solving and the consultation activity. To make the program go, you must have a high-level manager do the conference leading job. He holds regularly scheduled sessions on subjects of his own choosing with all the managers reporting to him. Sometimes he may use the help of staff people for preparation, but your superior supervisor must present and thoroughly support all the material which he gives to subordinate managers.

You will find the line-conducted conferences can be used appropriately for any sized organization. For instance, Martin Schwartz, chairman and president of NATPAC, a frozen-food processor headquartered in New York City,

[1] Sloan, Alfred P., Jr.: *My Years With General Motors,* p. 435

regularly meets with about twenty-five of his employees in the evenings in a New York hotel suite to study good management. NATPAC started business thirteen years ago with one plant, six employees, and $9,000. Today it has eleven subsidiaries, four plants, 225 employees, and an annual sales volume of $5 million.

> NATPAC has been able to obtain executives almost entirely from within its own ranks. And in a period of steadily rising costs, it has kept its operating expenses almost at the same level they were five years ago. According to Schwartz: "Most of the success of our company to date is attributable to the fact that we've had people who were ready to step into key positions as those positions opened up.[1]

Just imagine how effectively NATPAC's management improvement program dispels the common criticism of a training program conducted by a staff department which is often expressed in words such as these, "What you say sounds good, but my boss doesn't believe in this kind of stuff."

Line-conducted, conference-type education for managers in organizations large or small must be presented by a management official of the company with sufficient authority so that the supervisors to whom he is talking can accept his statements with confidence.

In a relatively short time after such a program is initiated, you will find these sessions become excellent tools for direct communication. Information is not only passed downward more easily and often, but a two-way exchange is encouraged. Lower level supervisors have a means of bringing up problems and asking questions which they may have found difficult to discuss on the job in the course of a regular day's work.

Mr. Schwartz finds, "Employees are sometimes reticent when he discusses on-the-job problems with them in his office. In class, however, he can get closer to them." [2]

If you are the manager conducting the development sessions, you will find that it is essential for you to make some thorough preparation before the meetings. The effort and the actual presentation is a broadening developmental medium for you which is not easily duplicated in any other way. You learn to correctly handle unexpected questions; the training facilitates logical reasoning processes. You gain a better insight into supervisors' attitudes and what causes them, and you become more acutely aware of problems while uncovering possible answers.

The line-conducted conference method encourages your whole group to work toward a common goal. Regularly scheduled sessions in which all your unit's or department's supervisors hear about problems of related mutual concern cultivate an appreciation of each other's difficulties. A better understanding of another's troubles leads to a healthier attitude of wanting to help. Such an association improves interdepartmental coordination and, after a short time, a

[1] McKamy, Kent, Editor: *Business Management,* May 1965, p. 60
[2] Ibid., p. 62

closely knit comradery develops which is beneficial to the entire organization. This type of education is of minimum expense and is a most effective way of emphasizing job problems and general principles, and implementing meaningful communications. Because of its very practical importance, the conferences should be an on-the-job educational activity; one for which the supervisor is allowed time from his regular duties to attend. If working requirements make it impossible, such sessions should be conducted outside the manager's regular work hours. Then, textbooks, instructional aids, and a place to conduct the sessions become the only out-of-pocket costs.

Benefits from Company-Conducted Miscellaneous Educational Programs

All companies have special educational needs arising from the nature of their business, products, diversification, and geographical locations. For instance: 1. A nation-wide corporation with multi-plant operations needs periodic report and progress meetings for selected managers in order to: (a) benefit from the experience of others, (b) better coordinate efforts toward a common goal, (c) develop a pride in the enterprise.

2. Emergency type of education, such as uniform use of a company-wide employee performance rating: (a) an immediate and intensive educational effort will help resolve the problem. (b) All managers get the same information by this method. (c) The responsible manager can be held accountable for correct performance after such instructions.

How to Obtain Greater Returns from Your Premanagement Education Program

If you and your organization are to fully benefit from the knowledge potential of your employees, you need a recognizable and usable means of selecting and training prospective first-level managers.

First, set some generally agreed upon standard for selection. You can use: (a) a minimum I.Q. score, (b) the recommendation of selected levels of line managers, (c) age, experience, years of service.

Second, make sure employees know the company is interested in superior individuals as possible managers: (a) You can urge a deserving employee to apply, (b) give some general publicity to promotions.

Third, have an educational course tailored to your needs: (a) the length of time, (b) method of instruction, (c) the material to be included, (b) who is to do the job.

Fourth, it is good practice to make certain that no promises are made to an employee when he enrolls in the course about the possibilities of appoint-

ment as a manager. In fact, it is a good idea to purposely graduate from your course more employees than will be appointed to a manager's job.

Experience shows that line management likes to make a choice and, even when such employees are not promoted into management, they: (a) show a greater appreciation of management problems by being more cooperative, (b) tend to remain with the company longer than employees not given the training, (c) tend to raise the general educational level of your employees.

Finding and Using Outside-the-Business Aids

Supplementing the list of specifically recommended programs for strengthening your broad knowledge, additional leadership power sources include: (a) the Advanced Management Courses conducted by leading universities throughout the country as well as an excellent series of meetings offered by the American Management Association. This general education is designed for the upper executive level of management and is a live-in program which normally varies in length from four to six weeks.

(b) The National Training Laboratory is another general type program for managers. Sessions are conducted at Arden House, Harriman, New York and Bethel, Maine, with some on the West Coast and at least two in the middle section of the country.

(c) Too numerous to name are the short orientation, workshop, and informational conferences and meetings ranging from one, three or five days to a couple of weeks duration. These can be conducted within the company by specialist employees or hired experts. They may include attendees from one company or several. The American Management Association makes a specialty of these programs as do many colleges, universities, and management consultants.

All these formalized broadening mediums are supported by Randall's thoughtful analysis when he said:

> To solve the great questions (of our time) requires a knowledge of psychology, of economics, of law, of communications, and many other areas of thought which are essential parts of the liberal arts curriculum. . . . Business does not employ a young man for what he knows, but rather for his proven capacity to learn. . . . The clear mind, the inquiring mind—these are the qualities that industry seeks.[1]

Experience indicates that these programs yield such specific helps as 1. new ideas for improved operation on the job, 2. broadening your resources for continuing research into helpful areas, 3. enabling you to make a direct comparison of operating methods used by other successful companies, 4. strengthens your get-along-with-others skills, 5. gives you a fresh look at what you as a manager ought to be emphasizing in your thinking about your job.

[1] Randall, Clarence B.: *A Businessman Looks at the Liberal Arts*, pp. 20-23

How to Benefit from Informal Company-Encouraged Education

Since good managers are leaders, with only a minimum of encouragement you and your associates will exercise the initiative to form such worthwhile group endeavors as: 1. a management club which devotes a portion of its efforts to the self-improvement of members through educational lectures and study groups, and special inducement to its members to further their education. 2. Speech and toastmaster's clubs which provide a forum, to give members experience in organizing words and thoughts as well as practice in speaking to groups. 3. Investment clubs, which supply an intriguing means of acquainting you and your associates with stock market operations. Rather than an attempt to make money, this is an unusual way for you to learn about growth, investment, and high-yield stocks and bonds. The experience should give you a better knowledge of the money market and its importance to corporation finance and investments.

How to Make Your Work in Public Affairs Repay You Three-Fold

You can expand your general knowledge horizon by actively serving in leadership roles with such worthwhile community activities as Chambers of Commerce, YMCA, Junior Achievement, city-wide professional clubs, service clubs, political organizations, church work, school boards, and United Funds. If you work at it, both you and your company will obtain a three-way benefit:

First: You increase your management skills. Intensive, wide-spread opinion surveys among practical-minded managers reveal the general opinion that such experiences: (a) Challenge your persuasive skills in a situation where the structure of an authoritative organization cannot be used as a crutch. (b) Improve your ability to communicate. (c) Emphasize the importance of self-discipline.

Second: (a) Such opportunities for service often enable a company to retain on its payroll a person of rare ability or skills who would otherwise transfer to another location or company. (b) The total community value of these activities is an important consideration in attracting high caliber employees. (c) Such activities foster a climate which invites new industry to your locality.

Third: (a) Such actions sell your company to the community, state, and nation. As H. Bruce Palmer, president of NICB, said, "People prefer to spend their money with the company which is a good citizen as well as a producer." [1] (b) Your valuable services raise the public's esteem for management as a profession. (c) Your work helps to preserve the free enterprise system and our way of life. (d) As Donald Kirk David, when he was Dean of the Harvard Graduate

[1] *The Wall Street Journal,* Dallas, Texas, September 22, 1965, Roger Ricklefs: Good Works, Inc.

School of Business Administration, said, "Far too many businessmen have secluded themselves with their own groups without opening their minds to what is happening around, without appreciating the social and political and economic responsibilities of business leaders." [1]

After reviewing the numerous suggested ways to help you increase your knowledge reservoir, assist you in becoming a better leader and secure the other mentioned benefits, some overworked executives have said, "But a manager can't spend all his time on such services." Of course, it must be agreed that you as a manager are hired to see that your company profits from the sale of its goods and/or services.

The answer as to how much time and effort you can properly devote to community services is to be found in planning for public affairs. You must realistically weigh the expected benefits against its costs and make a judgment decision. Admittedly, many of the benefits are of an intangible nature and may not bear immediate fruit, so it is a decision for which the pay-off will come sometime in the future. As you strive to develop yourself as a more productive manager, remember these thoughts suggested by Clarence B. Randall:

> Few problems in the field of management can be solved by reference to physical standards, or by laboratory methods of analysis and testing. Most of the problems would be just the same had the atom never been split. They require not knowledge of the nature of matter, but a clear mind, the power of logical analysis, wisdom and a talent for communication.[2]

Learning More and Using It Better

1. *Work at the job of gaining more knowledge about your present assignment as well as studying projected future needs.*
2. a. *Be sure to make use of both second- and first-hand learning methods.*
   b. *Recognize the relationship between increased education and greater general prosperity.*
   c. *Test your knowledge in your everyday work.*
   d. *Strive to make your knowledge the "for-sure" kind.*
   e. *Welcome the increased competition for your job by becoming a better professional manager.*
3. *General-knowledge studies prepare you for promotion opportunities, enable your superiors to build a better performing organization, and strengthen your company's competitive position.*
4. *Develop a full-service improvement program for your managers.*
5. *Use consultations to improve individuals, small groups, and your entire organization.*

[1] Rautenstrauch and Villers: op.cit., p. 435
[2] Randall, op.cit., p. 7

6. *Appreciate that conducting line-management conferences develops both you as a leader and your subordinates in a practical and economical fashion.*
7. *Try to select and develop all employees who display exceptional potential for management.*
8. *Be ready for emergency and specialized types of educational programs.*
9. *Encourage informal education among your managers through clubs and associations.*
10. *Examine your activities in public affairs and get the total benefits you should from those efforts.*

Chapter 15: How to Establish Your Right to Lead

"This is the way we are going to do it," is a statement you as the boss must sometimes make. If you are a manager, growing in leadership, your followers welcome the help such a positive decision gives them when they are uncertain about which course to pursue, and deciding the correct action is beyond their depth. When a subordinate is unsure because he thinks he is short of necessary information, when he is fearful of the results which may come from the various alternates he sees, when he just can't come up with answers, then he must look to his boss to bail him out.

Whatever your management position, the people reporting to you are often in this dilemma. Here is where your efforts to increase your most intangible personal management abilities—the ones we define as motivating, influencing, guiding, and encouraging others—pays off. You must also include the quality best described as your personal attraction for others because, as you become a better manager, you have to provide help for your subordinates in time of crisis. You have to be ready to say "yes" and "no" when others falter. Frederick L. Hovde, when president of Purdue University, once remarked, "Often in conferences with department heads I have said, 'those of you who deal with the exact sciences—physics, chemistry, mechanics, mathematics, etc.,—don't have problems comparable to those who deal with people and their reactions. There is where the real problems are found.' " Establishing your right to lead is admittedly a difficult part of your job because more and more it is becoming necessary for the manager to prove his right to be out in front. With greater frequency, followers are insisting that you give them some solid evidence of real leadership. If you are going to stand out from the crowd and direct the actions of other people, you have a very difficult but most fascinating job.

You must develop your own power sources in the "attraction for" category so that your followers step out confidently under your direction even when the results of the actions which they are taking are fog-shrouded.

When your subordinate says that you "always know just the right thing to do at the right time," you have arrived as manager in this very difficult performance area. Inspiring confidence in your leadership is insurance against being unexpectedly confronted with a complete breakdown of morale, the need for an immediate organizational change, or a stoppage of production which could have been avoided if you had been informed in time to correct the difficulty.

Values in Improving Your Ability to Do the Right Thing at the Right Time

"Nuts," was Brigadier General Anthony McAuliffe's reply to the German general's demand that the battered 10,000 besieged paratroopers of the 101st Airborne Division at Bastogne, Belgium, surrender to the surrounding 45,000 crack panzer troops supported by efficient tiger tanks December 22, 1944. His leadership decision rang through contemporary history because of its bold impertinence. The 101st held fast, preventing Field Marshal Von Rundstedt from turning the American's line and prolonging the war.

Hundreds of soldiers, responding to a leader in whom they had confidence, followed the right decision to their death. Of course, an army needs more stringent discipline than is present or even desirable in a management organization because, in becoming a better manager, your aim is to develop willing followers. You can further your purpose by improving your own personal appeal to the people you seek to lead and your ability to inspire loyal confidence in them. "Though he likes to believe otherwise, man behaves more in terms of his feelings than his rational thinking." [1] Do the things which show your subordinate that you understand him, respect his personal dignity and appreciate his individual worth.

Here is an actual series of circumstances pointing out the importance of laying a solid foundation in order to obtain the benefits of subordinate recognition. In a very busy manufacturing company, an office department was managed by a supervisor we will call A. Reporting to A were B and C. On the first level under B's direction were D, E, and F; and under C were G, H, and I. The department employed mostly women to handle the timekeeping, payroll, typing, and employment records. A reported to a division manager titled X. All these managers had held their present positions for many years. The depart-

[1] Levinson, *What is Mental Health?* p. 24

ment met its commitments. If anybody got excited about a new way of speeding up the record keeping or any other even minor improvement, the veteran employees wisely nodded, saying, "He just bought himself a transfer to another department." The watchword of A's operation was stability. X was a great believer in complete delegation; therefore, subordinate A directed his department without interference.

As chance would have it, one day while A was crossing the street he was knocked down and killed by a truck. This opened up a problem because when X recommended to his boss Y, the plant manager, that B should step up to A's former position, Y asked for a report on B's supervisory qualifications. X suddenly realized that he didn't know very much about the management in this particular department.

In an effort to quickly overcome his own negligence, X had some heart-to-heart talks with not only B and C but the other six managers as well. To his amazement, one of the first things that X learned was that A was a martinet in his stringent control of the department. No one was allowed to even question one of his orders. He inspired fear in all his subordinates, causing them to quake whenever he issued a directive and to refrain from even suggesting any thought which might rock the boat.

X quickly decided that he needed to know all the subordinate supervisors in the department better. As a result of his review, he concluded that a complete reorganization of the department management was needed. D was given A's job. G and F were raised to B and C's former positions. B decided to take early retirement, and C took a first-level manager's assignment. E and I were reduced to hourly rated jobs, and two younger Comers were brought up from the ranks to replace them. H was continued in his same position.

When X proposed all these drastic changes to Y, his boss, his superior thought a long time before giving his approval. If you were in Y's position, would you have agreed to these organizational shifts? Which of these managers must accept the greatest blame for the conditions which convinced X that a reorganization was necessary? What is one of the first things you must do before you can seriously consider inspiring, guiding, helping, or encouraging others?

In this example, certainly Y and X are to blame for poor management practices. By not knowing any more than they did about their subordinates, how could they favorably influence the behavior of these people? In addition, A and B were remiss in allowing conditions to persist without any strong protests. You should also look at the actions of the first-level managers; they cannot be absolved of blame because they, too, went along with the poor leadership emphasis on status quo.

As a manager, you can't expect to do the right thing at the right time unless you know a great deal more than Y, X, or A about the people reporting to you. If you assume that B and C knew their subordinates' wishes, needs, and desires, then they must be strongly criticized for lack of leadership spirit and ingenuity to carry through a determined purpose.

Substantially the same fault could be found with the performance of the six first-level managers although X apparently saw different degrees of incompetence in the individuals making up the group, as you may judge from the reorganization assignments.

How to Use Appeals to Emotions for Leadership Results

Be a take-charge kind of guy. Know where you are going and be on your way. People will not only admire but follow you when they think you know where you are going.

Napoleon, Hitler, Mussolini, and even Castro succeeded in attracting followers far out of proportion to their leadership ability, as history either has or is proving. All these international, pseudo crime-does-payers stood before the people they wished to lead in great confidence, shouting, "This is a great cause. Come with me and accomplish goals that are within your grasp." As a manager, you can be the kind of person that modern employees expect their boss to be: 1. Always give your subordinate your full attention when he wants to talk with you. If time is not available, schedule some and reserve it for him. Be sure your secretary knows that your subordinate is an important person; don't have your conversation interrupted by telephone calls or other people running in and out of your office. 2. Build up your subordinate; don't tear him down. When he makes a mistake, be careful of the words you use to tell him about it. If he is a good employee, he feels worse about the error than you do, so a confidence-building appeal to emotion is in order. 3. Talk with subordinates. You must have the help of his best performance, and you'll not get it if the two of you don't have easy communications. A lower-level manager said, "My boss is such a sharply intelligent guy that I used to dread saying anything to him for fear of being thought stupid. You know how I overcame it? I just forced myself to talk with him at every opportunity whether what I said was smart or not. The result was that he had to talk back. Now we both have a better understanding of each other." You can successfully employ this idea on all management levels. 4. Be humble enough to learn from others. Even though you may know a great deal more about a subject than your subordinate, listen for new information and new thoughts. It'll help you and encourage the speaker to think more deeply about his work as well as assist him to attack his problems with greater vigor. 5. Let the people reporting to you see that you have confidence in their ability to do important work. Have confidence in yourself, and when you bet on a subordinate make it clear that you are putting your "roll" on him to win. Don't get in the way of or slow up a subordinate who's on the move in the right direction by "over-managing." Give him freedom to fly as far and as fast as he can when in your calculated judgment it is safe to do so.

How to Get Results Through Appeals to Practical Self-Interest

The emotions and idealism which is so much a part of assisting you to be a modern successful manager must be backed up with realism. Just as water seeks its own level, so will your career in management tend toward the average or mediocre to the extent that you use *only* emotional motivators, guiders, directors. To develop day-in-and-day-out loyal followers, you must give the people reporting to you some red meat in the form of concrete rewards to chew on at frequent intervals, such as pay raises, status promotions and attainable opportunities to grow.

1. *Let your subordinates know you recognize that material things, such as money, talk pretty loud* to a fellow whom you expect to take over an accountability load and run with it. Be frank if you are over your merit raise budget and one of your subordinates deserves more money. Talking with him about the situation will help. Be careful about making promises for the future; the man's performance or circumstances may change.

2. *Get yourself the reputation as a manager who goes to bat for his subordinates.* Give them credit at every opportunity. Don't let them be criticized by others without a rebuttal. If you know of a better job opening in some other section of the company for which your subordinate can qualify, be sure to tell him about it. "Manager migration is already more widespread than many people realize. In its special survey, *Steel* found that twenty-two percent of its middle management respondents were hired away from other firms; and an equal number declared: 'We're not sure we'll be with our present employers five years from now.' "[1] So do everything you can to assure your good men that they have a future with your company.

3. *Set fair standards, make sure they are understood, and insist that everyone meet them.* Avoid the slightest hint of favoritism. You can't afford to compromise by accepting sloppy performance if a subordinate isn't doing the job and can't be motivated to improve even with training. The kindest thing for the worker, as well as the best action for your organization, is to replace him.

Winston Churchill made many enemies in his career largely because he had a compelling desire to get his leadership job accomplished. Violet Bonham Carter, describing Churchill's early years, in an intimate portrait said, "Above all, his vitality was irrepressible. His gusto for life, combined with a massive self-confidence and a delight in decision, made him intolerable to the second-rate."[2] As you gain experience as a manager, you learn that some of your subordinates will dislike you at times, maybe all the time, but you must have

[1] Campbell, Walter J., Editor: "Where Are the Take-Charge Guys?" *Steel,* January 3, 1966, pp. 106-107

[2] Carter, Violet Bonham: "An Intimate Portrait," *Saturday Review,* May 29, 1965, p. 33

their respect. In order to have subordinates look to you for direction, you must strongly want to be out in front and do the things which are not always easy, such as following the rules that you expect subordinates to abide by; working harder yourself than the employee is asked to work; exercising patience and self-control; and making personal sacrifices when the job needs special attention. These are a few examples which indicate the importance of setting and meeting performance standards in improving as a professional manager.

Most mature adults realize they can't expect to get something for nothing. Consequently, subordinates usually take a special pride in following a manager who refuses to accept inferior work. Even though they might not openly admit it, they know that superior personal performance is in their own best interest. Emerson wrote, *Our chief want in life is somebody who shall make us do what we can.*

How You Can Benefit from the Right Image

A recent television show used a full hour of prime time to dig up all the unsavory past actions of property owners and their agents against unprotected and poorly educated workmen. One of these long-ago incidents played up was the Homestead strike violence at the Carnegie Steel Company near Pittsburgh in 1892. A pay cut and the refusal to recognize a union by an executive of the company, Henry C. Frick, resulted in a pitched battle between the strikers and a company-hired force of Pinkerton operators. Guns and clubs caused the death of some twenty people with scores more injured.

The plant was closed for four months. Frick was burned in effigy and finally shot and stabbed by an anarchist named Berkman. The State Militia, 8,000 strong, established martial law; and the mills reopened in late November of that year. The special TV show gave exceptional emphasis to the horror of the general public at this, as it was called, clash of property rights and organized employees.

After the strike, Charles M. Schwab as superintendent of the steel mill and one of the first practicing professional managers began devoting his career to creating a better understanding between the managers of that day and the workmen.

In the show mentioned, other TV scenes, with appropriate mournful music, stressed the long hours and grimy working conditions which left a strong impression of a lack of sensitivity and even inhumanity by managers in industry.

You should be concerned about these slaps at your chosen field of endeavor. Whatever your position, it's your job to sell the value of the function by which you live. A successful, professional man must command respect because of the service he renders. Doctors, lawyers, accountants, and teachers are very conscious of the integrity of both themselves and others in their profession because they realize that "one bad apple in the barrel can do a lot of harm to all the others." You should be equally diligent in working for a similar high regard and acceptance of your profession as a manager.

Several writers, columnists, and speakers have reported that careers in business are routine, conformist, uninspiring, materialistic, lacking in opportunity for public service, and unchallenging to idealists. It is said that the poorest students enroll in business school and, even from this substandard group, business and industry are not getting a fair share of the graduates. Roger M. Blough, chairman of the board and chief executive officer of the United States Steel Corporation, writing in the *Harvard Business Review,* said:

> In 1964 Dartmouth reported of 640 men who graduated, 200 took business careers in accounting, advertising, finance, industrial administration, and insurance. Another 227 were headed for related careers, such as architecture, aviation, forestry, journalism, and corporate law. The remaining 213 planned nonbusiness careers. . . . The Council for Financial Aid to Education recently reported the findings of a study it had made of the backgrounds of the two top executives in each of America's 100 largest corporations. (Facts sheet "Study of College Backgrounds of Top Two Executives in America's Largest 100 Business Corporations.") This study revealed that, in 1955, 61% of these executives were college graduates, with 17% having earned advanced degrees. And by 1964 the figures had risen to 75% and 26% respectively. This is an increase of nearly 23% in college graduates and of about 53% in those holding advanced degrees—all in a period of ten years.[1]

So there are some things which can be said in favor of business which may get lost in the more sensational criticisms which seem designed to downgrade the image of business and industry.

You have a duty to challenge any of these misconceptions which young intellectuals may get from TV shows, plays, movies, and paperbacks. Remember, it is your profession and one in which you can truly be proud. Whenever you have an opportunity, you should contribute any possible help to colleges and universities so that the real business story gets over to the students.

To the extent that you are able to help build the right image for managers, you will: 1. gain greater self-satisfaction from your work, 2. earn more money, 3. receive more recognition both outside and inside your organization, 4. be able to contribute more to your company and your community, 5. attract better people into the profession.

How to Take Advantage of Your Unlimited Opportunities as a Manager

Today's effort is toward group cooperation and away from the individualism which characterized the period through the early 1900's in business and industry. In the late 19th and early 20th century, John D. Rockefeller was the Standard Oil; J. P. Morgan was the Morgan Bank; Joseph Pulitzer was the *New*

[1] Blough, "Business Can Satisfy the Young Intellectual," *Harvard Business Review,* January-February, 1966, pp. 50-51

York World; Samuel Gompers was the organized labor movement; and Henry Ford was the Ford automobile. In the late 1960's, while the top leaders of such great corporations as Boeing, U.S. Steel, General Electric and General Motors are well known, their individual identities are not as singularly all inclusive as in earlier times.

Size and diversity make it impossible for one man to personally control all of the activities of today's great corporate endeavors. There is an ever-increasing need for more and better leadership at every level of management.

You must improve as a manager if you are to gain from the rising demand in your profession. This requires some *faiths* on your part; the *first* of which is a conviction that individuals can learn practices, skills, and ways of working which will help you become a better supervisor. You must believe that industrial and business leadership is important work.

A second faith: You must believe that there is an effective pattern of personal leadership conduct which can be adapted to your individual personality. Sir Winston Churchill, called the greatest manager of our time, following the crisis which began in 1940, demonstrated several essential steps in this pattern. First, he obtained the understanding of the free people he led by working long and hard on his broadcasts, his speeches in the House, and his messages to and consultations with Roosevelt. Secondly, Churchill showed his sympathy for people. On one occasion after a heavy air raid by the enemy, as he walked through the shattered East End of London where some little homes had stood, a woman among the spectators who had gathered to cheer him touched her friend on the arm as she said, "Look, Mary, he's crying." Then she added, "He really cares." [1]

The great wartime prime minister also made decisions, held to them tenaciously, and exhibited a desire for dominance. The successful supervisor "... is not expected to dictate, but to dominate through leadership. Several studies have employed measures of dominance and report a positive relationship with effectiveness. However it is entirely possible that extreme dominance ... may be detrimental to effectiveness as a manager." [2] Again, here is evidence of a caution or the need for using judgment in attempting to guide others. As leadership tools, Churchill also used his reputation as a leader and the importance of successfully accomplishing his assignment. This enabled him to attract and keep good men and generate unbeatable enthusiasm.

A third faith which you need in striving toward better personal leadership is the conviction that managers develop themselves. You must believe that managers are not born with all the skills, qualities and abilities needed to step up to this complex job. However, even if a personality change is required, remember it can be done. A well-known example is that of Saul (later St. Paul)

[1] Urwick, *The Greatest Manager of Our Time,* pp. 42-44
[2] Mahoney, op.cit., p. 196

who, three days after his experience on the Damascus road, was a different man than he was before.

As a rising executive you realize the management of modern business encompasses a great many different areas of importance. The requirements are so complex that a day-to-day routine method of managing is inadequate even in the smallest and simplest business, largely "... because deterioration is what happens, normally—that is, unless somebody counteracts it. There is need for a systematic and purposeful program. There is need to reduce the almost limitless possible tasks to a manageable number. There is need to concentrate scarce resources on the greatest opportunities and results. There is need to do the few right things, and do them with excellence." [1]

As you work toward mastery in support of these basic faiths, you are putting yourself in a position to benefit from the boundless potential present in your demanding profession.

"Watch-For's" in Striving Toward Your Leadership Aims

To be a better manager, you have to marshal all your faculties in a concerted direction toward a specific goal and also be aware of some of the obstacles in the way of accomplishing your objectives. *The first "watch-for"* is to realize that both parties to your superior-subordinate relationship take a position to serve their own purpose. Consciously or otherwise this posture is intended to help each of you get what he thinks he wants.

Professor William H. Newman of the Columbia University Graduate School of Business wrote:

> An individual takes an action when the satisfactions he derives from doing so outweigh the discomforts and sacrifices that are involved. This does not mean that people behave in a rational manner based on logical analysis; far from it. Motives that are strong today may be weak tomorrow. Habit and inertia play a large part. Expectations and fears may be ungrounded.... Nevertheless, to the individual the tugs and pulls are real and he responds to them.[2]

A second "watch-for" is "ego-involved attitudes," or topics which are for many people crucial to their self-images and central to numerous related attitudes. Some of the most common are racism and religious beliefs. Ego-involved attitudes are important to you as you try to get ahead because such positions are particularly hard to change, as reflected in both the manager's actions and those of the people reporting to him.

This leads to *the third "watch-for;"* namely, changes must occur if improvement is to be made. New ideas, new methods, better ways of producing more products and/or services of higher quality at lower cost must be put into

[1] Drucker, *Managing for Results*, p. 131
[2] Newman, *Administrative Action*, p. 446

practice. Business and industry of necessity are highly dynamic. You have to sense, control, and administer change in others and be a leader capable and willing to change yourself. During the recent years of adjustment, one myth which has been effectively exploded is that "as an executive grows older, his resistance to change becomes greater." In industry after industry and situation upon situation, the older and more experienced managers have taken the lead to initiate and cope with changes. For proof, just note the ages of the top leaders in our front-ranked corporations today.

Forget the fallacy and direct your energy and attention to encouraging improvement at all management levels. In order to survive in the increasingly difficult competitive crisis ahead, you and your organization must translate capacity for change within your management into creative performance. To tap the potential, it must be understood that:

1. *Every individual has change potential.* An interesting example of such a change is related by Emile Capouya in his review of "The Autobiography of Malcolm X":

> From his own account, it is clear that Malcolm X was shattered and renewed by the experience of religious awakening. The absolute character of his conversion is testified to by the uncompromising puritanism of his later life. The addict and thief made of himself a monument of sobriety and disciplined energy. Most impressive of all, under the stimulus of religious conviction Malcolm's intellect unfolded. In prison, the functionally illiterate graduate of Lansing High School taught himself to read and write, taught himself to study history, sociology, and political theory, taught himself to speak.[1]

2. *It is to the company's interest to purposefully accelerate change potential.* Just think of the implications of predicted changes: "World population to double in forty years. The U.S. gross national product to double in fifteen years. Scientific research to double in just ten years." [2] You as a growing manager must be thinking about these developments as they will affect your company and its future as well as your own.

3. *Here is a project worthy of thoughtful attention.*

4. *Some way must be found to encourage the individual to accept responsibility for his own self-development.*

These ideas and actions are fundamental to building a better future for yourself as a KNOW-and-DO manager.

Recognize that you as well as supervisors at all levels are plagued with varying degrees of what can be called "the closed-mind affliction." Rigidity toward change grows somewhat logically out of past successes. You understand-

[1] Capouya, Emile: "A Brief Return From Mecca," *Saturday Review*, November 20, 1965, pp. 42-3

[2] See Irwin, Patrick H. and Frank W. Langham, Jr.: "The Change Seekers," *Harvard Business Review*, January-February, 1966, p. 81

ably seek situations and occasions in which you can continue to practice those things which have been useful in the past. This safe feeling, supported by lethargy, fear of failure or both, encourages a closed mind to reject new opportunities, ideas and attitudes. However, don't be too discouraged because there is a value in both the open and closed types of minds. An open mind seeks new ideas to replace those previously practiced, and such thinking is essential to keeping the enterprise alive under modern, competitive conditions, while the only value of the closed mind is to serve as a brake on management decisions needing a second look.

Fortunately, both types of minds can be trained into actions of value to your organization. Of course, as a modern manager interested in developing your subordinates, you must first identify the tendency of your subordinate supervisor toward either an open or closed mind. As a creative manager capable of valuable contributions to your organization, you can counteract any feeling which he may develop concerning lack of appreciation for his ideas, skills, and methods of operating. You must keep challenging the open-minded supervisor. In handling the obstructionist tactics of the closed-minded supervisor, review your decisions, confirm or even alter your decisions, but do not permit such objections to unnecessarily delay or cause you to abandon productive ideas.

Use Sincerity to Improve Your Management "Pulling Power"

Whatever your position in your company management organization, strive to make sure that your performance reflects your true personality in an open and sincere fashion. Remember that a real leader does not attract followers by tricks, subterfuge, or manipulation. You will succeed or fail in the personal power source area of your profession by display of evident ability, in "pulling qualities," and use of straight-forward management strategic skills. One of the things to which you must dedicate yourself is sincerity. An at-home feeling by all employees generates a constructive working atmosphere. Your most consistently productive subordinates have confidence in your leadership. Why is this true? Because they feel they know you. Assurance comes from experience and subordinates develop a secure feeling from an understanding of the boss: a certain knowledge of support in right actions and punishment in wrong actions. Watch the difficulties which occur for other managers when subordinates are not sure of their backing. As a natural result, an individual becomes over-conservative, passes the buck, and friction with loss of productivity is inevitable. You must set unit objectives, preferably in cooperation with your subordinate, but clearly understood regardless of how they are set. These goals then become targets for accomplishment.

Some over-clever managers pride themselves on spectacular short-run results through manipulation. Their actions are very seldom entirely dishonest or wholly intentional. Often it is simply a case of not informing the subordinate of what is expected or what he can look forward to if he decides to violate some rule. Thus, when the superior takes a subordinate to task, the subordinate with some justification sees it as a bad experience. Confidence which the superior may have taken a long time to build can be quickly destroyed.

Keep firmly in mind the fact that the quality of sincerity is something that cannot be faked by people in close association. Your subordinates know whether you care anything about them and whether you are honest with them or not. I once knew a very successful plant superintendent whose favorite saying was that dogs knew whether people cared anything about them—whether they were honest with them or not. He said you could turn a dog loose in a room of strangers and the dog would go up to the people in that room who liked dogs, and "people are as smart as dogs."

Using Another's Point of View to Get Better Management Results

In your department, section, or group, an atmosphere of mutual respect among all managers and workmen is a real advantage. To establish such a climate, you must use a great deal of self-control. Often you cannot do all the things you might like to do or maybe all the things you might once have done, and further, you have to use some of the general principles of good relationships.

One of the more essential of these facts of life is that *"All people like to feel important."* Your subordinate badly needs assurance that the job he is doing is worthwhile and that he as an individual amounts to something. You can even say that your subordinate will not be fully productive unless he does have the assurance that he is in some ways a special person.

One of the better ways to keep in mind the importance of the other person is to mentally put yourself in his shoes. Look at your idea from his viewpoint and when you talk to him, talk to him from his viewpoint. Henry Ford once said, "If there is any one secret to success, it lies in the ability to get the other person's view and see things from his angle as well as your own."

You should not lose sight of the fact that this is a means of acquiring additional knowledge; however, you as a rising manager need to be careful that you do not get trapped into believing that management is primarily just an accumulation of knowledge. Howard Thurston, the great magician, was once asked if the secret of his success was because he had superior knowledge of magic. He answered *no,* stating that hundreds of books have been written about legerdemain and scores of people knew as much as he did about it. Thurston felt his success was due in the main to two qualities: *first, hard work* involving practice which enabled him to project his personality across the footlights, and *second, he had a genuine interest in people.* For instance, he said some magicians would approach an audience with the attitude, "Yah! Bunch of suckers out there, a bunch of hicks!" Thurston's method was entirely different. Every time he had a performance, before he entered the stage he consciously said, "I am grateful because these people come to see me. They make it possible for me to earn my living in a very agreeable way. I am going to give them the very best I possibly can." Idealistic, maybe, but this is the formula used by one of the most famous operators of all time in his chosen field.

To be a better manager, you have to become genuinely interested in other people. One hundred years before the birth of Christ, the Roman poet, Publius Syrus, said, "We are interested in others when they are interested in us." The great Abraham Lincoln said, "Everyone likes a compliment." William James, the philosopher, said, "The deepest principal in human nature is the craving to be appreciated." Notice that the word is "craving" and not "wish" or "desire." Alfred Lunt, the actor, said, "There is nothing I need so much as nourishment for my self-esteem."

Early in this century, a famous philosopher-economist named Thornstein Veblen, who is credited with having a strong influence on the thinking of an entire generation, published a book entitled *The Theory of the Leisure Class.* In his book Veblen says that the driving force for any man is "the propensity to emulation." These words simply mean that a person wishes to look well in comparison with his neighbor; the individual endeavoring to assert his own importance, which is a personal need that you as a developing manager must recognize and respect.

Be Careful When You Use the Great Destroyer

Both you and your subordinate lose when your management actions arouse defensive behavior. Far more often than you realize, a threat, intentional or otherwise, prevents your getting top performance from the people reporting to you. To be a better manager, you must recognize that unfavorable emotions—resentment, antagonism, and anger—can easily be aroused in your subordinate or an associate by criticism. This means the tearing-down kind of criticism. The effect can be bad even though you are trying your best to be helpful. In your managing, remember that an important principle of human relations is that *nobody likes to be criticized.* Now you can say that a person ought to listen to criticism, appreciate it, and welcome it. It is a way in which he can make an improvement so he ought to like it, but he doesn't. He is a creature of emotion —prejudiced, proud, and vain. These things are true of me and they are probably true of you.

Aside from being America's first great merchant, John Wanamaker was a very distinguished citizen. He was Postmaster General of the United States, and he had a lot of horse sense. This is the sense a horse has that keeps him from betting on a man. He wrote so wisely, he has often been called the modern Benjamin Franklin. Among his writing we find, "I learned 30 years ago that it was foolish to scold. I have enough trouble overcoming my own limitations without fretting over the fact that God has not seen fit to distribute evenly the gift of intelligence."

Nobody knows all the answers to all the problems of good human relations, but of one thing you can be sure. The answer is *not criticism.* Consider a moment what you do when you criticize someone. In effect you are saying, "I am going to show you where you are wrong." What is the normal reaction to this? "The h--l you are!" There are very few exceptions. People just do not like to be *criticized.*

Take the following situation. Any one of you go home tomorrow night and your wife meets you at the door and she says, "Honey, I was down the street today and I bought myself a new hat. Now tell me honestly—what do you think of it?" You had better be careful. She doesn't want criticism; she wants praise and, furthermore, you had better give it to her.

Consider this thought. Many good relationships are cemented through the simple expedient of overlooking minor errors and mistakes of other people which do not make any difference anyway. You are all familiar with the kind of person who very diligently searches and digs until he finds that "i" that is not dotted or the "t" that is not crossed, and then he very gleefully runs over to you and says, "Yah! Yah! Yah! You have made a mistake!" *DO NOT DO IT.*

As Lord Chesterfield, the famous English wit of the nineteenth century, advised his son, "Be wiser than other people if you can, but do not tell them so." Samuel Johnson said, "God himself, sir, does not propose to judge a man until the end of his days. Why should you and I?"

But as a good, down-to-earth, practical manager, you may say, "It is my job to tell people about their shortcomings. I have to correct them and point out their mistakes. It is part of my responsibility."

Ask yourself these questions: Is it really my job? Wouldn't it be better to keep reminding myself that my primary function is to get better total performance from every person in my group? Am I finding fault with a subordinate just to show how smart I am? Will what I am about to say help or hinder another person in future, continuous, long-term job performance? After you have carefully considered these questions, perhaps you will conclude that there is no safe way to use criticism, the great destroyer. If you still feel you must use it, be sure you know what you are doing and be careful when you do it. The whole world is moving forward. Each individual is demanding more for himself. You see it every day. If you are going to be a leader of these people, you must establish your right to be out in front by developing and using your personal power sources and by being a better performer in both the general and functional areas of your profession.

Ways to Establish Your Right to Lead

1. *Learn to do the right thing at the right time:*
   a. *Be decisive.*
   b. *Know the people reporting to you.*
   c. *Work at your job with judgment.*
2. *Make use of emotional appeals:*
   a. *Give attention to your subordinates.*
   b. *Build up everyone reporting to you.*
   c. *Talk with all whom you expect to be productive.*
   d. *Learn from others.*
   e. *Show confidence in your subordinates.*
3. *Use appeals to practical self-interest:*
   a. *Don't keep your knowledge of the importance of these motivators a secret.*
   b. *Support your subordinates all the time.*
   c. *Set consistent working standards.*
4. *Build up the image of management as a proud profession.*
5. *Use your opportunities as a manager:*
   a. *Guide others into doing a better job.*
   b. *Develop your own personal leadership pattern fitted to your personality.*
   c. *Stay off the down-hill slide.*
6. *Avoid the stumbling blocks of:*
   a. *failure to recognize that your subordinate's performance must be rewarded*
   b. *dangers in ego-involved attitudes*
   c. *a lack of appreciation of the need for changes.*
7. *Improve your pulling power with sincerity:*
   a. *Be honest.*
   b. *Don't put up a front.*
   c. *Avoid any semblance of manipulation.*
8. *Get the other person's point of view:*
   a. *Help others feel important.*
   b. *Express a genuine interest in others.*
9. *Use criticism—the great destroyer—with care:*
   a. *It is your job to get consistently better total job performance from those reporting to you.*
   b. *Nobody likes a fault-finder.*
   c. *If you* must, *make it as impersonal as possible, in private, accurate, and with the honest intent to help the receiver.*

BIBLIOGRAPHY

Beishline, John R., *Military Management for National Defense,* p. 42. New York: Prentice-Hall, Inc., 1950.

Bittel, Lester R., *Management By Exception,* pp. 267-68. New York: McGraw-Hill Book Company, 1964.

Bliven, Bruce, "Your Brain's Unrealized Powers," pp. 58-62. *Reader's Digest,* Vol. 69, October 1956. Pleasantville, New York: The Reader's Digest Association, Inc.

Blough, Roger M., "Business Can Satisfy the Young Intellectual," pp. 50-51. *Harvard Business Review,* January-February 1966. Soldiers Field, Boston.

Bross, Irwin D. J., *Design for Decision,* p. 15. New York: The Macmillan Company, © 1953.

Business Week. References to the April 20, 1963 and August 31, 1963 issues of *Business Week* by special permission. Copyrighted © 1963 by McGraw-Hill, Inc.

Campbell, Walter J., ed., "Where Are the Take-Charge Guys?" pp. 106-107. *Steel,* 1-3-66. Cleveland: The Penton Publishing Co.

Capouya, Emile, "A Brief Return From Mecca," pp. 42-43. *Saturday Review,* 11-20-65. New York: Saturday Review, Inc.

Carter, Violet Bonham, "An Intimate Portrait," p. 33. *Saturday Review,* 5-29-65. New York: Saturday Review, Inc.

Catton, Bruce. *This Hallowed Ground,* p. 168. Copyright © 1955, 1956 by Bruce Catton. Reprinted by permission of Doubleday & Company, Inc.

Cerami, Charles A., *How to Solve Management Problems,* p. 120. Englewood Cliffs, N.J.: Prentice-Hall, Inc., 1957.

Chesterton, James D., "The Maverick Manager," pp. 38-39. *Personnel,* September-October 1965. New York: American Management Association.

Committee for Economic Development, "Raising Low Incomes Through Improved Education," pp. 16, 19. September 1965. New York.

Cooper, Joseph D., *The Art of Decision Making,* pp. 119-120. Copyright © 1961 by Joseph D. Cooper. Reprinted by permission of Doubleday & Company, Inc.

Drucker, Peter F., "Big Business and the National Purpose," p. 50. *Harvard Business Review,* March-April 1962. Soldiers Field, Boston.

———, *Managing for Results,* pp. 226-27, 131. New York: Harper & Row, 1964.

———, *The Practice of Management,* p. 6. New York: Harper & Brothers, 1956.

Dubin, Robert, *Human Relations in Administration,* pp. 167, 232. Englewood Cliffs, N.J.: Prentice-Hall, Inc., 1961.

Economic Almanac (1964), pp. 273, 32-33, 72, 123, 77. New York: National Industrial Conference Board.

First National City Bank, *Monthly Economic Letter,* pp. 94-95. August 1965. New York.

Gaudet, Dr. Frederick J., "Seven Places to Watch Your Step" from "How To Get To Be An Executive," *Changing Times,* Vol. 10, No. 5, May 1956, The Kiplinger Washington Editors, Inc., Washington, D.C.

Gellerman, Saul W., *Motivation and Productivity,* pp. 139, 95-96. New York: American Management Association, 1963.

Gibran, Kahlil, *The Prophet,* p. 28. Alfred A. Knopf, N.Y., 1958, Copyright 1923 by Kahlil Gibran, Renewal copyright 1951 by Administrators C. T. A. of Kahlil Gibran Estate, and Mary G. Gibran.

Goetz, Billy E., *Management Planning and Control,* p. 27. New York: McGraw-Hill Book Company, Inc., 1949.

Golden, L. L. L., "Not by Divine Right," p. 129. *Saturday Review,* 9-18-65. New York: Saturday Review, Inc.

Gray, J. Stanley, *Psychology in Human Affairs,* p. 553. New York: McGraw-Hill Book Company, Inc., 1946.

Greenewalt, Crawford H., "Sensing Who Can Command," pp. 40, 110. *Nation's Business,* October 1965. Washington, D.C.: Chamber of Commerce of the United States.

———, *The Uncommon Man,* p. 32. New York: McGraw-Hill Book Company, Inc., 1959.

Hawley, Cameron, *Cash McCall,* pp. 355, 357-59. Boston: Houghton Mifflin Company, 1955.

Hoslett, Schuyler Dean, ed., *Human Factors in Management,* p. 109. New York: Harper & Brothers, 1951.

Irwin, Patrick H. and Frank W. Langham, Jr., "The Change Seekers," p. 81. *Harvard Business Review,* January-February 1966. Soldiers Field, Boston.

Jennings, Eugene Emerson, "It Takes Two to Reach the Top," p. 202. *Nation's Business,* November 1961. Washington, D.C.: Chamber of Commerce of the United States.

Joseph, Albert M., "How to Write Better." Reprinted *Business Management* (formerly *Management Methods*), 1960, Management Magazines, Inc., Greenwich, Conn.

Kennedy, Robert F., "A Peak Worthy of the President," p. 9. *National Geographic Magazine,* July 1965. From a longer quotation by James Ramsey Ullman, *The Age of Mountaineering,* p. 319.

Koontz, Harold and Cyril O'Donnell, *Principles of Management,* p. 279. New York: McGraw-Hill Book Company, Inc., 1955.

Leavitt, Harold J., *Managerial Psychology,* p. 164. Copyright 1958 by The University of Chicago, Published 1958. First Phoenix Edition 1962. Seventh Impression 1962. Composed and printed by The University of Chicago Press, Chicago, Illinois, U.S.A., 1959.

Levinson, Harry, "What is Mental Health?" p. 24. *Think,* March-April 1965, published by IBM. Pleasantville, N.Y.: The Reader's Digest Association, Inc.

Likert, Rensis and Samuel P. Hayes, Jr., eds., "Some Applications of Behavioural Research," p. 62. Switzerland: UNESCO, 1957.

Mahoney, Thomas A., *Building the Executive Team,* pp. 125, 189-90, 195-96. Englewood Cliffs, N.J.: Prentice-Hall, Inc., 1961.

Mann, D. J., "Providing for Present and Future Management Needs," p. 27. *Personnel,* July-August 1965. New York: American Management Association.

Mansfield, Harold, *Billion Dollar Battle,* pp. 171-72. New York: David McKay Company, Inc., 1965.

McGuire, Joseph W., *Business and Society,* pp. 300, 167. New York: McGraw-Hill Book Company, Inc., 1963.

McKamy, Kent, ed., "This President Runs His Own Management Development Program," pp. 60, 62. *Business Management,* May 1965. Greenwich, Conn.: Management Magazines, Inc.

Merrill, Harwood F., *Management News,* p. 5. April 1965. New York: American Management Association.

Michelon, L. C., *Basic Economics,* p. 70. Cleveland: The World Publishing Co., 1960.

Miller, Dr. Louis, et al., "An Evaluation of Two Procedures Designed to Improve Employee Attitudes and Performance." Crotonville, N.Y.: General Electric, 1964.

Newman, William H., *Administrative Action,* pp. 326-27, 203, 446. Englewood Cliffs, N.J.: Prentice-Hall, Inc., 1955.

Odiorne, George S., *How Managers Make Things Happen,* pp. 50, 53. Englewood Cliffs, N.J.: Prentice-Hall, Inc.

———, "Management Motivation Muddle," p. 31. *Michigan Business Review,* March 1965. Ann Arbor, Michigan: The University of Michigan.

———, "The End of Leisure," p. 119. *Adult Leadership,* October 1965. Washington, D.C.: Adult Education Association of the U.S.A.

Packard, Vance, *The Pyramid Climbers,* pp. 206, 6. New York: McGraw-Hill Book Company, Inc., 1962.

———, *The Status Seekers,* pp. 28, 42-43. New York: David McKay Company, Inc., 1959.

Potter, David M., *People of Plenty,* p. 89. Copyright 1954 by The University of Chicago, all rights reserved, Published 1954. Composed and printed by The University of Chicago Press, Chicago, Illinois, U.S.A.

Quinn, John R., "Sure-fire Ways to Stunt Your Subordinates' Growth." *Personnel,* January-February 1963. New York: American Management Association.

Randall, Clarence B., "A Businessman Looks at the Liberal Arts," pp. 7, 20-23. *The Fund for Adult Education,* 1957. Copyright American Foundation for Continuing Education.

Rathe, Alex W., ed., *Gantt on Management,* pp. 113-15. New York: American Management Association and the American Society of Mechanical Engineers, 1961. Cambridge: Riverside Press.

Rautenstrauch, Walter and Raymond Villers, *The Economics of Industrial Management,* pp. 72, 435. New York: Funk & Wagnalls Co., 1957.

Riegel, John W., *Management, Labor and Technological Change,* p. 55. Ann Arbor: The University of Michigan Press, 1942.

Roadmaps of Industry, No. 1526, July 15, 1965. New York: National Industrial Conference Board.

Sloan, Alfred P., Jr., *My Years With General Motors,* p. 435. Garden City, N.Y.: Doubleday & Company, Inc., 1964.

Smiddy, Harold F., "Integrating and Motivating for Effective Performance," p. 22. Crotonville, N.Y.: General Electric Company, 2-18-55.

Spence, Clark C., *The Sinews of American Capitalism,* p. 1. New York: Hill & Wang, Inc., 1964.

Terry, George R., *Principles of Management,* Third Edition, pp. 413, 300. Homewood, Illinois: Richard D. Irwin, Inc., 1960.

The Wall Street Journal (Dallas, Texas), 9-22-65. Roger Ricklefs, "Good Works, Inc."

The Wall Street Journal (Dallas, Texas), 11-26-65, p. 1. Washington Wire Column.

The Wall Street Journal (Dallas, Texas), 12-1-65, p. 16.

The Wichita Eagle, 2-2-65. Sylvia Porter column.

The Wichita Eagle, 12-4-65. "David Lawrence's View."

The Wichita Sunday Eagle and The Wichita Beacon, 8-22-65, p. A2. UPI Release, Morganfield, Ky.

Urwick, Lyndall F., "How the Organization Affects the Man," p. 4. General Management Series Publication No. 189, "The Man in Management: a Personal View." New York: American Management Association.

———, "The Greatest Manager of Our Time," pp. 42-44. *Management Review,* March 1965. New York: American Management Association.

Whyte, William H., Jr., *The Organization Man,* pp. 7, 52. © 1956 by William H. Whyte, Jr. Published by Simon and Schuster, Inc. Rockefeller Center, 630 Fifth Avenue, New York 20, N.Y.

Wickens, Delos D. and Donald R. Meyer, *Psychology,* p. 354. New York: Dryden Press, 1955. By permission of Holt, Rinehart and Winston, Inc.

Worthy, James C., "Manpower Inventory and Planning," 12-17-64, p. 2. Industrial Management Program, Oklahoma State University, Stillwater.